Cultural Studies and Environment, Revisited

The environment is perhaps most misunderstood as a static place, somewhere "out there," separated from the practices of our everyday lives. Given this assumption, environmental movements and concerns have remained mostly marginalized or denigrated in Anglo-Australian-American cultural studies publications, conferences, and presentations. Recent global developments have made changing this oversight and, at times, direct resistance to engaging environmental concerns a new priority. This edited collection illustrates an appreciation of the dynamic, palpable, and significant ways the environment permeates culture (and vice versa), as well as a collective commitment to the ways that cultural studies has more to offer—and to learn from—taking environmental matters to heart. Like foundational categories of identity, economics, and historical context, this collection reminds us why the environment is and should be considered relevant to any work done in the name of "cultural studies." Including research from four continents and across media, the authors offer insights on timely topics such as food, tourism, human/animal relations, forests, queer theory, indigenous rights, and water.

This book was published as a special issue of *Cultural Studies*.

Phaedra C. Pezzullo is an Associate Professor in the Department of Communication and Culture, and adjunct faculty of Cultural Studies and American Studies at Indiana University, Bloomington, USA. She authored *Toxic Tourism: Rhetorics of Pollution, Travel, and Environmental Justice* (University of Alabama, 2007) and co-edited *Environmental Justice and Environmentalism: The Social Justice Challenge to the Environmental Movement* (MIT Press, 2007).

Cultural Studies and Environment, Revisited

Edited by
Phaedra C. Pezzullo

LONDON AND NEW YORK

First published 2011
by Routledge
2 Park Square, Milton Park, Abingdon, Oxfordshire OX14 4RN

Simultaneously published in the USA and Canada
by Routledge
711 Third Avenue, New York, NY 10017

First issued in paperback 2014

Routledge is an imprint of the Taylor and Francis Group, an informa business

© 2011 Taylor & Francis

This book is a reproduction of *Cultural Studies*, 22.3-4. The Publisher requests that those citing this book use the bibliographical details of the journal issue on which the book is based.

Typeset in Times New Roman by Taylor & Francis Books

All rights reserved. No part of this book may be reprinted or reproduced or utilised in any form or by any electronic, mechanical, or other means, now known or hereafter invented, including photocopying and recording, or in any information storage or retrieval system, without permission in writing from the publishers.

British Library Cataloguing in Publication Data
A catalogue record for this book is available from the British Library

ISBN 978-0-415-61313-2 (hbk)

ISBN 978-1-138-87955-3 (pbk)

Disclaimer
The publisher would like to make readers aware that the chapters in this book are referred to as articles as they had been in the special issue. The publisher accepts responsibility for any inconsistencies that may have arisen in the course of preparing this volume for print.

Contents

1. Overture: the most complicated word
   Phaedra C. Pezzullo — 1

2. Speculative visions and imaginary meals: food and the environment in (post-apocalyptic) science fiction films
   Jean P. Retzinger — 9

3. Tourism, race and the state of nature: on the bio-poetics of government
   Margaret Werry — 31

4. Forest, flows and identities in Finland's information society
   Eeva Berglund — 52

5. Cat and mouse: iconographics of Nature and Desire
   Jody Berland — 71

6. Queering ecocultural studies
   Catriona Mortimer-Sandilands — 95

7. Resisting ecocultural studies
   Jennifer Daryl Slack — 117

8. From water crisis to water culture
   Dr. Vandana Shiva, an interview by Andy Opel — 138

Notes on Contributors — 150
Index — 152

Phaedra C. Pezzullo

OVERTURE

The most complicated word

> We need different ideas because we need different relationships.
> (Williams 1980, p. 85)

> But you know, grandson, this world is fragile.
> (Silko 1977, p. 35)

> And when nature is heard as nonsense, (its) music will sound through, unhampered. Again, nature will be heard.
> (Minh-ha 1996, p. 102)

'Nature,' or to what I will refer more broadly as 'the environment,' is perhaps most misunderstood as a static place, somewhere 'out there,' somehow beyond or separated from the practices of everyday life. All too often, when the environment is reduced to a place, we tend to assume it signifies the country, and forget it also refers to the city. We imply that it is static, and not dynamic. We take it for granted, and turn our attention elsewhere. Under industrial, colonial, developmental, and other arrogant influences unwilling to appreciate its fragility or to listen to its complex composition, the environment often falls prey to what Renaldo Rosaldo (1989) calls an 'imperialist nostalgia,' in which 'people destroy their environment and then worship nature' (p. 108).

The environment, of course, is neither pure nor obsolete. Rather, it both exceeds the cultural and invokes a performative, heterogeneous discourse that shapes our entire lives. More than a location, *the environment is what it does* materially and symbolically. Yes, it is where we stand and where we lie down; however, it also heats and cools us. It provides us light at night. It fuels our cars, buses, trains, and airplanes. It permeates every pore of our flesh, DNA strand in our genetic make up, and identity written on and through our bodies. It involves processes with and without us that we still do not – and may never – comprehend.

Over a decade ago in this journal, an issue dedicated to environmental matters was edited by Jody Berland and Jennifer Daryl Slack, signaling the challenging array of scholarly research approaches, critical perspectives, and political stakes involved in exploring this field of research by engaging a range of themes, such as community, technology, water, ecofeminism, Earth Day, the weather, and computer simulations of global warming.[1] Since then, a small handful of cultural studies scholars has provided rich insights into how we might continue to identify, interpret, and intervene within and on behalf of the environment. Eschewing universal abstractions and skeptical of grand proclamations, these creative endeavors tend to be grounded in specific cultural and ecological contexts, while acknowledging that such perspectives shift, like ecosystems themselves, over time and space. Perhaps the most notable indicator of change has been the introduction of 'the environment' itself into the lexicon of cultural studies. For example, in *Keywords*, Raymond Williams' (1976) includes an entry on 'nature' and astutely observes, more than culture itself, 'Nature is the most complicated word in the [English] language' (p. 219). Three decades later, in the revised text, *New Keywords*, the term 'nature' (that notably cites Williams' earlier claim) is accompanied by a separate entry by Jennifer Daryl Slack (2005) on 'environment/ecology,' one that further complicates how these terms 'developed to assert different conceptions of separation and connection' (p. 106).[2]

Yet, for the most part, the environment remains marginalized within cultural studies publications, conferences, and conversations. Put more bluntly, it is unclear whether or not cultural studies actually is ready or equipped to engage the environment. As Jody Berland (unpublished address 2005) suggests, there seem to be at least three fundamental limitations of cultural studies – as some still currently practice it – that might suggest the roots of this reluctance: (1) an emphasis on the logic of representation that reinforces a dualism between nature and culture; (2) a resistance to critiquing consumption in any context; and (3) a resilient legacy from the Sokal affair and 'science wars' that continues to make some of us fear engaging and border-crossing into questions of science.[3] Further, I would add two points. First, it is telling that cultural studies scholars are more likely to publish criticisms about environmental movements or struggles than we are to take seriously environmental critiques. For me, at least, it is disappointing and disconcerting when cultural studies practitioners tend to dis-articulate the project of cultural studies from environmental politics, rather than making linkages and alliances between the two. Second, the environment stubbornly appears ghettoized in cultural studies, the purview of only those of us who identify as environmentalists or who make the environment one of our primary areas of research – as if one can or should talk about topics such as popular culture, technology, government policy, or global flows without mentioning environmental dimensions as part of the analysis. Like foundational categories such as identity, economics, and historical context, the environment is and should be considered relevant to any research done in the name of 'cultural studies.'[4]

Given this unfortunate lack of a robust response to the last special issue on the environment in this journal, it seems timely once again to revisit and to re-imagine these research trajectories, in order to avoid stagnating in our evasion of environmental matters and risking the political and theoretical integrity of the practice of cultural studies itself. As such, this volume of *Cultural Studies* wishes to animate, rather then delimit our appreciation of the environment as vital to the past, present, and future of cultural studies.

Despite calls to the contrary in the US, this collection of international voices testifies that a eulogy for environmental movements and the environment itself is vastly premature and based on a narrow definition of each. Evidence of the vitality of the environment and those who speak for it may be found in the traces of local and transnational practices across the globe, suggesting both the possibilities and the limitations of language and human agency. As such, each contribution illustrates an appreciation of the dynamic, palpable, and significant ways the environment permeates culture (and vice versa), as well as a collective commitment to the ways that cultural studies has more to offer – and to learn from – taking environmental matters to heart. Motivated by specific contexts and practices, each articulates the environment as only one factor driving her analysis. In other words, although the environment is vital to their practice of cultural studies, each argues how the environment is connected with broader cultural, political, and ethical concerns, such as popular practices, marginalized identities, and the project of cultural studies itself. Overall, they offer a diverse – and, hopefully, inspiring – range of more ethical and sustainable possibilities within and beyond cultural studies.

As an overture for this provocative collection of voices, I offer the following 'brief excursions' (Pollock 1998) or riffs echoing some more familiar melodies and dropping hints of some notes of the harmonies just beginning to be heard in an attempt to invoke the kinetic and consequential spirit I have been describing.

Environments spatialize and temporalize. Multiple and sometimes contradictory social relations. Materially constituted and symbolically operating. Geographically-bound and politically-infused (Massey 1994). Biotic and abiotic ways of operating. Territories created by bird songs (Deleuze & Guattari, 1987). Communication routes established by beavers and cod fish (Innis 1930, 1940).

Articulations of identity (always are) constituted *in situ*. Even when, as Gloria Anzaldùa (1987) writes, some of us become turtles, voluntarily or involuntarily carrying 'home' on our backs (p. 43). In these contact zones, technological 'fixes' sometimes fail and unstable frontiers often appear simultaneously tangible and mystical.

Environments blur boundaries. When our tongues taste cocoa melting from the heat of our mouths. When our noses smell fresh peaches and mangos at the market. When our necks feel a chill on a winter's day. When our eyes dwell on a photograph of a cat we have not met – and we smile. When our ears hear a horse whisper to us. When we find ourselves in the *intermezzo* of life (Minh-ha 1996) – and also in the *crescendos* and the *diminuendos*. When we imagine local/global communities – including extraterrestrial ones. When norms are queered. False binaries and dualistic borders are obscured and complicated by rhizomes, cyborgs, and actor networks.

Environments elude. In those moments when we desperately and, sometimes, compulsively use Doppler radar to attempt to predict the weather or Global Information Systems to try to track and to forecast forest fires. In the glimpse of a bird quickly flying out of our line of sight. In our own bodies when we attempt to conceive a child and discover human-made toxins have polluted our breast milk and created our low sperm counts. And in the illnesses like SARS, mad cow disease, and avian flu, which plague us suddenly and unexpectedly – though undoubtedly. Like the green fire extinguishing in a dying wolf's eyes or the sense of time a mountain must know (Leopold 1949), it reminds those of us who will listen how relatively fleeting and fragile our own existence is.

Environments charm. As sure as the seasons change, tides ebb and wane, blossoms bloom, and winds whisper through trees. As long as our thirsts are quenched, our stomachs filled, and our homes are built. As soon as we inhale and exhale, dress and undress. We find its movements and colors indispensable to the magic and poetics of our lives. Speaking to our many needs and desires, we relish the ways it can 'fuse function, feeling, and meaning' (Spirn 1998, p. 3).

Environments nourish. Inspiring spiritual refuge and rejuvenation through sacred mountains, sublime canyons, or calming bodies of water. Promising the freedom to roam, climb, swim, dance, relax, and tour. Redefining economic discourse in our everyday experiences with gardens, parks, farms, homes, jobs, and schools. Providing materials to build everything from skyscrapers to paper. Fostering popular articulations to entertain and to educate us across every media technology from board games (Opel 2002) to IMAX (Acland 1998). Whether inspiring grotesque projections of the unfamiliar future or picturesque nostalgic fantasies, we are captivated by the affective and intimate intensity of the environment. This is why a silent spring is so shocking to imagine.

Environments kill. Tsunamis drown. Hurricanes devastate. Earthquakes demolish. Lead paint deforms. Pesticides destroy. Species die. People murder. Corporations pollute. Accidents – even nuclear ones – happen. Environmental movements and discourses have been articulated to racist agendas (Ross 1994, 1996, 1998, Cronon 1996, Hage 1998, Morris 1998, Moore *et al.* 2003), economically elitist politics (Helvarg 2004, Kennedy 2004), individualized politics at the expense of structural change (Grossberg 1992, Davis 1997), and essentialist notions of sex, gender, and sexuality (Domosh & Seager 2001, Massey 1994, Stabile 1994). Neo-conservatives relish opportunities to frame these hurtful and divisive linkages as universal, necessary, and inevitable. The damage, at times, feels irreparable.

Environments provoke. Governments to war. Authors to write. Activists to protest. Directors to film. Musicians to sing. Engineers to build. Scientists to experiment. People to consume. These acts are uneven and often unequal. Economically. Nationally. Globally. Questions arise. How can we enact long overdue global treaties to prevent further damage from global warming? What if we stopped placing the disproportionate burden of solid and hazardous waste on indigenous, people of color, and poor communities? When will drinkable water and breathable air become appreciated as human rights and not privileges? Is Wangari Maathai's honor of receiving the Nobel Peace Prize a sign that the world is beginning to recognize the link between sustainable environments and democratic movements? Questions continue.

Environments haunt. Our memories. With smells. With sounds. With tastes. With events. Our bodies. In scars. In growth. In pain. In love. Our mattering maps. Of who we once were. Of who we are. Of who we want to be. And, most certainly, (in) the pages that follow ...

Acknowledgements

The author wishes to thank Jody Berland, Rachel Hall, and Ted Striphas for their feedback on this preface, which was sent to the volume contributors in anticipation of their own work in the summer of 2005 and then, in turn, edited again in the summer of 2006 to help foster linkages between the diverse voices gathered here.

Notes

1   *Cultural Studies*, volume 8, issue 1, 1994. That same year, another noteworthy special issue dedicated to the environment was published: *Australian Journal of Communication*, volume 1, issue 3, 1994.
2   I favor the term 'environment' because it is more encompassing and less alienating than 'nature,' admitting to the inextricable linkage between people and the Earth. Arturo Escobar (1995) rightly notes, however, that there is a risk in this move in so far as, taken to an extreme degree, the environmental turn may become distorted as a justification for an anthropocentric view of agency and contribute to a belief in nature merely as a passive 'appendage to the environment' (p. 196).
3   Jody Berland, 'What is environmental cultural studies?,' Cultural Environmental Studies Symposium, York University, unpublished address 2005, cited with permission from author.
4   In this sense, I read Jennifer Daryl Slack and Laurie Anne Whitt's (1992) call for developing a more specialized 'ecoculturalist theoretical perspective' as an invitation to transform how we appreciate and articulate the broader project of cultural studies (as they do, from the historical roots until today), rather than as an attempt to develop a specialized branch that can continue to be marginalized and taken-for-granted. Slack revisits and embellishes on this point in her essay published in this volume, adding five points of her own to this overture's working list of why the environment remains far too marginalized in cultural studies.

References

Acland, C. R. (1998) 'IMAX technology and the tourist gaze', *Cultural Studies*, vol. 12, no. 3, pp. 429–445.
Anzaldùa, G. (1987) *Borderlands/La Frontera: The New Mestiza*, San Francisco, CA, Aunt Lute Books.
Cronon, W. (1996) *Uncommon Ground: Rethinking the Human Place in Nature*, New York, W. W. Norton & Company.
Davis, S. G. (1997) *Spectacular Nature: Corporate Culture and the Sea World Experience*, Berkeley, CA, University of California Press.
Deleuze, G. & Guattari, F. (1987) *A Thousand Plateaus: Capitalism & Schizophrenia*, Minneapolis, MN, University of Minnesota Press.

Domosh, M. & Seager, J. (2001) *Putting Women in Place: Feminist Geographers Make Sense of the World*, New York, Guilford Press.
Escobar, A. (1995) *Encountering Development: The Making and Unmaking of the Third World*, Princeton Princeton, NJ, University Press.
Grossberg, L. (1992) *We Gotta Get Out of this Place: Popular Conservatism and Postmodern Culture*, London, Routledge.
Hage, G. (1998) *White Nation: Fantasies of White Supremacy in a Multicultural Society*, Annandale, NSW, Pluto Press.
Helvarg, D. (2004) *The War Against the Greens: The "Wise-Use" Movement, the New Right, and the Browning of America*, revised updated edn, Boulder, CO, Johnson Books.
Innis, H. A. (1930) *The Fur Trade in Canada*, New Haven, CT, Yale University Press.
Innis, H. A. (1940) *The Cod Fisheries: The History of an International Economy*, Toronto, University of Toronto Press.
Kennedy, R. F. Jr (2004) *Crimes Against Nature: How George W. Bush and His Corporate Pals Are Plundering the Country and Hijacking Our Democracy*, New York, HarperCollins.
Leopold, A. (1949) *A Sand County Almanac*, Oxford, Oxford University Press.
Massey, D. (1994) *Space, Place, and Gender*, Minneapolis, MN, University of Minnesota Press.
Minh-ha, T. T. (1996) 'Nature's r: a musical swoon', in *Futurenatural*, eds G. Robertson et al., London, Routledge, pp. 86–104.
Moore, D. S., Pandian, A. & Kosek, J. (2003) *Race, Nature, and the Politics of Difference*, Durham, NC, Duke University Press.
Morris, M. (1998) *Too Soon Too Late: History in Popular Culture*, Bloomington, IN, Indiana University Press.
Opel, A. (2002) 'Monopoly™ the national parks edition: reading neo-liberal simulacra', in *Enviropop: Studies in Environmental Rhetoric and Popular Culture*, eds M. Meister & P. M. Japp, Westport, CT, Praeger, pp. 31–44.
Pollock, D. (1998) 'Chapter five: performing writing', in *The Ends of Performance*, eds P. Phelan & J. Lane, New York, New York University Press, pp. 73–103.
Rosaldo, R. (1989) 'Imperialist nostalgia', *Representations*, vol. 26, pp. 107–122.
Ross, A. (1994) *The Chicago Gangster Theory of Life: Nature's Debt to Society*, New York, Verso.
Ross, A. (1996) 'The future is a risky business', in *Futurenatural*, eds G. Robertson et al., London, Routledge, pp. 7–21.
Ross, A. (1998) *Real Love: In Pursuit of Cultural Justice*, New York, New York University Press.
Silko, L. M. (1977) *Ceremony*, New York, Penguin Books.
Slack, J. D. (2005) 'Environment/ecology', in *New Keywords: A Revised Vocabulary of Culture and Society*, eds T. Bennett, L. Grossberg & M. Morris, Malden, MA, Blackwell, pp. 106–109.

Slack, J. D. & Whitt, L. A. (1992) 'Ethics and cultural studies', in *Cultural Studies*, eds L. Grossberg, C. Nelson & P. Treichler, New York, Routledge, pp. 571–592.

Spirn, A. W. (1998) *The Language of Landscape*, New Haven, CT, Yale University Press.

Stabile, C. A. (1994) *Feminism and the Technological Fix*, Manchester, Manchester University Press.

Williams, R. (1976) *Keywords: A Vocabulary of Culture and Society*, Oxford, Oxford University Press.

Williams, R. (1980) *Problems in Materialism and Culture*, London, Verso.

Jean P. Retzinger

SPECULATIVE VISIONS AND IMAGINARY MEALS

Food and the environment in (post-apocalyptic) science fiction films

> *As speculative visions, science fiction films reveal the dreams and the anxieties of the present. This essay focuses on food scenes in science fiction films depicting the future on a post-apocalyptic earth to explore the commentary they offer on the health of the environment (including humans). Familiar and unfamiliar foods, prepared, shared, denied, and eaten illuminate popular perceptions about nature, technology, and humanity. In this analysis, food is imagined not only as a necessary sustenance for corporeal needs, but also as a liminal cultural symbol of life and death, nature and culture, human and non-human. Such projections of food, whether dramatic or parodic, help illustrate competing claims of nostalgia, progress, failure, control, alienation, and excess.*

In 1902, Georges Melies married science fiction to the fledgling art of motion pictures with his 14-minute film *La Voyage dans la Lune* (*A Trip to the Moon*). Its fanciful painted backdrops, scantily clad actresses, and imaginative narrative (which both critiqued the conservative science of its day and portrayed a hostile encounter between earthlings and the Selenite inhabitants of the moon) earned Melies an enthusiastic audience. More than a century later, science fiction remains an immensely popular film genre, accounting for five of the films listed among the Top Ten 'Box Office Champions' of all time (Campbell *et al.* 2006, p. 229).[1] With their dazzling special effects and futuristic fantasies, science fiction films perhaps best illustrate Marshall McLuhan's (1964) observation that a movie 'is not only a supreme expression of mechanism, but paradoxically it offers as product the most magical of consumer commodities, namely dreams' (p. 254).

Science fiction cinema inhabits the realm of imagination, offering us glimpses of the world as it might be – whether in an alternate present or a possible future, on earth, in space, or on a distant planet. In addition to being termed a 'speculative' genre (Merril 1954, Hendershot 1999, Seed 1999, King & Krzywinska 2000), science fiction has also been described as a 'degraded' film genre (Hendershot 1999) in which cultural fears are expressed, sometimes explicitly, and sometimes on a metaphorical level. Regardless of the era or setting depicted, a science fiction film reveals most firmly the dreams and anxieties that mark its own present.[2] Fredric Jameson (1982), in fact, argues that science fiction dramatizes 'our incapacity to imagine the future' (p. 153).

Science fiction incursions into the dreamworld are reigned in by the requirement that its narratives must be made to seem wholly possible, creating an interplay between the unfamiliar and the recognizable, or estrangement and cognition in Darko Suvin's (1979) words. Science fiction restructures and defamiliarizes our experience of the present as Jameson (1982) notes, yet it is a genre insistent upon explanations, populated by characters offering instruction and edification. The premise of a work of science fiction 'requires material, physical rationalization, rather than a supernatural or arbitrary one. This grounding of SF [science fiction] in the material rather than the supernatural becomes one of its key features' (Roberts 2000, p. 5). The insistence on materiality in science fiction leads many films to address humans' biological as well as social and psychological needs. Science fiction films pose fundamental questions about what it means to be human. While other genres may only need to demonstrate humanity as opposed to villainy, science fiction is often forced to differentiate the human from the machine (robot or cyborg) and from the (other-worldly) alien as well.

In many science fiction films, these differences are amplified in food scenes. Familiar foods serve as an anchor in an altered world (evoking both nostalgia and parody), whereas unfamiliar food may become one of the clearest measures of how far we have journeyed from the present. In nearly every instance where food is prepared, shared, and eaten in science fiction films, it aids in what Vivian Sobchack (1988) describes as science fiction's central theme: a 'poetic mapping of social relations as they are created and changed by new technological modes of "being-in-the-world" ' (p. 229).

Both on and off screen, food literally 'places' us in the world, both through its materiality and its meanings. In its materiality, food forces attention to the body; in its many psychological and social meanings, food preferences and the rituals of eating help reveal the shadings of gender, class, ethnicity, power, and community (Telotte 1985, Boswell 1990, Dorfman 1992, Barr 1996, Bell & Valentine 1997, Fernandez-Armesto 2002, Ferry 2003, Bower 2004).[3] For food not only shapes our bodies, but it structures our lives, fashioning daily rituals and helping mark significant rites of passage. Food connects us to others — both directly, through shared meals, and culturally, through shared 'tastes.' Parley Anne Boswell (1990) notes that food is a staple of film properties in nearly all genres. 'Audiences respond to food, to eating, to dining scenes because we all understand something about food – we all eat' (p. 7). Mary Anne Schofield (1989) argues that food in literature 'articulates in concrete terms what is often vague, internal, abstract' (quoted in Boswell 1990, p. 7). Depictions of meals in films serve as shorthand that often allows audiences to better understand individual characters through their relationship to food and characters' relationships with others in interactions taking place over food.[4]

Food not only signifies the needs of the individual, biological body and the grammar of a particular society and culture, but it also represents the interplay of nature and technology. Food at once serves as our most fundamental connection to the environment (as all food represents in one form or another sun, soil, water, and seeds transformed into sustenance) and, simultaneously, illustrates our indebtedness to science and technology. Technology's role in the foods we eat has become increasingly evident in the decades following World War II in the mass-produced, processed, packaged foods that line grocery store shelves and fill kitchen cupboards and refrigerators. Yet even fruits and vegetables, 'even the "wild" berry from the bramble,' as Fernandez-Armesto (2002) points out, are the products of technology, 'the result of generations or eons of selective breeding' (p. 2).[5] Food, then, as Atkinson (1983) argues, 'is a liminal substance; it stands as a bridging substance between nature and culture, the human and the natural, the outside and the inside' (quoted in Bell & Valentine 1997, p. 44). In Raymond Williams' terms, food links 'in a mutual necessity of profit and power' the country and the city, as 'a city eats what its country neighbors have grown' (1973, pp. 50–51). Food, I would add, also bridges the living and the dead: that which gives us life – whether a cow or a carrot – must first be killed, thus adding a moral/ethical component to our eating. Its liminality makes food a device well-suited to science fiction, which interrogates all of these oppositions or dualities, and is 'often at its most interesting when the lines become blurred' (King & Krzywinska 2000, p. 11).[6]

The more than two dozen science fiction films discussed in this essay have in common their attempts to depict future life on earth; most, though not all, fall within the sub-category of post-apocalyptic cinema.[7] Many of these films were made in the 1970s, a decade in which a wide range of environmental issues gained widespread attention and sympathy. These same and additional environmental concerns continue to find their way into contemporary science fiction cinema. The dystopian visions these films portray originate from the failures of the past: humanity's inability to balance its relationship with the environment, technology, or both. My examination of the many food scenes found in these films explores the ways in which food, situated in the interstices between nature, culture, science, and technology, helps to answer some of the most fundamental and persistent questions asked in science fiction films: What does it mean to be human? What role should science and technology occupy in our lives? What responsibilities do we hold toward each other and towards the earth? The presence of food at the critical junctures in which the familiar and the strange, the past, present, and future all collide lends materiality to the answers being worked out on screen. Hunger takes both literal and metaphorical form in science fiction films, arising from scarcity and uncertainty alike. Yet the act of eating rarely satiates a character. More often, the actions taken to assuage hunger further strain the relationships of humans to each other, to the environment, and to technology, provoking even greater anxieties. Science fiction food scenes help obscure, expose, perpetuate, and challenge the divisions of culture and nature.

Familiar foods in unfamiliar settings

Science fiction represents 'a literature of ideas predicated on some substantive difference or differences between the world described and the world in which readers [viewers] actually live' (Roberts 2000, p. 3). But those differences must be bridged to some extent in order for viewers to enter into and understand the world depicted on the screen. Robert Scholes (1979) employs the term 'fabulation' to describe 'fiction that offers us a world clearly and radically discontinuous from the one we know, yet returns to confront the known world in some cognitive way' (p. 2). Fabulation, then, requires that fantasy be 'melded with the mundane' (Roberts 1979, p. 21), the extraordinary with the ordinary, for science fiction narratives to be believable. Food scenes provide an opportunity for such unstable juxtapositions in which the food itself, the setting, or the interactions that take place over food can each in turn provide either the familiar anchor or the fantasy element. These juxtapositions serve as one way in which science fiction films can and often do offer a critique of contemporary culture. But such critiques are not always as progressive as one might assume or hope.

When characters eat familiar, contemporary foods in futuristic settings, food typically represents the world that has been lost. Although many people presume that science fiction is a genre that looks to the future, Adam Roberts (2000) argues that, in fact, most science fiction texts are more interested in the way things have been; science fiction uses the trappings of fantasy to explore age-old issues. Roberts argues that the chief mode of science fiction is not prophesy but nostalgia (2000, p. 33). Nostalgia, however, is notoriously unstable. The past is illusory; what we long for may never have existed.

When Neo (Keanu Reeves) visits the Oracle (Gloria Foster) for the first time in *The Matrix* (1999), for example, she welcomes him into her homey kitchen, its walls, counters, cabinets, and appliances, saturated in warm and comforting shades of green and orange. The Oracle inhabits an illusory world, yet represents the archetypal nurturing mother, offering solace in the form of food. At the close of their conversation, the Oracle urges Neo to take one of her freshly baked cookies and assures him, 'I promise you by the time you're done eating it, you'll feel right as rain.' Of course, viewers are as aware as Neo that neither the kitchen nor the cookie exist – and the Oracle herself assumes a residual memory identity that is also fictitious. But Neo eats the cookie (and with it the promise that he will find the inner strength he needs) while we consume the normative gender depictions the scene relies upon. As David Seed (1999) notes, science fiction novels and films 'are not producing arbitrary fantasy but rather reworking key metaphors and narratives already circulating in the culture' (p. 2). Amidst filmic uncertainty about what is real and what is illusion, the familiarity of food and the stereotypes of gender offer stability and comfort.

The less the world of the future resembles our own present, the more that food seems deployed as a bridge, not simply to the present but to an even more distant past. This seems particularly true of films in which environmental crises have reconfigured the world. In a bleak setting, familiar foods take on the role of 'comfort foods' quite literally – and offer a means of clinging to a former world. The opening sequence of *Soylent Green* (1973) offers a visual history of earth's collapse, beginning with a slow black and white photographic montage of pastoral scenes and then speeding forward into an increasingly urbanized and industrialized landscape – in which technology ultimately transforms cities into waste heaps of detritus. Of all the films discussed in this essay, *Soylent Green* is most explicitly about food. Food not only figures into several lengthy scenes, but it is central to the anxieties about the future at the heart of the film. In an early scene, the film's protagonist, an investigator named Thorn (Charlton Heston), visits a black market grocery store – where a single stalk of celery and two small apples are rung up for a total of $219. And then a cut of beef is revealed – so exotic and fantastical that no price is ever named. We understand immediately that only the very privileged can afford such luxuries, and then only rarely. The mass of humanity subsists on a mysterious diet of soylent green. When Thorn and his partner Sol (Edward G. Robinson) sit down to their dinner of salad (ironically flavorless-looking iceberg lettuce and a small, pale tomato) and beef stew, the older man reveals that it has been years since he's tasted anything like it; Thorn admits these flavors are all new to him. Yet both men revel in the sensory experience and seem to derive equal pleasure from the flavors – for one, familiar, for the other, exotic – they taste. For Sol, this meal operates much like Proust's madeleine, evoking another world, another time. Yet Thorn's response reminds us that nostalgia need not be grounded in memory. An imagined past is every bit as powerful as a remembered one.

Nostalgia may seem unsurprising in a film depicting destruction and loss, but it appears as well in films that depict a dramatically altered future arising as the result of technological 'progress.' Here food scenes still offer a bridge to the past, and food again provides 'comfort' amidst anxieties about the future. Unlike most of the films treated in the essay, *Minority Report* (2003) depicts neither a post-apocalyptic nor clearly dystopian future. Instead the film offers a glimpse of a near-future world in which technology has eliminated many problems – but imperfectly. Murder has been eradicated, thanks to the efforts of the pre-crime detectives who arrest and incarcerate individuals intent on homicide before the crime can occur. Detective John Anderton (Tom Cruise) ends up fleeing for his own life when he is charged with a pre-crime: the imminent murder of a man he has never met. In the elaborate, special effects saturated chase scene that follows the revelation of his impending crime, Anderton, clinging to the backs of police officers equipped with individually propelled flight suits, crashes through a window into an apartment, disrupting a family's dinner preparations. Eight hamburgers are lined up neatly on an electric grill in a kitchen that looks remarkably familiar despite the technological wizardry that appears to have transformed virtually every other space in this high-tech, awe-inspiring future world. More stable than even the appearance of the kitchen itself, though, is the depiction of this family: a plump and vaguely ethnic-looking mother who screams in distress, two cowering children, and an older, silent and emotionally unresponsive father figure, who sits impassively throughout the scene as strangers invade his apartment, pummel each other, set the dinner on fire, knock over a bowl, and finally crash through the ceiling into the apartment above. A similar juxtaposition is repeated in the second apartment, where the family (father, mother, son, and daughter) sits in perfect harmony around a dining room table, their food in bowls arrayed before them. The scenes are clearly played for humor, relying on the juxtapositioning of the ordinary with the extraordinary. But these families, meant to seem familiar, are strangely anachronistic, belonging more to an earlier era than our own. The meals prepared in these scenes are already something of an anomaly – as are the nuclear families who are gathered together to share them. The film ends up relaying an odd warning – not just about the possibility of technology going awry in the future, but reminding us of the world we have already lost. The juxtaposition of past and future conspire to offer a conservative rather than progressive critique of the present. Nostalgia in science fiction acts not only to normalize the present, but to enshrine it (however illusory its vision of the present may be). This is as true for the agricultural and industrial practices and policies that undergird contemporary food production as for gender relations acted out over that food. (For it is difficult to imagine how current agricultural practices can be sustained at all, let alone in a super-saturated and paved-over technological future with a teeming US population.) Both are not only left unexamined, they are bathed in the warm glow of nostalgia.

While present-day, familiar food served up in an imaginary future can provide material expression for nostalgic longings for the past, it can also provide fodder for parody. Humor serves as one means of disrupting nostalgia for the past/present and the foods that signify them. If familiarity can offer comfort, it can also breed contempt – or at least serve as the punchline for jokes understood around the world in a global film economy. Mass-produced foods make an easy target, and McDonald's, as the most obvious symbol of American fast food, figures into a few futuristic food scenes, although not in the form of product placements. In *Battlefield Earth: A Saga of the Year 3000* (2000), Jonnie (Barry Pepper) is guided through the ruins of a former city. The two men who lead him forward describe with awe the 'golden arches' that once adorned the city where food magically appeared. *The Fifth Element* (1997) delights in parody in its food scenes set in New York City in the year 2214. Early in the film, the police officers assigned to pursue the protagonist and taxi driver Corbin Dallas (Bruce Willis) and his alien fare Leeloo (Milla Jovovich) choose to stop for lunch instead. The bright red backdrop and golden arches of McDonald's are instantly recognizable – despite their being painted across the entire face of a skyscraper – with the police car hovering in mid-air several stories above the ground. The boxed food and giant drinks in paper cups identified as 'two golden menus' look comfortably familiar as well, while all around cars and trucks zip through the air. Later, in the same film, we watch the protagonist eating at a noodle shop staffed by an elderly Chinese man (in a scene perhaps crafted in homage to the noodle shop scene in *Blade Runner*). We presume he is dining out (despite a message for him arriving via a tube partway through the meal) – until the camera pulls back to reveal the restaurant as a floating Chinese junk (another symbol of a distant past) detaching itself from the side of Dallas' apartment and sailing off in the air, presumably to serve another customer. Ethnic, like gender, stereotypes remain deeply entrenched in these science fiction visions of the future.

Parody, ironically, suggests the impossibility of fundamental change. Although the technologies of food delivery may be altered in unpredictable ways, these parodic visions of the future insist that corporate behemoths and individual entrepreneurs alike will persist, continuing to feed us the foods we crave. Thus parody, while calling attention to the peculiarities of the present, also reifies them. We are asked to smile at absurdity, not critique it. A psychiatrist in *The Lathe of Heaven* (1980) taking a sip of vending machine coffee pronounces it 'dreadful' adding, 'Well, we've eliminated war and hunger. We still can't come up with a good cup of coffee.' *The Last Man* (1999) (a post-apocalyptic film which only tenuously qualifies as science fiction), depicts the actions of the last three survivors in America. It is unclear – even to the survivors – what caused the destruction of human life on earth, whether nuclear weapons or biological warfare. In any case, the city of Los Angeles remains largely intact; occasional bodies litter the streets and store aisles. The three survivors gather food from grocery stores, while the protagonist (David Arnott) records his days on film, noting to the camera as he places boxes of packaged goods into his grocery cart, 'It's amazing how long this stuff stays fresh.' In a scene at the close of the film, he holds up a jar of peanut butter striped with jelly – and comments that he will leave the film he has created next to it. Such a product, he observes, is certain to inspire attention and awe among the next race to follow humans on the planet, thus ensuring his film will be discovered. Humor rebuffs nostalgia, but revels as well in the familiarity that makes nostalgia possible.

At times, though, nostalgia is turned completely on its head and references to the past provide more horror than comfort. The illusionary qualities of nostalgia are explicitly evoked and critiqued. In *A Boy and His Dog* (1975), the post-nuclear world of the future is divided in two. Those who remain above ground ferret out a bleak existence by scavenging for (leftover, canned) food in the desert-like landscape. Others have retreated underground, recreating the former world in a garish, nightmare version of small town America in the 1950s. In many respects, the 'future' depicted in the film is actually one of clashing pasts: primitive, nomadic hunter-gatherers versus a repressive, patriarchal (and sterile) society. Vic, the 'boy' of the title (Don Johnson), ultimately traverses both worlds and is at home in neither. He is largely ignorant of the past (except for the history lessons taught him by his dog) and distrustful of the future. The canned food he eats mirrors his isolation and disconnect from both nature and human culture. In a desolate present, with both the past and the future discredited, the world shrinks to the bonds between a boy and his dog. Visions of community are rendered as barbarous as the desperate actions of individuals seeking only to satisfy their own immediate hunger and desires. Despair and disbelief trump nostalgia.

Using familiar foods in science fiction films set in the future arises not from the screenwriters' or directors' lack of imagination. Such foods serve specific – though diverse – needs and help give material form to abstract ideas. In representing the past (and the viewers' own present), these foods may offer easier access to the cultural messages served up alongside them. Such foods typically help make the future itself seem more familiar and comforting, reassuring us that all is not yet lost, nor need it be. But the presence of such foods in worlds paved over and dense with technology obscures human dependence on nature. The liminal bridging of nature and culture is severed.

Unfamiliar foods in alienated settings

Unfamiliar foods in science fiction film scenes communicate a different set of messages. In discussing the 'alienation of the familiar,' Vivian Sobchack (1987) notes that small budget, pessimistic science fiction films, 'quietly and grayly ... turn the familiar into the alien, visually subvert the known and comfortable, and alter the world we take for granted into something we mistrust' (p. 109). While Sobchack focuses primarily on the role of landscapes, unfamiliar foods function in much the same way (and at even lower costs). Strange foods help emphasize the strangeness of the future — and serve as a warning of what may be in store for us. For David Seed (1999), science fiction narratives of nuclear holocaust 'perform a role of negative prophesy where dreaded outcomes are envisaged and therefore hopefully deferred, in such a way that the reader or viewer is induced to ponder on present signs of danger' (p. 9). Threats to the food supply represent only one of these 'dreaded outcomes,' but because food can speak so vividly to both short-term and long-term human needs and environmental changes, the search for food amidst a world of scarcity is a frequent motif in post-apocalyptic science fiction. Most post-apocalyptic films portray only the relatively short-term aftermath of nuclear destruction [as in *The Omega Man* (1971), *A Boy and His Dog* (1975), *The Road Warrior/Mad Max 2* (1982), *Testament* (1983), *The Aftermath* (1985)], thus permitting the film's characters to subsist on scavenged canned goods. Their efforts to obtain these foods as well as their refusal or willingness to share these meager goods with others helps illustrate the delicate balance among humans, technology, and the environment that food represents. The competing values of independence and equality, self-sufficiency and community are variously celebrated and contested in the future (as in the present), juxtaposed uneasily in the rituals of eating. The 'negative prophecy' Seed (1999) describes, though, applies as well to changes wrought by other causes: global warming, over-population, and pollution. Many science fiction films depicting changes produced by these crises must invent futuristic foods that represent longer term solutions to humans' demand for a steady food supply.

Unfamiliar foods, in fact, so readily register as a fabulation, a novelty, that they may serve as one of the first clear signals that the future is a strangely altered place. When the shape or color of food served betrays our expectations, food can indicate more profound changes to the culture as a whole, which lie buried under the surface. Neither the urban landscape nor the interiors of the bureaucratic world of the future depicted in *Brazil* (1985) register at first glance as unusual. The settings all seem vaguely familiar, albeit somewhat dreary. The technologies of the future assume slightly odd forms: heating and cooling ducts everywhere, tiny, individual-sized automobiles, and fully automated, but badly malfunctioning, kitchen appliances. But it is the food itself — or at least the dishes served in an upscale restaurant — that represents the profound differences between this vision of the future and the world we inhabit. In a scene read by Janet Staiger (1999) as a critique of the 'false appearance of options in a choiceless social order' (p. 115), the protagonist Sam (Jonathan Pryce) meets his mother (Katherine Helmond), her friend Mrs Alma Terrain (Barbara Hicks), and Mrs Terrain's daughter Shirley (Kathryn Pogson) at an elegant restaurant for lunch. The four diners are presented with large, box-like menus that light up when opened to reveal glowing color photos of the various menu items. Sam orders a steak – rare, but in asking for the item by name instead of by number he violates etiquette and enrages a waiter who hisses, 'Say the number please. You have to say the number.' When their meals arrive seconds after being ordered (braised veal in wine sauce, duck a l'orange, crevette a la mayonnaise, and steak), each plate looks remarkably alike once its silver cover is removed: three scoops of a paste-like substance varying only slightly in shades of green or tan. At the center of each plate, a color photograph of the 'original' food item is affixed to an elegant silver card holder. The human interactions that take place over this (interrupted) meal prove equally strange, heightening the 'postmodern sense of powerlessness and dysfunction' analyzed by Laurel Forster (2004), p. 261).

Even when the exterior world of an imagined future is unsettling in its differences, food scenes can further amplify what is altered as well as what is unchanged. The stark, all-white settings of both the work and home environments in George Lucas's first film *THX 1138* (1970) renders the future as cold and sterile. The food glimpsed there matches it perfectly: a single small, off-white rectangular item, served unheated. The only familiar elements in this food scene are the couple's exaggeratedly stereotyped interactions. When THX 1138 (Robert Duvall) returns home from work, his partner, LUH 3417 (Maggie McOmie), is in the kitchen, 'preparing' a meal and asking if he wants to eat. He refuses even to answer, retreating silently to a separate room to watch 3D holograms (TV) in solitude. Unfamiliar foods signal a world radically changed, with both nature and culture in jeopardy. An environment unable to produce recognizable foods seems to threaten cultural ties as well, leaving its populace hungry for human connections to help sustain them.

When hunger takes a literal rather than metaphorical form, it propels actions that serve to define what it is to be human – or to be inhuman. Food (and water) scarcity leads both to brutality and kindness in science fiction films such as *The Omega Man* (1971), *A Boy and His Dog* (1975), *The Road Warrior/Mad Max 2* (1982), *Testament* (1983), *The Aftermath* (1985), and *Tank Girl* (1995). A world thrown into chaos and violence is often softened by scenes of generosity and nurturing that take place over food.

The food of the future most often glimpsed in such scenes can only be described as 'gruel.' The very form of gruel, an indistinct and homogenous substance, serves as a visual metaphor for the role that food frequently adopts in these films: both symbol and facilitator of equality and community. Taking an off-white hue in *The Matrix*, the gruel is dispensed from a spigot and described as 'a single-celled protein combined with synthetic aminos, vitamins, and minerals. Everything the body needs.' Or at least that's how the character Dozer (Anthony Ray Parker) describes it. Other characters refer to it as 'runny eggs,' 'a bowl of snot,' and 'tasty wheat.' (This later description engenders a soliloquy about the uncertainty of any flavors or tastes. 'You have to wonder really: How did the machines know what tasty wheat tastes like? Maybe they got it wrong.') For one character, Cypher (Joe Pantoliano), this 'same goddamned goop every day' inspires his treachery, as he trades it in (and promises to betray his shipmates) for the illusion of fine dining and the taste of a steak back in the comforting delusion of the matrix. Yet the scene is carefully structured and shot to emphasize the crew's equality (regardless of race or gender differences), and the very act of their dining together signals a sense of community, including Neo's newfound membership aboard the ship.[8]

Gruel extruded into troughs for the man-animal prisoners in *Battlefield Earth* (2000) (in which humans are an endangered, but not highly prized, species) serves as an explicit vehicle for a lesson in equality. The protagonist Jonnie battles a fellow prisoner in order to end the tyranny of rank and order — and to allow everyone to eat equal shares of the same gruel simultaneously. The survivors hiding from machines in the post-apocalyptic world of *The Terminator* (1984) in 2029 share a meal of gruel as do the remaining inhabitants of New York City, terrorized by the Eurac forces in *2019: After the Fall of New York* (1983). Residents in the post-apocalyptic future of *The Postman* (1997) (resembling a nineteenth century past) eat thin soup in freedom and pasty gruel and white bread as captured prisoners. Gruel even appears as a destabilizing joke in an early scene in *The Island* (2005) — but the scene takes on further meaning when Delta 2 Jordan (Scarlet Johanson) shares her breakfast bacon with Lincoln 6 Echo (Ewan MacGregor) signifying their 'proximity' and emerging human consciousness. The act of sharing food serves as a sign of shared humanity. The more meager and sparse the food, the more poignant these scenes of cooperation and communal meals become.

If food helps to establish community at times, it must be noted that its opposite is also possible: exclusion from the intimate circle surrounding shared food. In a sepia-toned scene in *Gattaca* (1998), the eldest son, Vincent (Ethan Hawke) reveals his estrangement from his family during a dinner scene in which his parents and brother are gathered around the dining room table while he sits alone, absorbed in a book on space travel. Vincent's hunger is deflected away from food; he finds no sustenance of any sort within the family circle. This scene, in some ways reminiscent of those in *Minority Report*, seems initially to offer a nostalgic and anachronistic rendering of the past — except for this detail: the past depicted is no more 'perfect' than the highly technologized future this film explores.

Such exclusions enacted over food also call attention to the individual body. While the sheer physicality of the human (animal) body and what we already are provokes fear in horror films, science fiction explores fears about what we may become — though holding out the promise that such an end is not inevitable. Fear in science fiction, then, is often a fear that we may 'lose contact with our bodies' (Sobchack 1987, p. 39), and that we will become dehumanized not by becoming more animalistic, but by becoming more machine-like. As Laurel Forster (2004) observes, 'the body in science fiction is a deliberately targeted zone' (p. 353), but this holds as true for alien and cyborg bodies as for human ones. Fascination with the 'other' engenders attention to the body, for science fiction, as Roberts (2000) notes, is in 'some central sense about the encounter with difference' (p. 28) — whether as aliens, cyborgs, or even the altered human body (shrunken, enlarged, 'snatched,' and invaded).

Moral articulations of consumption and production

Films from a wide variety of genres include scenes depicting food preferences and practices to help illustrate cultural or individual difference. Difference can be (and frequently is) depicted for laughs, but science fiction offers opportunities to explore more fundamental and profound differences and to pose moral and ethical dilemmas through both the consumption and production of food. Food carries life and death consequences — for the eater and the eaten. Science fiction films, in those few occasions when they address food explicitly, exploit this tension.

Food preferences — or even the ability to eat at all — may be used to distinguish human from alien or human from cyborg, thus further defining what it is to be human. Such distinctions provide humor in *Battlefield Earth* (2000) when the alien commander Terl (John Travolta) confidently determines that raw rats are earthlings' favorite food after the starving protagonist Jonnie temporarily 'escapes' the work camp/prison and devours one.[9] The aliens of *Battlefield Earth*, in contrast, sip glowing chartreuse drinks at a bar and are never witnessed eating. Food also is used to differentiate the cyborg star (Peter Weller) of *Robocop* (1987). Though upon his transformation into the perfect crime fighter, the Robocop bears little resemblance to his human counterparts, food still is called upon to further distinguish him. Thus, when the newly fashioned Robocop is first introduced at the police precinct, one of the first questions asked is: 'How does he eat?' The explanation from his inventor/creator is immediately forthcoming, 'His digestive system is extremely simple. This processor dispenses a rudimentary paste that sustains his organic systems.' As he speaks, we witness a machine extrude a thick brown sludge that plops into a small paper cup. One of the officers dips a finger into the paste, samples it, and declares, 'Tastes like babyfood.' Food, thus, serves to inform viewers that the Robocop is not purely a machine; he retains some human characteristics, however rudimentary. Despite his tremendous strength and power, he is childlike in his innocence. The Robocop is burdened with neither memories nor emotions, and, though he eats, he does not partake in the sensual pleasures of food and the camaraderie it allows.[10] His is not a diet of coffee and donuts shared with fellow officers.

Food in these instances is an added, but not strictly necessary, device that differentiates humans from an 'other.' When appearances are deceptively similar, food particularly serves as a clear biological marker of humanity. Sitting, but not eating, together for meals illuminates the lack of full communion between the cyborg child David (Haley Joel Osment) and his adoptive parents in Steven Spielberg's *Artificial Intelligence: AI* (2001). The film opens with a voiceover describing the environmental and social crises that have reconfigured earth: global warming, cities underwater, people displaced and starved in poorer countries, and strict regulation of pregnancies in richer nations – 'which is why,' the narrative continues, 'robots who were never hungry and who did not consume resources beyond their first manufacture were so essential an economic link in the chainmail of society.' Yet, David is hungry. Though he hungers for love and acceptance, scenes at the family table (over a breakfast and three different dinners) most clearly illustrate his unsatisfied cravings. When the real son returns (miraculously recovered from a coma), David is further estranged. Taunted by his adoptive brother at the dinner table, longing for affection, and desiring above all to become a 'real boy,' he stuffs his mouth with bright green cooked spinach. The family watches in horror as his face slowly begins to melt, his cyborg circuitry disrupted. Hunger blurs distinctions between humans and the other, and the cyborg body is betrayed by food.

Moral lessons surrounding food are worked out not only within the rituals of consumption, but also in relation to food production. Few glimpses of agriculture or other explanations of the sources of food exist in science fiction films, lending those rare exceptions added significance.[11] In two films, agricultural labor is explicitly linked with virtue, evoking a Jeffersonian ideal.[12] *Silent Running* (1971) places an astronaut named Lowell (Bruce Dern) in space tending to three domes containing the last remnants of forests and gardens from a now completely denuded earth. Orders are given to destroy the domes (and thus all plant life) in order to return the spacecraft to commercial use. After hearing the news, Lowell harvests a cantaloupe and tries to persuade his shipmates to disobey the orders and leave the domes intact. Their argument is displaced onto the food each eats: Lowell's cantaloupe (which his shipmates claim 'stinks') and the dried, synthetic 'crap' which the others are content to consume. While one shipmate mocks the cantaloupe as 'real food' 'growing out of the dirt,' another asks, 'What's the big deal? I can't see the difference between that and this [pointing to the synthetic food on the table] anyway.' Lowell responds,

> The difference is that I grew it. That's what the difference is. That I picked it and I fixed it. And it has a taste and it has some color. And it has a smell. And it calls back a time when there were flowers all over the earth, and there were valleys, and there were plains of tall green grass that you could lie down in and that you could go to sleep in. And there

were blue skies. And there were things growing all over the earth — not just in some domed enclosures blasted some millions of miles out into space.

Virtue is made tangible in the sensory experiences of taste, smell, and sight afforded by the literal fruits of one's labor. And morality is tested in the choice between fidelity to human laws or to nature. Technology (the spacecraft itself as well as the three robots, Huey, Dewey, and Louie) ultimately allows for the preservation of nature and the continuation of agricultural labor.

The inventor and time traveler George (Rod Taylor) in *The Time Machine* (1960) stops in the year 802701 to discover a world he describes as 'one vast garden without any sign of weeds or briars. Trees and vines laden with fruit of strange shapes and colors. Nature tamed completely and more bountiful than ever before. At last I'd found a paradise.' But his questions to the Eloi about the source of their food and clothing receive only vague answers:

> George: Doesn't anybody work?
> Eloi Man: No.
> George (pointing to a bowl of fruit): Where did that come from?
> Eloi man: It grows. It always grows.
> George: Yes, I know. But it must be cultivated, planted, and nurtured.

The Eloi's innocence is matched by their passivity, complicating the concepts of virtue and paradise itself. Though the Eloi's peacefulness and beauty clearly are preferred to the brutality and coarseness of the apelike Morlocks, their dependence makes them vulnerable. They become victims of the Morlocks' rapacious appetites for power and food. The Eloi, it turns out, are the crop being cultivated by the Morlocks.

In conversations between Vic and his dog in *A Boy and His Dog*, 'over the hill' represents both the past and the future — a spatial and temporal alternate to the bleak present the two inhabit. Yet, as the following dialogue makes clear, past and future alike are mere fantasies to Vic; his milieu is the present, no matter how dispiriting.

> Dog: Your continued, narrow-minded refusal to believe in over the hill is possibly costing us a better life, you know.
> Vic: Over the hill, my ass.
> Dog: Well, when do we start looking for it again?
> Vic: As soon as I can get my heart started. I know what you mean. Over the hill where the deer and the antelope play and it's warm and clean and we can relax and have fun and grow food right out of the ground. How do you like that pipe-dream?
> Dog: It's called farming.

Vic: Oh, I believe you. And they also have a great crop of clothes and guns and gorgeous chicks. Now tell me how you saw the whole wonderful thing with your baby blues.
Dog: I never said I saw it. I said I heard about it.

In such a future, agriculture exists purely as a (residual) 'urban legend,' a matter of hearsay unsupported by direct observation or experience.[13] In the largely amoral world of the present (devastated by environmental crises and subsequent societal collapse), agricultural production holds no more virtue than any other option. This point is made clear in the final scenes of the film when Vic, in order to save his dog's life, feeds him the woman Vic has followed into the underworld and back out again. The morality of food 'production' and consumption become tangled with ideas of loyalty, betrayal, expedience. Though Vic refuses the meal himself, he has clearly unseated the 'natural' order of things.

When food moves from the periphery (offering insight into characters and their relationships with each other) to the center (becoming the locus of fear) in science fiction films, food represents the whole of a culture's entangled relationship with both nature and technology. Our ignorance of both leaves us vulnerable. Science fiction exploits this vulnerability by exaggerating food's liminality, breaking down the boundaries and taboos along the food chain we imagine to be firmly in place, and challenging our conceptions of what it is to be human. Ignorance of food production can prove deadly, not just distasteful. What merely had been monotonous processed food becomes a source of horror when Thorn in *Soylent Green* learns that the mysterious food he and his fellow citizens have been eating is made of human corpses. In response, Thorn runs through the streets of New York City (famously) shouting, 'It's people. Soylent green is people.' The grim world he inhabited turns into a nightmare with the (unwitting) violation of the ultimate food taboo. Cannibalism is meant to represent the complete breakdown of the social order and an offense against natural law.[14] The delicate balance of nature, culture, and technology that food represents is shattered; they collide and collapse, turning food from sustenance to symbol of our fall from grace.

Aftertaste

Hunger — for food, but also for power, stability, love, knowledge, certainty — fuels many of the actions in post-apocalyptic films. The foods eaten, the rituals of eating, the settings in which eating occurs may all shift shape in response to social, political, technological, or environmental changes. Thus food helps illustrate the competing claims of past and present, nostalgia and progress, memory and desire, familiarity and difference. Food, as necessity, amplifies and sharpens the significance of these many issues and the choices made to satiate our needs and our desires.

For many contemporary social critics, US systems of food production already have entered the realm of nightmarish science fiction. Scientists not only have engineered ways to splice a fish gene into a tomato and a toxic bacterium into a corn plant (and patent their seeds), but such creations have been let loose upon the world. While many farmers may adopt such technologies willingly, others' farm fields have been unwittingly invaded, not from outer space, but by windblown pollens contaminating their crops. Grocery store shelves are lined with foods containing ingredients derived from genetically modified organisms (GMOs), unlabelled and unrecognized by most consumers.[15] While most of the nation's fruits and vegetables come from fields heavily saturated with pesticides in California, processed foods derive most of their flavor, as Eric Schlosser (2001) reveals, from factories in New Jersey. The rural 'heartland' of America, meanwhile, has in large measure been swallowed up by corporate 'factory farms' raising vast fields of monocultural crops and the compressed wastelands of cattle feedlots and hog confinement operations, thick with sewage and stench, leaving its residents alienated and impoverished.[16] Such agricultural practices, far removed from urban population centers and carried out under the banner of efficiency in our names, are for the most part rendered invisible. Our alienation from nature and, thus, from the foods we eat means that, as Raymond Williams (1980) notes, 'we find it very difficult to recognize all the products of our own activities. We recognize some of the products, and call others by-products; but the slag-heap is as real a product as the coal' (p. 83). In this regard, soil erosion, water depletion and pollution, pesticide contamination, and even rising rates of heart disease and obesity should become recognized as products of modern 'conventional' agriculture.[17]

As Elpeth Probyn (2000) has noted, the materiality of eating can help 'draw out alternative ways of thinking about an ethics of existence, ways of living informed by both the rawness of a visceral engagement with the world, and a sense of restraint in the face of excess' (p. 3). While science fiction films rarely wrestle with the ethics of food production, they do with some frequency explore moral aspects of food consumption. Whether motivated by nostalgia for an illusory past or fear arising from an uncertain present, science fiction cinema ultimately argues for moderation in all things. We must eat, but unchecked appetites pose a danger to earth and to its inhabitants. In warning, science fiction films offer a glimpse of the future in which our hunger and rapaciousness threaten to destroy us, eating away at our souls and our bodies alike.

Acknowledgements

The author would like to thank Phaedra Pezzullo for her encouragement and many helpful suggestions from this essay's beginnings (at the 2003 National Communication Association Convention) to its final draft.

Notes

1 These films, spanning a nearly 30-year time period, are #2. *Star Wars* (1977), #4. *E.T.: The Extra-Terrestrial* (1982), #5. *Star Wars: The Phantom Menace* (1999), #7. *The Lord of the Rings: The Return of the King* (2003), and #10. *Jurassic Park* (1993) (p. 229).

2 Kuhn (1999) notes, 'overviews of the genre, for example, very often adopt a historical approach in which science fiction's thematic preoccupations are tracked alongside social events and attitudes prominent at the time the work first appeared' (p. 3). These preoccupations and concerns often take the form of explorations of environmental crises, matched to each era's own set of anxieties. In the 1950s, fears of radioactive fallout spawned mutants: *It Came from Beneath the Sea* (1955), *Them!* (1954), *The Incredible Shrinking Man* (1957), *The Attack of the 50 Foot Woman* (1958). By the 1970s, when nuclear holocaust seemed poised to extinguish all life on earth, films responded with opening shots of mushroom clouds and a world thrown into chaos: *The Omega Man* (1971), *A Boy and His Dog* (1975), *Testament* (1983), *The Aftermath* (1985), *The Lathe of Heaven* (1986), *The Terminator* (1984), *Terminator 2: Judgment Day* (1991). Biological weaponry ravaged cities and citizens in *Twelve Monkeys* (1995), *The Postman* (1997), and *The Last Man* (1999). Widespread pollution forces the creation of the domed city that becomes both refuge and prison in *Logan's Run* (1976) and the spaceship greenhouses containing the last remnants of earth's forests in *Silent Running* (1971). Pollution and overpopulation result in the grim New York cityscape of *Soylent Green* (1973) and the dreary Los Angeles of *Blade Runner* (1982). Toxins causing widespread sterility refigure life in *The Handmaid's Tale* (1990). Greenhouse gases and global climate change altered the worlds found in *Waterworld* (1995), *Artificial Intelligence: AI* (2001), and *The Day After Tomorrow* (2004).

3 Scholarly attention to food in film only recently has begun to flourish. Telotte (1985) argues the persistent images of food and appetite in film noir suggests an underlying critique of society in post-World War II America and an anxiety about consumerism. Boswell (1990) concludes that the abundance of food popular Hollywood films is used to set up a direct contrast; it becomes a sign of 'spiritual famine,' exposing other yearnings that are not so easily filled. 'Hollywood's America,' argues Boswell, 'is forever the land of plenty, and Americans are forever uncomfortably hungry amidst an abundance of food' (1990, p. 21). Dorfman's (1992) exploration of the 'carnal kitchen' in American popular culture examines scenes in which

intimacy and seduction are entangled with food preparation and consumption. Barr (1996) uses food scenes in films to explore ethnicity, specifically the ways in food choices and dining scenes help to relay information about Jewish identity, culture, and assimilation. See also Poole (1999), Ferry (2003), and Bower (2004).

4   Not all science fiction films treat the subject of food, though such occasional absences are surprising. See *Logan's Run* (1976).

5   The role of technology in Americans' food system is visible as well in the technologies used to plant, cultivate, and harvest foods, as well as the extensive infrastructure used to transport and deliver food. See Berry (1997).

6   Forster (2004) raises a similar point, noting 'there are many points of convergence between food and science fiction, making food such a helpful point of illustration for metaphor and exemplification of social concerns' (p. 253). Forster identifies only two points of convergence: the body and technology. A third could be also added: the environment. The three are deeply entangled.

7   I have excluded futuristic science fiction films set in space or on distant planets. My interest lies in what films have to say about this planet and its environmental conditions — with food serving as one important means of measuring the health of natural conditions and technological systems. One exception is my discussion of *Silent Running* (1971), for the plot is driven by the destruction of the earthly environment and the effort to preserve what remains of nature.

8   A detailed analysis of this scene is found in Cimagala (2005).

9   Food scarcity and hunger offer films an opportunity to examine humanity on another level: teasing out what constitutes proper, or at least permissible, food. To assuage their hunger, characters ingest bugs (*Twelve Monkeys*), rats raw (*Battlefield Earth*), rats roasted over open fires (*2019: After the Fall of New York*), and canned dog food (*The Road Warrior*).

10 Tellingly, when the Robocop is injured, his partner nurses him back to health, bringing him three jars of babyfood. Though she willingly assumes the role of nurturing mother caring for a sick child, the Robocop refuses his part. He has regained memory of his past, and this humanizing element causes him to reject the food. Later, he sets the jars atop each other in a small pyramid and shoots them (and the smiling face of a young boy on their label) one by one. His childlike innocence has been lost.

11 The following two science fiction films also make reference to agriculture: *Tank Girl* (1995) (a glimpse of a hydroponic garden helps explain the source of food) and *Sleeper* (1973) (a comic garden of gigantic fruits and vegetables lying on bare ground, attached by hoses to a central source of nutrients).

12 Jefferson (1787/1954) argued, 'Those who labour in the earth are the chosen people of God, if ever he had a chosen people, whose breasts he has made his peculiar deposit for substantial and genuine virtue ... Corruption of morals ... is the mark set on those, who not looking up to heaven, to

their own soil and industry, as does the husbandman, for their subsistence, depend for it on the casualties and caprice of customers. Dependence begets subservience and venality, suffocates the germ of virtue, and prepares fit tools for the designs of ambition' (pp. 164–165).

13   With fewer than two percent of the American population currently engaged in agricultural labor, Vic's understanding of farming may, in fact, parallel that of most contemporary Americans living at a distance from the farm fields and orchards which supply their food (and their cotton, wool, silk, linen, and hemp clothes). The mirror image of 'urban legends' may be the rural stories circulated among farmers about 'city slickers' who look for potatoes growing above ground, etc.

14   A more compelling reading of the logic of cannibalism is found in Fernandez-Armesto (2002), who regards it as a 'ritual practiced not for a meal, but for its meaning' (p. 27). He argues that cannibalism arises out of a desire for self-transformation, in which human flesh – like many other foods – are eaten in the hopes that they will pass on their virtue.

15   For further reading on GMOs, see Teitel and Wilson (1999), Rifkin (1998), and Lappe and Bailey (1998).

16   Recommended sources on the social consequences of contemporary agricultural policy and practices include Berry (1997) and Davidson (1996).

17   On links between food and health (especially obesity), see Nestle (2002), Critser (2003), and Schlosser (2001).

References

Barr, T. (1996) 'Eating Kosher, staying closer', *Journal of Popular Film & Television*, vol. 24, no. 3, pp. 134–144.

Bell, D. & Valentine, G. (1997) *Consuming Geographies: We Are Where We Eat*, London, Routledge.

Berry, W. (1997) *The Unsettling of America: Culture & Agriculture*, San Francisco, CA, Sierra Club Books.

Boswell, P. A. (1990) 'Hungry in the land of plenty: food in Hollywood films', in *Beyond the Stars III: The Material World in American Popular Film*, eds P. Loukides & L. K. Fuller, Bowling Green, OH, Bowling Green State University Popular Press, pp. 7–23.

Bower, A. L. (2004) *Reel Food: Essays on Food and Film*, New York, Routledge.

Campbell, R., Martin, C. R. & Fabos, B. (2006) *Media & Culture 5: An Introduction to Mass Communication*, Boston, MA, Bedford/St Martin's.

Cimagala, B. (2005) 'Why does everything taste like chicken? Food representation in *The Matrix*', unpublished manuscript, April 2005.

Critser, G. (2003) *Fat Land: How Americans Became the Fattest People in the World*, Boston, MA, Houghton Mifflin.

Davidson, O. G. (1996) *Broken Heartland: The Rise of America's Rural Ghetto*, expanded edn, Iowa City, IA, University of Iowa Press.

Dorfman, C. (1992) 'The garden of eating: the carnal kitchen in contemporary American culture', *Feminist Issues*, vol. 12, no. 1, pp. 21–38.
Fernandez-Armesto, F. (2002) *Near a Thousand Tables: A History of Food*, New York, Free Press.
Ferry, J. (2003) *Food in Film: A Culinary Performance of Communication*, New York, Routledge.
Forster, L. (2004) 'Futuristic foodways: the metaphorical meaning of food in science fiction films', in *Reel Food: Essays on Food and Film*, ed. A. L. Bower, New York, Routledge, pp. 251–265.
Hendershot, C. (1999) *Paranoia, the Bomb, and 1950s Science Fiction Films*, Bowling Green, OH, Bowling Green State University Popular Press.
Jameson, F. (1982) 'Progress versus utopia; or, can we imagine the future', *Science-Fiction Studies*, vol. 9, no. 2, pp. 147–158.
Jefferson, T. (1954) *Notes on the State of Virginia,*, ed. William Peden, W. W Norton & Company, New York. (Originally published 1787).
King, G. & Krzywinska, T. (2000) *Science Fiction Cinema: From Outerspace to Cyberspace*, London, Wallflower.
Kuhn, A. (ed.) (1999) *Alien Zone II: The Spaces of Science Fiction*, London, Verso.
Lappe, M. & Bailey, B. (1998) *Against the Grain: Biotechnology and the Corporate Takeover of Your Food*, Monroe, ME, Common Courage Press.
McLuhan, M. (1964) *Understanding Media: The Extensions of Man*, New York, Signet.
Merril, J. (1954) *Beyond the Barriers of Space and Time*, New York, Random House.
Nestle, M. (2002) *Food Politics: How the Food Industry Influences Nutrition and Health*, Berkeley, CA, University of California Press.
Poole, G. (1999) *Reel Meals, Set Meals*, Sydney, NSW, Currency Press.
Probyn, E. (2000) *Carnal Appetites: Food, Sex, Identity*, London, Routledge.
Rifkin, J. (1998) *The Biotech Century: Harvesting the Gene and Remaking the World*, New York, Putnam.
Roberts, A. (2000) *Science Fiction*, London, Routledge.
Schlosser, E. (2001) *Fast Food Nation: The Dark Side of the All-American Meal*, Boston, MA, Houghton Mifflin.
Scholes, R. (1979) *Fabulation and Metafiction*, Urbana, IL, University of Illinois Press.
Seed, D. (1999) *American Science Fiction and the Cold War: Literature and Film*, Chicago, IL, Fitzroy Dearborn.
Sobchack, V. (1987) *Screening Space: The American Science Fiction Film*, 2nd edn, New York, Ungar.
Sobchack, V. (1988) 'Science fiction', in *Handbook of American Film Genres*, ed. W. D. Gehring, Westport, CT, Greenwood Press.
Staiger, J. (1999) 'Future noir: contemporary representations of visionary cities', in *Alien Zone II: The Spaces of Science Fiction*, ed. A. Kuhn, London, Verso.
Suvin, D. (1979) *Metamorphoses of Science Fiction: On the Poetics and History of a Literary Genre*, New Haven, CT, Yale University Press.
Teitel, M. & Wilson, K. A. (1999) *Genetically Engineered Food: Changing the Nature of Nature*, Rochester, VT, Park Street Press.

Telotte, J. P. (1985) A consuming passion: food and film noir', *Georgia Review*, vol. 39 no. 2, pp. 397–410.
Williams, R. (1973) *The City and the Country*, New York, Oxford University Press.
Williams, R. (1980) *Problems of Materialism and Culture: Selected Essays*, London, Verso.

Filmography

2019: After the Fall of New York (1983) Dir. Martin Dolman, Nuova Dania Cinematografica Medusa.
The Aftermath (1985) Dir. Steve Barkett, Nautilus Film Company.
Artificial Intelligence: AI (2001) Dir. Steven Spielberg, DreamWorks Pictures.
The Attack of the 50 Foot Woman (1958) Dir. Nathan Hertz, Allied Artists.
Battlefield Earth: A Saga of the Year 3000 (2000) Dir. Roger Christian, Warner Brothers.
Blade Runner (1982) Dir. Ridley Scott, Warner Brothers.
A Boy and His Dog (1975) Dir. L. Q. Jones, Independent.
Brazil (1985) Dir. Terry Gilliam, Universal.
The Day After Tomorrow (2004) Dir. Roland Emmerich, Fox.
E.T.: The Extra-Terrestrial (1982) Dir. Steven Spielberg, Universal.
The Fifth Element (1997) Dir. Luc Besson, Columbia Tristar.
Gattaca (1998) Dir. Andrew Niccol, Columbia Tristar.
The Handmaid's Tale (1990) Dir. Volker Schlondorff, Virgin-Miramax.
The Incredible Shrinking Man (1957) Dir. Jack Arnold, Universal.
The Island (2005) Dir. Michael Bay, DreamWorks Pictures.
It Came from Beneath the Sea (1955) Dir. Robert Gordon, Columbia.
Jurassic Park (1993) Dir. Steven Spielberg, Universal.
The Last Man (1999) Dir. Harry Ralston, Lion's Gate.
The Lathe of Heaven (1986) Dir. David Loxton and Fred Barzyk, Thirteen/WNET New York.
Logan's Run (1976) Dir. Michael Anderson, MGM.
The Lord of the Rings: The Return of the King (2003) Dir. Peter Jackson, New Line Cinema.
The Matrix (1999) Dir. Andy Wachowski and Larry Wachowski, Warner Brothers.
Minority Report (2003) Dir. Steven Spielberg, DreamWorks Pictures.
The Omega Man (1971) Dir. Boris Sagal, Warner Brothers.
The Postman (1997) Dir. Kevin Costner, Warner Brothers.
The Road Warrior/Mad Max 2 (1982) Dir. George Miller, Warner Brothers.
Robocop (1987) Dir. Paul Verhoeven, Orion.
Silent Running (1971) Dir. Douglas Trumbull, Universal.
Sleeper (1973) Dir. Woody Allen, United Artists.
Soylent Green (1973) Dir. Richard Fleischer, MGM.
Star Wars (1977), Dir. George Lucas, Lucasfilm Ltd. and Twentieth Century Fox.
Star Wars: The Phantom Menace (1999), Dir. George Lucas, Lucasfilm Ltd. and Twentieth Century Fox.

Tank Girl (1995) Dir. Rachel Talalay, MGM.
The Terminator (1984) Dir. James Cameron, Orion.
Terminator 2: Judgment Day (1991) Dir. James Cameron, Le Studio Canal +
Testament (1983) Dir. Lynne Littman, Paramount.
Them! (1954) Dir. Gordon Douglas, Warner Brothers.
THX 1138 (1970) Dir. George Lucas, Warner Brothers.
The Time Machine (1960) Dir. George Pal, MGM.
Twelve Monkeys (1995) Dir. Terry Gilliam, Universal.
Waterworld (1995) Dir. Kevin Reynolds, Universal.

Margaret Werry

TOURISM, RACE AND THE STATE OF NATURE

On the bio-poetics of government

The ethno-historical study of tourism can lend a new focus to the theorization of governmentality, demonstrating the ways in which it rests on the systemic, performative, and affective interpenetration of human and environmental bios ('nature'), built form, economy, and the technologies of the state. This paper examines Rotorua, a tourism centre in New Zealand at the turn of the twentieth century, suggesting that it operated as a laboratory for the forms of political rationality associated with the emerging liberal state, in particular those concerned with race. It analyzes town planning and environmental engineering initiatives, the medical discourses relating to the spa complex constructed by the government, and tourists' accounts of the geo-thermal attractions of the area. In each of these cases, tourism was oriented towards the production of white subjects, and the 'liberalization' of Māori populations, through reflexive work on what Foucault called the 'conduct of conduct.' In each of these cases, bio-political imperatives relied on a repertoire of bio-poetical performances, investing the subject imaginatively in forms of conduct that are viscerally embodied, expressive, creative, improvisatory, and even eroticized. Where the literature of governmentality focuses predominantly on the rationalities, technologies, and generalized institutional loci of bio-politics, attending ethno-historically to tourism attunes us to its affective registers, performative repertoires, its intimate relationship with locality and spatiality, and the symbolic (a)logics through which it achieves its purchase on the immanently political territory of natural life.

They called it the netherworld. Situated in the isolated heart of the North Island of New Zealand, the spa-town and ethnic tourism enclave of Rotorua was at once a wonderland and a hell-hole. The tiny settler township, and the Māori villages of Whakarewarewa and Ōhinemutu that adjoined it, were built atop an active volcanic plateau, where sulphurous steam rose from gaping cracks in the ground, and luminous pools of mineral tinted water or mud bubbled away in residents' back yards. To the late Victorian eye it was a space in which nature was uncannily, violently present in its most elemental form, enfolded with human society in ways that fascinated and beguiled. Even as its mineral waters were enlisted to heal, cure, and pamper, to cook and clean, even as the alternately sublime and pastoral landscapes delighted the eye, Nature's titanic forces seemed to threaten the tourist with annihilation at every footstep. Yet, Rotorua was also a space in which colonial modernity reigned triumphant, channeling the geothermal energy, 'civilizing the wilderness' of native vegetation, and erecting a thriving, profitable enterprise on their remains (Ginders 1890, p. 5).

The Rotorua region was New Zealand's first major nationalized leisure site. Between the 1880s and 1914, the administration of this self-governing, ex-British colony expropriated large tracts of Māori land ('for the good of the people of the world'), built a railway to the region, constructed first a township, then an entire spa complex, and tirelessly promoted them all to the burgeoning middle classes of the colony-becoming-nation, and the cosmopolite public beyond. Historians call the period that saw Rotorua's ascendance as a tourist destination New Zealand's Liberal Era. It was a period of intense state-making, that operated on three inter-related fronts to extend the fabric of government: territorially (wresting land into private title, converting 'unproductive' or marginal tracts — many of them the basis of Māori communal livelihood — into agricultural 'productivity' or other uses, such as tourism); administratively (with state involvement in most arenas of capital accumulation, as for instance, in the founding of the Department of Tourism and Health Resorts that managed the 'government town' of Rotorua and its surrounding attractions); and socially (intervening in citizen's lives with the instatement of nationalized health and education provisions, social welfare programs, and universal suffrage). Māori, comprising 10 percent of the national population at the beginning of this period and experiencing population growth for the first time since colonization, fit uneasily into this liberal trajectory. While experiencing few of its benefits, they were the focus of many of its imperatives: policies and discourses aimed to incorporate Māori into liberal (if proletarian) citizenship, and responded to tenacious Māori resistance to such transformations. It was in this context that tourists to Rotorua came to see not pristine native life but, as the self-appointed ethnographers of colonial modernity, to study the process of transition in what was (inaccurately) presented as a last bastion of Māori society, living — with a certain poetic irony — on the brink of 'natural' annihilation.

This paper approaches Rotorua as it was represented by those turn-of-the-century tourists, as a space both extraordinary and *intra*-ordinary, exotic and paradigmatic: a space that activated both the most arcane reaches of cultural and creative imagination and the most pragmatic reflections on the processes and principles of liberal government. It argues that an examination of such tourist sites — particularly those evolving around and enfolded with Nature as their object — can lend a new focus to the theorization of governmentality. To the New Zealand (NZ) state, Rotorua tourism was an instrument of regional development, an export industry, and a national 'branding' strategy, but — like many similar tourist enclaves in nascent states — it possessed a symbolic significance that dwarfed these economistic rationales. Rotorua's spa complex, its geological wonders, and its Māori inhabitation, together operated as a laboratory of sorts, a crucible for the forms of political rationality associated with the liberal state, in particular those concerned with race. It was a site in which state, societal, market, human and non-human actors met in concentrated and recursive work on what Foucault called the 'conduct of conduct': those disciplinary technologies whereby individuals self-constitute as the sovereign subjects of rule, and which both produce and regulate that entity — the social body — which the state undertakes to manage. Tourism, I want to suggest, is a significant and revealing instance of this *'art of government'* not only because it forges such ramified networks, and focuses their energies on subjectivization at the level of the bodily conduct, but because it reveals, precisely, the pivotal importance of *art* to these processes. From bio-political imperatives tourism evolves a repertoire of bio-poetical performances, investing the subject imaginatively in forms of conduct that are viscerally embodied, expressive, creative, improvisatory, and even eroticized. Where the literature of governmentality focuses predominantly on the rationalities, technologies, and generalized institutional loci of bio-politics, attending ethno-historically to tourism attunes us to its affective registers, performative repertoires, its intimate relationship with locality and spatiality, and the symbolic (a)logics through which it achieves its purchase on the immanently political territory of natural life.

The following moves through three interwoven facets of touristic bio-politics in Rotorua, each bearing on the production of racial subjects through the systemic, performative, and affective interpenetration of human and environmental *bios* ('nature'), built form, economy, and the technologies of the state. The first of these is the sanitary reform of Māori dwellings (and perforce their labor and lifeways) in the native villages of Ōhinemutu and Whakarewarewa. The second is the architecture of and treatments undertaken in the spa complex built by the state at Rotorua, where the thermal features of the land were quite literally applied in the leisured re-formation of predominantly white bodies. The third site is the practice of landscape tourism in the thermal reserves of the area, a ritual of racial formation in which tourists enacted psychotopographic dramas of interaction with an anthropomorphized and racialized Nature.

My method is ethno-historical, attending to ways in which governmental processes were not only devised and implemented, but lived and understood, performatively elaborated and viscerally experienced by their agents. In the first two sections, I read statements of intention, strategy, and diagnosis by policy-makers, commentators, and experts working in and around the leisure industries in New Zealand. Rather than attending to outcomes, I analyze the relationship between the material and metonymic dimensions of the procedures they advocate in planning for the wellbeing of tourist, Māori, and 'national' populations, for what they reveal about the environmental logic of race. In the final section, I examine the testimony of tourists themselves, as they – in that hermeneutic circle common to travel accounts – both interpret their intimate spatial experiences for a dispersed public, and write the scripts for subsequent tourists' spatial practices and interpretations. Tourist attractions and institutions, of course, are inherently ethnographic: they represent culture in its reflexive mode, orienting bodies and space towards an anticipated interpretive gaze through staging meaningful signs, object lessons, and exemplary instances. My account, then, is necessarily compounded: it is an ethnography and a study of ethnographic meaning-making. It is an interpretive analysis of governmental analytics, techniques, and practices, at the same time as it is a reading of governmentality's performance at Rotorua, by which I mean the ways in which it was staged, enacted, and reflected upon by the range of agents – tourists, civil servants, entrepreneurs, citizens, experts – on and through whom it operated.[1]

Sanitizing space, managing difference, reforming bodies

The state investment in Rotorua tourism was fuelled at its outset by an almost textbook agenda of bio-political engineering. In the popular as well as the official imaginary, the development of the spa and town was a national prerogative not only for its fiscal benefit as a touristic 'gold mine' to the colony, but also as the precursor to a fully nationalized public health service.[2] Such a service, it was argued, would fulfill the liberal mandate of productivity, by returning the cripple (a 'burden to society') to the ranks of the nation's 'industrial army,' while rationalized recreation would similarly be a boon to the emerging national bourgeoisie, the 'fagged men of business' who would be restored by their bathing and sightseeing (Tramp 1899, p. 4). This framing of the population at large as an assemblage to be managed through techniques aimed at 'welfare' was entirely congruent with the logic of governmentality identified by Foucault in his 1978 lecture at the Collège de France (Foucault 1978/1991, see also Foucault 1994a,b). The lecture traces the genealogy of the modern conception of government as having its object in the augmentation of security, prosperity, productivity, health, and longevity of a population, pointing to the early modern turn away from the goal of exercising authority over a territory, and towards an ethic of pastoral care (or policing) that assumed and integrated 'the care of the natural life of individuals into its centre' (Agamben 1998, p. 5). The subsequent liberal articulation of governmentality took to government at a distance, concerning itself not with the individual, but with operations that attended to the biological processes of the social body, at level of 'population' (made newly apprehensible, qua population, through technologies of measurement, perception, and surveillance). Animated by what Barry *et al.* (1996) have termed a 'naturalist' conception of the social, liberal governmentality envisaged this assemblage as a norm-governed entity, and aimed to minimize direct intervention in order to allow social equilibria to function undisturbed. Instead, governmentality focused its transformative energies on environment and infrastructure, but in such a way as to penetrate the social body at the level of the subject through technologies of the self: molding the forms of practical expertise, or conduct, through which individuals might enter into relation with 'those things that are wealth,' and shaping the 'desires, aspirations, interests, and beliefs' (Dean 1999, p. 11) that bring the individual to bind his/her identity to the state.

What the governmentalized state framed as benefaction, then, was always also an operation of regulation that aimed to transform individual habitus and dispositions, and through them, social and economic life itself. In the case of Rotorua, the national production of wealth, and the welfare and efficient mobilization of labor throughout the colony were objects taken up not only by the state, but by a range of agents and agencies (Māori and settler reform organizations, commercial tourism entrepreneurs, tourists themselves, health workers, local boosterists, and cultural commentators) throughout which this bio-political drive was dispersed. Detached from totalizing forms of rule, the governmental impetus operated at a distance (in eminently liberal form), through the apparatus of the tourism industry. Significantly, the problem around which this network of agencies constellated – or rather the phenomenon that their constellation transformed into a problem – was the management of ethnic life.

Everywhere in the nation during this era, Māori lifeways came under the fire of state, semi-state, and civic organizations – both Māori and settler – rallying to a reforming cry that championed liberal norms among the indigenous community. Reformers advocated for nuclear family life, rather than the tribal loyalties or extended kin groups that dominated Māori social and economic organization. 'Independence,' (meaning the private ownership and accumulation of capital, rather than the distribution of income amongst the community and communal ownership of tracts of tribal land), was likewise a common catch-cry, while calls for 'temperance' anchored attempts to instill regularity in both labor and consumption practices in a population that resisted the spatio-temporal dictates of waged labor in favor of the fluid demands of tribal festivities and seasonal needs. In so far as the persistence of Māori lifeways presented an obstacle to the ideal, deterritorializing vision of settler capitalism, tourism appeared to offer a laboratory solution: where elsewhere in the nation traditional Māori landholding, communalism, and tribal life were considered an impediment to progress and productivity, in the context of tourism, indices of Māori difference could be rendered productive as spectacle. Yet their very conspicuousness brought them under redoubled pressure to conform to practical rationalities (and racial norms) of liberal citizenship, to act as a model for and index of Māori modernization elsewhere in the nation.

In the Rotorua villages of Ōhinemutu and Whakarewarewa, adjacent to the spa and township, this bio-political imperative coagulated around the issue of spatial practice – particularly as it was conditioned by the built form of the villages – and drew its moral force from a concern for public health. Were the one-roomed Māori dwellings dens of pestilence where stagnant air lurked, and families lived in morally and physically unhygienic proximity with each other? Was the lack of, light, air, circulation indicated by the absence of windows and raised foundations acceptable, or did the houses need to be 'opened up'? It was generally acknowledged that the waste removal services (of both night soil and garbage) were inadequate, but were these problems compounded by the disorganization of Ōhinemutu, in particular, which lacked clear demarcations between private and public property, and hence a clear means for attributing responsibility for cleanliness?[3] Such concerns were not unique to the Rotorua villages, stemming in part from the emerging health service's response to epidemics (of typhoid and influenza, for example) that had taken a disproportionate toll on Māori communities (Lange 1999). As in these other contexts, the discourse worked to detach this perceived lack of hygiene from actual evidence of poverty, framing it instead as the 'natural' product of faulty organization, and indicative of Māori resistance to the vivifying currents of modernity (Osborne 1996). Like the dwellings themselves, Māori collectivities were considered to be sluggish and festering, lacking transparency to the regulatory gaze of government. Housing reform promised to tool such practical technologies as drains, for example, to the production of Māori as liberal-citizen-subjects: they would promote privacy, but suture private units to a broader civic and state infrastructure that penetrated them, enabling both inflow and outflow. As in similar urban planning and public health discourse in the UK, what was at stake was 'not so much a normalization of vital capacities but the regulation of their normativity via the medium of environmental regulation; to free, so to speak, a space for vital normativity through minimum standardization of the environment' (Osborne 1996, p. 116).

What was unique about the political dramaturgy of Rotorua's cleanliness campaign, however, was that it allied tourist aesthetics with governmental surveillance to both rationalize and strategize a more general, nationalized intervention into ethnic space. In the place of the customary expert mechanisms of anthropology, sociology, or medicine this strategy implanted the visualizing apparatus of tourism as the mode of 'knowledge, expertise, and calculation that [might] render human beings thinkable in such a manner as to make them amenable' to the intervention of administrative techniques (Inda 2005, p. 2). Tourism's techniques of observation, like the state's, produced material inscriptions (screeds of travel accounts, guides and photography, rather than white papers or reports) that documented the 'data' of Māori life, its natural laws, customs, and norms, and usefully (for the state) posing such surveillance not as penetration or imposition but as incitement. The two modes of perception converged in the demand that Māori at once preserve the aesthetic character of native life (the population's source of wealth and value to the state, as the lifeblood of ethnic tourism at Rotorua) while transforming its material practice and thus the conditions of its visibility. This, it was felt, might provide the model for nationwide reform. The local Māori Health Officer, together with colleagues from the Young Māori Party (a reform-oriented, pan-tribal, Māori political advocacy group) and the local representative of the government Department of Tourist and Health Resorts (to all intents, the *de facto* mayor of the town), crafted a plan to convert the dwellings of Ōhinemutu into a 'model village,' exemplifying modern, hygienic, 'reasonable' Māori architecture.[4] The homes would have several rooms (separating the functions of domestic life, as well as the members of the − implicitly nuclear − family), several windows, raised foundations, running water, and drains, but their exteriors would retain the design features that made Māori *whare* so 'picturesque' to the tourist eye, and pleasing to their inhabitants. As desiring subjects − subjects desiring the growth, prosperity, and mobility promised by a share in the tourism industry, and the security promised by hygienic environments − it was presumed that Māori would naturally undertake this reorganization of the ethos and practical ground of ethnic life.

A similar impulse was at play in the environmental operations undertaken by the state on the grounds of the new government Sanatorium, but in ways that expose the asymmetries of liberalism's political rationality played out across the terrain of ethnic difference. Here, the state's engineers also undertook the spatio-cultural conquest of a nature that was cast as unnatural. To the colonial eye, the area appeared a 'veritable wilderness' of 'barren plains and dry brown hills' (Weekly Press, 16 August 1889, p. 21) 'through which few dared wander, lest the crust beneath their feet should break and bring them to an awful doom' (Bullock 1897, p. 3). As in the Māori villages, the mandate of security and hygiene was pursued through both aesthetic and practical technologies that were seen to be making the environment 'safe' for settlers and tourists, a refuge not only from an alien environment but also from the ordeals of industrial modernity. What resulted in the Sanatorium Reserve was an orderly combination of arbors, drives, and croquet lawns, tea pavilions, flower beds, and artificial ponds — the archetypal requisites of late Victorian bourgeois 'rational recreation' — while the spa facility itself was a vast edifice constructed in English half-timbered style, that bespoke the symmetry, solidity, order of 'Home' (i.e. Great Britain). It, like the new Māori homes, was 'clean and inviting,' airy, well ventilated and well lit.[5] And to the physical culture of disciplined bodies in healthful spaces was matched the artistic culture of moral and aesthetic discipline, as statuary with biblical and classical themes peppered the interior, and native plants were reinstated in the beds by the walks, isolated, captioned, and regularly pruned. In so far as native bodies took a place in this environment, it was in a similarly deracinated form: the tea kiosk, for example, built in 1902 near the tennis-court and bowling green, featured Māori ornamentation in its architecture, suggested Māori social tradition in its name (Te Runanga, or 'the meeting'), and was staffed by 'prettily dressed Native girls acting as attendants' [*Appendices to the Journals of the House of Representatives (AJHR)* H.2, 1903, p. vii].

Ethically and ethnically 'incomplete' subjects

The core systematicity incarnated in such tourist spaces articulates environment, economy, built form, technology, the body politic and the bodies of political subjects, producing a complex of alignments and translations, linkages and relays between them in the work of leisure and pleasure. At Rotorua, the character of these networks as at once metaphorical and material, molecular and molar, corporeally intimate and administratively actionable was made most explicit in the technologies implemented in the spa itself, where the scientific (and often bizarrely theatrical) operations of balneology were brought to bear upon the invalid and tourist body alike. While governmental procedures managed, re-formed, and valorized the natural life of Māoridom outside the spa, inside it, they worked to materialize the conduct of whiteness that embodied hygienic liberal subject- and state-hood. According to Toby Miller and George Yúdice, such cultural policy produces a radical indeterminacy in its political subjects: 'it finds, serves, and nurtures a sense of belonging, through educational and other cultural regimens that are predicated on an insufficiency of the individual against the benevolent historical backdrop of the sovereign state' (2002, p. 17). The ethical incompleteness of the subject of governmentality to which Miller and Yúdice allude — the sense that it had to be repaired, cultivated, cultured by the state — was also an ethnic incompleteness, an implicitly white citizenship that was the focus of continuous reformative intervention. Where a racially determined body politic was nominated in the aesthetics of the spa architecture, it was also the referent for the bodies to be treated in the institution, subjected to and extended by technologies aimed at regulating flow, system efficiency, and productivity.

The appointment of Dr Wohlmann in 1901, as director of the spa marked the government's commitment to the medical philosophy of balneology, a state-of-the-art therapeutic science that involved a highly managed regime of bathing, rest, exercise, the application and consumption of naturally occurring mineral waters, and the stimulation of the body by natural means (massage, alterations in temperature and light levels) as well as technological ones, principally electro-therapy. This complex system in which the Nature was brought to act upon the body, also bore the much more evangelical and reformist imprint of the hydropathy and physical culture movements (Cayleff 1987). All three were premised on a similar naturalist discourse, taking bathing as part of a holistic health regimen that addressed the ills of urban modernity (gout, neuralgia, and so on), and aimed to restore a natural state of balance, equilibrium and purity through its treatments. In the spa, government technicians applied the most advanced developments in balneological technology to this end, investing heavily in, for example, the 'mechanico-therapeutic' exercise equipment developed by Dr Zander of Stockholm (that mathematically regulated movement to individual requirements, orchestrating active and passive movements of 'every joint in the body'), and ingenious electrical apparates that applied currents to stimulate bodily processes (*AJHR* 1891, H.6, vol. III, p. 2). Balneology was structured by discourses of systemic efficiency, theorizing medical complaints of all sorts as the result of unnatural blockages of the flow of products – waste products or productive materials – within the hermetic system of the body. Its treatments claimed to make the body into a more efficient machine, expelling waste products more speedily, increasing circulation, invigorating 'sluggish organs,' aiding the absorption of 'abnormal' products, and stimulating the nerve endings of the skin (Ginders 1890, p. 5).

The construal of health as a state of activity, vigor, efficiency and cleanliness – the received attributes of whiteness – meant that its production through leisure practices was subtly mandated as a moral and political prerogative. When hyperbolic publicists quipped about the waters of Rotorua acting on 'all the ills to which flesh is heir,' their meaning was intentionally double, conjoining medical to moral intervention through the metonymical association of the physical body with the body politic (Ginders 1890, p. 1). Social hygeine, cultural purity, and economic vitality were discursively collapsed in claims such as those of Dr W.B. Hunter that after 'violations of the code of health (unwitting or otherwise)' that resulted in an imbalanced corporeal system, hydropathy depended on 'the inherent capacity of the economy for self-rectification, opportunity allowed it, and prefers this restoration by Nature herself, to any that the highest and most recondite art can supply.'[6] Recalling at once the language of eugenics and that of *laissez-faire* capitalism, the liberal ethos grounded its practical reason in a Nature from which it rigorously dissociated itself, and yet into which it was constantly interposed. When politician Peter Buck, or Te Rangihīroa (the Māori Health Officer for the Rotorua region between 1905 and 1909 and later Member of Parliament) accused parliamentarians of thinking of Māori 'merely as an appendage and a useless sort of appendage like a vermiform appendix,' his comment resonated with the equation drawn by the spa promoters between body, economy, race and hygiene, and pointed precisely to the racial limits to the quasi-organic integrity of the state imagined by Rotorua's touristic laboratory (Sorrenson 1986, p. 26). Māori were not only vestigially superfluous to the flows of the political and cultural economy, they were a potentially dangerous repository for infectious social waste.

Balneology was but one of a battery of 'intellectual and practical techniques and inventions' at Rotorua, 'via which civil society [was] brought into being as both distinct from political intervention and yet potentially alignable with political aspirations' (Barry et al. 1996, p. 9). In climatology, balneology's companion science, governmental agencies found a broader bio-political rationale for tourism itself. As a procedure for the production of environmental knowledge, climatology also motivated voluntary self-regulation through a species of systems-thinking that was particularly explicit in its correlation of leisure practice, liberal economy, and the moral legitimacy of racial subjects. The object of climatological practice, to which Wohlmann and his Tourist Department employers adhered, was to determine the best spatial venues for therapeutic relocation through an exhaustive analysis of everything from altitude and topographic features, to the composition of the air. Its diagnostics produced a kind of Herderian ethno-cartography which speculated on the prospects for white acclimatization, and on the environmentally determined capacities of indigenous populations (Livingstone 1994, Moore 1890). As climatologists Sir Hermann and F. Parkes Weber attested, 'the best climate for one race is not necessarily the best climate for another race' (1907, p. 299). In a liberal twist on the Herderian rule, however, it was the practice of mobility that was ultimately thought to be most closely allied with a sense of racial and moral viability on the part of the subject: 'Change within and without is an invariable rule of nature for the healthy organism, without which it rapidly becomes effete' (Wohlmann 1907, p. 4, see also Herbert 1921). Not just territorial occupation and development, but also labor and leisure mobility were mandated as mutually reinforcing praxes, tending towards both productivity and efficiency, and demanding a consistent attentiveness to environment.

The regime of practices elaborated at Rotorua points to governmentality's signature procedure: its continual problematization of the natural, its thoroughgoing transformation of the conduct of 'natural life,' and its instrumental reinstatement of this transformed 'nature,' framed a source of wealth and value to the state, yet independent of its operations. When liberal governmentality constitutes natural life (aka the social) as an entity outside the domain of the political (and thus independent of, and impermeable to the intervention it, in fact, performs), its doing so both belies and enables the flourishing networks being formed between technologies (architectural, medical, administrative), environment, economy, and population, the political and physical body. The process is similar to that characterized by Bruno Latour as the 'modern Constitution' whereby political thought cleaves Society and Nature, proliferating hybrids and networks between humans and non-humans — Society and Nature — even as it insists on discursively 'purifying' Nature of social influence, and Society of natural objects, effects, and phenomena (Latour 1991, 2004). The mediation of Nature and Society is the preserve of designated technicians (scientists, for example) and apparatuses of translation (laboratories) that produce facts and truths based on claims relating to inaccessible Nature. 'The critical power of the moderns,' Latour argues, 'lies in this double language: they can mobilize Nature at the heart of social relationships, even as they leave Nature infinitely remote from human beings; they are free to make and unmake their society, even as they render its laws ineluctable, necessary and absolute' (1991, p. 37). The centrality of Rotorua to the colonial nationalist imagination in the early part of the twentieth century might in part be accounted for by the fact that, in its analogic character, it allied these parallel liberal and modernist processes: while subjecting social formations to extensive technological intervention in the name of their 'natural' integrity, and while putting natural spaces (such as environments) to thoroughly social transformations in the name of their sociable and productive potential, touristic practice managed not only to retain the distinction between nature and society, the political and the social, but to obscure the fundamentally political character of their dissociation.

Psychotopographics and statehood

What interests me most here, however, are the political and practical rationalities that orchestrate the work of separation, and that in describing the organization of specific *forms* of the natural-social, adjudicate their viability with respect to political outcomes. A particularly neglected dimension of governmentality studies — even as that neglect is widely acknowledged — is the pivotal importance of race in these differentiations of bio-politics. If the racial, and particularly the colonial, Other has been most consistently identified with natural states or states of nature, it has also paradoxically been the focus of the most vigorous, even necro-political, incursions in the name of the security and prosperity of population (Inda 2005, Scott 2005). The production of Māori liberal subjects at Rotorua (both in direct bio-political intervention such as housing reform, and via the management of the 'native' environment with which they were identified), proceeded by way of moral and aesthetic delegitimation of their natural state, and its reconstruction as a second nature, marked by 'a domesticated nonconflictual "traditional" form of sociality and (inter)subjectivity' that was both privatized and mobile (Povinelli 2002, p. 6). It is important to note, however, that the bio-political program operated through its linkage to a bio-poetical program that performed this work of discrimination, as tourists themselves calibrated the limits to liberal toleration of other natures. Their moral and aesthetic discriminations, and their cultivation of affects of repugnance as well as repulsed fascination, flourished not just in ethnic tourism but in landscape tourism, as they trained their gaze on a Nature that was – to the Anglo eye – inherently unnatural. This unnatural nature imperiled or prohibited social life and necessitated technological management: ghosting the organic metaphor of society that presided over bio-political operations, the thermal landscape was imaged as a diseased body, potentially contaminating, noxious, violent and destructive in its processes. Yet it was actively preserved by the state and made available for profound, even pleasurable, imaginative investment, as the environmental ground on, in, and through which the racial normativity of liberal subjecthood might be produced.

At the government spa spatial discipline was clearly linked to racial prerogative, through the management and display of the native and the natural. The thermal phenomena that peppered the grounds – sulphurous fumeroles, bubbling hot springs, and boiling mud pools – were domesticated by the state's environmental engineers, framed by neatly bordered gravel paths, or channeled by mechanical subvention for the use in spa techniques.[7] However, in the neighboring untamed Māori thermal reserve of Whakarewarewa, the fabric of quotidian space opened to proscribed sensations, and affective experiences of visceral intensity. In all the guide, publicity, and travel literature, the spatial charge of the volcanic landscape was metaphorically linked to ideas about infection, bodily corruption, and the containment of violent natural forces. Ranged against the hegemony of Western bourgeois anxieties about waste management, body boundaries, and systemic equilibrium at the Rotorua spa, at Whakarewarewa a Rabellaisian 'wild and grotesque disorder' ruled (Elkington 1906, p. 91). In this havoc of personified geography, tourists imagined bodies that could not contain their unruly passions, could not manage their boundaries: the unleashed, animate presence of nature here represented an image of 'undifferentiated, unorganized, uncontrollable relations,' a travesty of the exclusionary boundaries of civilized order (Douglas 1966, p. 369). From the magnificent ejaculation of the Waimangu geyser, to the tiniest of gaseous emissions, descriptions of the thermal reserve were rife with dischargings, bubblings and stinkings, quiverings and palpitations, orifices and protuberances. Even the hot mud pool was described as a 'boiling filthy sore upon the earth,' 'struggling in an attempt to break its bounds and cover the earth with its filth' (Mansfield 1907/1978, p. 65). The common characterization of the space as the border of the 'nether regions' with the daylight world clearly had both a biblical and a bodily referent: the corporeal abject was never far from the touristic imagination.

In the excessive environment of Whakarewarewa, the disembodied, panoramic gaze that characterized the rhetoric of exploration and landscape appreciation gave way to a subject immersed in an environment that was experienced as profoundly alienating, profoundly inhospitable, full of potential perils and the threat of physical injury, and environment that willfully rejected their attempts at what Mary Louise Pratt (1992) has called the 'master of all I survey' position. The ears were 'suddenly assailed by fierce bubblings and sputterings,' hissing and hammering, while the feet battled the scorching silica and pumice underfoot, and eyes were blinded by clouds of steam (Dolman 1900, p. 126). The literary mechanisms of the accounts and guides produced the environmental experience as a participatory drama of racial encounter mediated by space, which, in its perceived excess, formed the basis for a sensuous and affective aversion to the phenomena of Māori life with which it was identified. This spatial identification was nearly uniform in the literature, enshrined in the name ('Māoriland') given to the area by tourist touts and publicists: in their foreignness to the Anglo-colonial eye, it was a 'natural transition' from Māori to geysers and other peculiar spectacles and sensations of the area. As the tourist body and this (un)natural body of the land and the Other converged, difference was intimately, physically sensed, and the work of moral and aesthetic delegitimation embodied. One tourist, for example, described her arrival by train in the area thus: 'besieged by a crowd of Māori children offering little baskets of hand-woven flax for sale. Such funny mites they were, in all shades of brown and pale yellow ... and creamy-tinted maidens with fuzzy masses of bronzy hair coquettishly tied at the neck ... But,' the writer goes on, 'insidiously an odour of extreme nastiness was creeping upon us, and with one accord we drew in our heads and exchanged eloquent glances' (Lowth 1906, p. 11). Only much later in the narrative is the reader informed that the odor is that of the sulphurous gases pervading the thermal area, rather than that of the Māori vendors. Again and again in this literature, spatial repulsion or even fear intrude on racial fascination, while disgust, aversion, and withdrawal are rehearsed incessantly, alongside a profound desire to repeat the contact.[8]

This bio-poetic spatial process might be described, after Karen Shimakawa, as one of 'national abjection,' the constitutive movement whereby 'the (racial) abject must continually be made present and jettisoned' to produce the citizen-subject and national body (2002, p. 160). Affects such as repugnance or fear test the moral obligation demanded by liberal citizenship (Povinelli 2002). But they also assay the constitution of the political subject itself, reminding of the fragile boundaries to that self-hood, and the inhuman materials that lie beyond. Whakarewarewa was a spatial frontier that staged a racial one, a definitional margin on which participatory performances were enacted to produce (raced) settler self-hood through facing down its annihilation. The 'tremulous pleasure' that tourists reported gaining from this uncanny spectacle (symptomatically described as 'repulsive, yet alluring') was partly that of allayed self-immolation (Dolman 1900, p. 125). Tourist habitus – the tourist's racialized sense of being spatially, perceptually, behaviorally 'at home' – demanded this continual test of its own limits. These could be small spatial experiments: daring to step on precariously thin, hollow sounding crust of the earth off the edge of the path, poking a stick into a cliff of sinter to create a steaming vent, leaping to one side as a blow hole explodes at one's feet. Or they could be profoundly affective psychotopographic dramas. The savage landscape coalesced around a series of nodes to which tourists were drawn in a state of heightened perceptual attention, guided by the 'scripts' provided by guiding and account literature.[9] These scripts described encounters with these spatial nodes as a sublime loss and recovery of self-presence: curiosity, sensual attraction, and 'spellbound' fascination proceeded through the loss of consciousness in spectatorial absorption; the narrator projects a loss of self-possession if s/he were to be brought into the presence of the unpresentable; sudden shock, repulsion and retreat follow, culminating in the renewed desire to return to the site, a repetition compulsion that was the ideal disposition melding the commercial imperatives of tourism with the psychic rewards of self-jeopardy.

> This cauldron is a most interesting object, exercising over some folks a fascination which grows with every visit. It is a natural spring of translucent water, boiling hot, but soft as silk ... its depth is practically measureless. You hang over its lip and gaze down, and down, into depths where purple shadows lurk ... and wonder how long you would be getting to Gehenna if you lost your balance. Then you start back with a spasm of fear, as your eyes are suddenly blinded by a hot puff from out the mist which the changing breeze has rolled your way. And then, perhaps, you leave somewhat hurriedly; but you will return again, and yet again, if you stay any time in Rotorua. (Bullock 1897, p.7)

Meshing such disturbing intimations with 'imperialist nostalgia' or the 'dying race' truisms that prevailed in assimilationist rhetoric (Rosaldo 1993), some tourists confessed to a 'feeling of relief' that the 'hot springs, mud geysers, volcanoes and *other things of like nature* were fast disappearing. Though we would not have missed them yet they were much too uncanny to be enjoyable.'[10]

Bio-poetics: making subjects, space, and states

In considering landscape tourism as a fundamental component of a bio-political program, this argument develops several propositions about the linkages between environment, tourism practice, governmentality, liberal subjectivity, and race — linkages that are unthinkable without attention to the bio-poetic dimensions of the bio-political.

The first of those relates to the performative and aesthetic character of the modes of conduct cultivated in tourism. That landscape tourism practice constitutes a practical rationality seems clear: it is a form of expertise that functions as a 'grid for the perception and evaluation of things,' that 'crystallize[s] into institutions' and 'inform[s] individual behavior' (Foucault 1980/1991, p. 81). Guide books acted, to all intents and purposes, as manuals of conduct, training in regimes of perception, modes of environmental and racial knowledge, and aesthetic discrimination, strict protocols and disciplines of engagement with space. As much as the medical program of balneology, or the administrative sciences of public health and city planning, tourism practice comprised 'an ensemble of arts and skills entailing the linking of thoughts, affects, forces, artifacts, and techniques that do not simply manufacture and manipulate, but which, more fundamentally order being, frame it, produce it, make it thinkable as a certain mode of existence that must be addressed in a particular way' (Rose 1998, p. 54). While the discourses and institutional apparates of tourism were a crucial aspect of this ensemble, its essence was in its enaction: tourism conduct was a repertoire of performance, an embodied and 'non-archival system of transfer,' that bodied forth an environmental disposition through 'restored behaviors' of strolling, gazing, bathing, inspecting, describing, and so on (Taylor 2003, p. xviii). But it was also performative in the Austinian sense that it produced the environmental effects, the racial and political reason, the Nature it named.

Understanding such practical rationalities as performative, rather than exclusively technical or expert systems, makes it possible to see their proximity to the technologies of the self which, according to Foucault, 'permit individuals to effect by their own means or with the help of others a certain number of operations on their own bodies and souls, thoughts, conduct, and way of being, so as to transform themselves in order to attain a certain state of happiness, purity, wisdom, perfection, or immortality' (Foucault 1988, quoted in Bennett 2003, p. 59) In other words, leisure performance practices not only order the world, but order the subject, producing the 'well tempered,' self-governing citizens of liberal modernity (Miller 1993). And they do so through primarily aesthetic procedures. Theorists such as Ian Hunter (1992) propose that aesthetics is at core concerned with subjectification, providing the materials for a continual ethical problematization of conduct and events that ultimately brings the self into being as the subject of an aesthetic experience. Landscape tourism might be understood as a vernacular, even bowdlerized, version of the process Hunter describes in relation to early nineteenth century philosophers of art, one concerned with the formation of society not as the 'organic expression of human self-actualization', but as the ethical presencing, in the subject, of the distinction between human and non-human, society and nature, the moral and the repugnant, a presencing that could only be accomplished through the persistent problematization of those boundaries (1992, p. 362).

The second of these propositions relates to the political rationalities produced in and through environment itself, as governmental modernity invests in 'the optimalization of its capabilities, the extortion of its forces ... its integration into systems of efficient and economic controls' (Foucault 1978, p. 139). While governmental analysis attends to the material milieux through and in which government occurs (Inda 2005, p. 11), it has also tended (in its emphasis on state-level systematicity, and the governmental aspects of media) to frame governmentality as an abstract and ordering imposition on those environments. The kind of historical ethnography of tourist sites and practices that I have undertaken here, however, suggests the improvisatory, performative nature of that engagement, framing governmentality as responsive to and symbiotic with locality and emplacement. Landscape, by definition, refers to a cultural elaboration upon space, not to space as a given (Carter 1988). Landscaping produces space, materially (as in the spa grounds) as well as discursively (as at Whakarewarewa), and tourism – despite its emphasis on the originality or authenticity of the natural – focuses our attention on the techniques through which that nature is actively 'worked up' (Lefebvre 1991). Tourist conduct – programs of nature worship that had been all modernity in formation, yet were ever alive to new materials – was integral to the interweaving of aesthetic and material, symbolic and spatial processes at Rotorua, its performance mediating between human and non-human agents, natural space and natural life. Governmental practices, then, produce the spaces of the state as much as they produce its subjects, and they do so under cover of the same naturalism that enables their transformations to take place 'at arms length' (Rose 1996, p. 40).

The third and final proposition concerns the centrality of affect to the political, and especially the racial rationalities of liberal governmentality. Governmental analysis's past neglect of questions of race, I would suggest, derives at least in part from its orientation around the paradigm of rationality. Analysts both presume and select for a level of systematicity in the governmental phenomena they observe, examining orderly, objective, inferential (if not always transparent) procedures of knowledge production and the methodical execution of governmental projects. While the classifications of race thinking can be seen to conform to rational procedures (however spurious the material grounds for those might be), the production of subjects who act and self-constitute on the basis of them requires a level of imaginative investment that operates well in excess of reason. In the case of late colonial New Zealand, liberal pluralism's establishment of a tacit racial norm required first an act of racial discrimination — the imposition of a local and specific rule of difference that established governmentality's targets. It aimed on the one hand to endow self-interested Māori subjects with 'a progressive desire for industry, regularity, and individual accomplishment', and on the other hand to instill in white subjects a vigilant, hygienic self-governance on the basis of which the settler economy would flourish, and in which the practice of rational recreation played a major part (Scott 2005, p. 31). If Māori were expected to follow the rational dictates of desire and self-interest, white tourists were to be goaded not by reason, but by the symbolic alogics of tourist poetics, the corporeal intensities — disgust, repugnance, pleasure — generated in the imaginative transaction between bodies and environment, social subjects and natural objects. These intensities expose the fundamentally irrational basis of the racial dimensions of political reason, its reliance on the 'fluctuating testimony of the senses or the deceptive judgment of the imagination as it botches things together' (Descartes, quoted in Lloyd 2005, p. 298).

For a brief two decades, at the height of New Zealand's moment of liberal state-formation, Rotorua — a small, isolated, marginal, anomalous, recent, and sparsely populated settlement — reigned as the emblem of the nation, an exemplary space or a national brand of sorts, instantly recognizable across the British Empire as the heart of the young dominion. I venture here that Rotorua owed this status to the density of the governmental apparatus that was elaborated there: it was a laboratory of liberal statehood — not a state of exception to the national norm, but a space of intensification, cross-semination, and innovation. Tourism in Rotorua performed the identity work of liberal statehood, essentially producing citizen-subjects through spatial dramas in which tourists were viscerally, affectively, corporeally invested (and invested with political subjectivity), and creatively allying 'interests, powers, objects, institutions and persons' in the pursuit of national welfare and prosperity (Barry *et al.* 1996, p. 11). The interlocking practices of ethnic tourism, health and nature tourism — normally analyzed as discrete fields — constituted a powerful technology for cultural policy to 'think' the relationship between race, economy, habitus, and territory, and citizens-in-the-making to perform it.

Notes

1   Notably absent is the perspective of local Māori, whose contestations and accommodations of governmental procedures I deal with elsewhere (Werry 2001).

2   A.S. Wohlmann to T.E. Donne, 11 December 1902, TO1/1901/5/10, NZ Archives. Such state benevolence was unevenly distributed across ethnic lines: institutionalized racism and cultural insensitivity (especially around issues of bodily *tapu*), policy discriminations, and geographical marginalization meant that Māori had little real access to these services (Lange 1999).

3   Elsewhere, I trace the emergence of this discourse in detail, through a reading of health education, urban reform, national census, Young Māori Party literature, and parliamentary debates (Werry 2001).

4   'By forming the roads, introducing proper drainage systems and reasonable sanitary conveniences, and by insisting on a reasonable form of Māori architecture in the villages ... the attraction of these villages to the tourists can be enormously increased.' Engineer in charge to superintendent, 19 September 1908, TO01-0044, NZ Archives. Sir Peter Buck (Te Rangi Hīroa) and Frederick Bennett (both Māori reformers) drafted plans for the 'ideal whare' (or Māori house) combining Māori architectural aesthetics with European prerogatives of structure and hygiene, and submitted them to the Young Māori Party conference (Te Aute College Students Association 1906, Young Māori Party 1909).

5   A.S. Wohlmann to Hon. J.G. Ward, Minister DTHR, 5 February 1903, TO1/1901/5/10, NZ Archives; A.S. Wohlmann, enclosure with T.E. Donne to Hon. R.J. Seddon, Premier, 14 February 1903, TO1/1901/5/10, NZ Archives.

6   'Hydropathy' by Dr W.B. Hunter reproduced in Muir (1900, n.p.).

7   One of the early spa directors, Camille Malfroy, in fact manufactured thermal attractions, including three geysers that he, tellingly, named 'Victoria' 'Nelly' and 'May,' and put into action on the Queen's birthday (*AJHR* 1891, C. 1, vol. I, p. 6., Malfroy 1892).

8   Anxieties also revolved around a perceived lack of spatial discipline, adhering even more closely to a racial analogy, and bespeaking alarm at the barely controlled violence of the natural. Where tourists personified thermal features as 'raging like all-possessed ... their centres in a wild tumult, and their hoarse mutterings suggestive only of a scrummage of demons,' their descriptions corresponded uncannily in structure, language and imagery to representations of Māori performances of the haka, or war chant (Elkington 1906, p. 91).

9   For discussion of the nature of the hermeneutic circle created by tour guides, their quality of being both prescriptive and descriptive of actual touristic performance, see Rojek (1994) and Werry (2001).

10 C.S. Phillips (née Brayton), 'Journal 1896–25,' MS Papers 961, ATL.

References

Agamben, G. (1998) *Homo Sacer: Sovereign Power and Bare Life*, trans. D. Heller-Roazen, Palo Alto, CA, Stanford University Press.

Barry, A., Osborne, T. & Rose, N. (1996) 'Introduction', in *Foucault and Political Reason: Liberalism, Neo-liberalism and Rationalities of Government*, eds A. Barry, T. Osborne & N. Rose, Chicago, IL, University of Chicago Press, pp. 1–18.

Bennett, T. (2003) 'Culture and governmentality', in *Foucault, Cultural Studies, and Governmentality*, eds J. Z. Bratich, J. Packer & C. McCarthy, Albany, NY, State University of New York Press, pp. 47–66.

Bullock, M. (1897) *The World's Sanatorium: A Sketch of Rotorua and its Environs*, Wellington, John Mackay, Government Printer.

Carter, P. (1988) *The Road to Botany Bay: An Essay in Spatial History*, London, Faber.

Cayleff, S. E. (1987) *Wash and Be Healed: The Water-cure Movement and Women's Health*, Philadelphia, PA, Temple University Press.

Dean, M. (1999) *Governmentality: Power and Rule in Modern Society*, London, Sage Publications.

Dolman, F. (1900) 'An infernal region', *English Illustrated Magazine*, May, pp. 122–127.

Douglas, M. (1966) *Purity and Danger: An Analysis of Concepts of Pollution and Taboo*, London, Kegan Paul.

Elkington, E. W. (1906) *Adrift in New Zealand*, London, John Murray.

Foucault, M. (1978) *The History of Sexuality. Volume 1: An Introduction*, trans. R. Hurley, New York, Vintage Books.

Foucault, M. (1988) 'Technologies of the self', in *Technologies of the Self: A Seminar with Michel Foucault*, eds L. H. Martin, H. Gutman & P. H. Hutton, London, Tavistock.

Foucault, M. (1991) 'Governmentality', in *The Foucault Effect: Studies in Governmentality*, eds G. Burchell, C. Gordon & P. Miller, Chicago, IL, University of Chicago Press, pp. 87–104. (Originally published 1978).

Foucault, M. (1991) 'Questions of method', in *The Foucault Effect: Studies in Governmentality*, eds G. Burchell, C. Gordon & P. Miller, Chicago, IL, University of Chicago Press, pp. 73–86. (Originally published 1980).

Foucault, M. (1994a) 'The Subject and Power', in *Power*, ed. J. Faubion, New York, The New Press, pp. 326–348.

Foucault, M. (1994b) 'The political technology of individuals', in *Power*, ed. J. Faubion, New York, The New Press, pp. 403–417.

Ginders, A. (1890) *The Thermal-Springs District of New Zealand and the Government Sanatorium at Rotorua*, Wellington, Government Printer.

Herbert, A. S. (1921) *The Hot Springs of New Zealand*, London, H.K. Lewis & Co. Ltd.

Hunter, I. (1992) 'Aesthetics and cultural studies', in *Cultural Studies*, eds L. Grossberg, C. Nelson & P. Treichler, London, Routledge, pp. 347–372.

Inda, J. X. (2005) 'Analytics of the modern: an introduction', in *Anthropologies of Modernity: Foucault, Governmentality, and Life Politics*, ed. J. X. Inda, Malden, MA, Blackwell, pp. 1–22.

Lange, R. (1999) *May the People Live: A History of Māori Health Development 1900–1920*, Auckland, Auckland University Press.

Latour, B. (1991) *We Have Never Been Modern*, trans. C. Porter, Hemel Hempstead, Harvester Wheatsheaf.
Latour, B. (2004) *Politics of Nature: How to Bring the Sciences into Democracy*, trans. C. Porter, Cambridge, MA, Harvard University Press.
Lefebvre, H. (1991) *The Production of Space*, trans. D. Nicholson-Smith, Oxford, Blackwell.
Livingstone, D. N. (1994) 'Climate's moral economy: science, race and place in post-Darwinian British and American geography', in *Geography and Empire*, eds A. Godlewska & N. Smith, Oxford, Blackwell, pp. 132–154.
Lloyd, G. (2005) 'Reason', in *New Keywords: A Revised Vocabulary of Culture and Society*, eds T. Bennett, L. Grossberg & M. Morris, Malden, MA, Blackwell.
Lowth, A. (1906) *Emerald Hours in New Zealand*, Christchurch, Witcombe and Tombs Ltd.
Malfroy, C. (1892) *Geyser-action at Rotorua, N.Z*, Wellington, Government Printing Office.
Mansfield, K. (1978) *The Urewera Notebook*, ed. I. A. Gordon, Oxford, Oxford University Press. (Originally published 1907).
Miller, T. (1993) *The Well-tempered Self: Citizenship, Culture, and the Postmodern Subject*, Baltimore, MD, Johns Hopkins University Press.
Miller, T. & Yúdice, G. (2002) *Cultural Policy*, London, Sage.
Moore, J. M. (1890) *New Zealand for the Emigrant, Invalid, and Tourist*, London, Sampson Low, Marston, Searle & Rivington.
Muir, J. (1900) *How to Take the Baths and Drinking Waters at Rotorua and Te Aroha*, Wellington, New Zealand Times Co.
Osborne, T. (1996) 'Security and vitality: drains, liberalism and power in the nineteenth century', in *Foucault and Political Reason: Liberalism, Neo-liberalism and Rationalities of Government*, eds A. Barry, T. Osborne & N. Rose, Chicago, IL, University of Chicago Press, pp. 99–122.
Povinelli, E. (2002) *The Cunning of Recognition: Indigenous Alterities and the Making of Australian Multiculturalism*, Durham, NC, Duke University Press.
Pratt, M. L. (1992) *Imperial Eyes: Travel Writing and Transculturation*, London, Routledge.
Rojek, C. (1994) *Ways of Escape: Modern Transformations in Leisure and Travel*, Lanham, MD, Rowman & Littlefield Publishers Inc.
Rosaldo, R. (1993) *Culture and Truth: The Remaking of Social Analysis*, Boston, MA, Beacon Press.
Rose, N. (1996) 'Governing "advanced" liberal democracies', in *Foucault and Political Reason: Liberalism, Neo-liberalism and Rationalities of Government*, eds A. Barry, T. Osborne & N. Rose, Chicago, IL, University of Chicago Press, pp. 37–64.
Rose, N. (1998) *Inventing Ourselves: Psychology, Power, and Personhood*, New York, Cambridge University Press.
Scott, D. (2005) Colonial governmentality, in *Anthropologies of Modernity: Foucault, Governmentality, and Life Politics*, ed. J. X. Inda, Malden, MA, Blackwell, pp. 23–49.

Shimakawa, K. (2002) *National Abjection: The Asian American Body Onstage*, Durham, NC, Duke University Press.

Sorrenson, M. P. K. (ed.) (1986) *Na to hoa aroha: From Your Dear Friend, Correspondence 1925–50, Sir Apirana Ngata and Te Rangi Hiroa (Sir Peter Buck)*, Auckland, Auckland University Press.

Taylor, D. (2003) *The Archive and the Repertoire: Performing Cultural Memory in the Americas*, Durham, NC, Duke University Press.

Te Aute College Students Association (1906) Report of the Tenth Conference held at Ōhinemutu, Rotorua, 25 December 1905 to 1 January 1906, Rotorua, Hot Lakes Chronicle.

Tramp Esq, A. (1899) 'Casual ramblings', *Auckland Weekly News*, 18 August.

Weber, Sir H. & Parkes Weber, F. (1907) *Climatotherapy and Balneotherapy: The Climates and Mineral Water Health Resorts (Spas) of Europe and North Africa, Including the General Principles of Climatotherapy and Balneotherapy, and Hints as to the Employment of Various Physical and Dietetic Methods*, 3rd edn, London, Smith, Elder, & Co.

Werry, M. (2001) *Tourism, Ethnicity and the Performance of New Zealand Nationalism, 1889–1914*, Evanston, IL, Doctoral Dissertation, Northwestern University.

Wohlmann, A. S. (1907) *The Mineral Waters and Health Resorts of New Zealand*, Wellington, Government Printer.

Young Māori Party, Southern Division (1909) Report of the Thirteenth Conference Ōhinemutu, Rotorua, 13–16 April, Gisborne, Gisborne Times.

Eeva Berglund

FOREST, FLOWS AND IDENTITIES IN FINLAND'S INFORMATION SOCIETY

Recent social theory has tended to celebrate boundary transgressions and flexibility. At the same time political thought has adopted the view from academic commentary, that the space of flows is now the dominant geographical logic. This essay proposes that such theoretical contributions might well be problematic from the point of view of progressive, liberatory and environmentally sustainable politics. This essay draws on social theory that neither ignores geography nor forgets nature, to make sense of some of the pressures of living with the information society's imperatives of mobility and flexibility in the Kainuu region of Finland. It also relates these to the promotion of branded regional identities in the information society. In resource-dependent regions like Kainuu, nature, culture and technology, even innovation, are broadly unproblematic elements of social reproduction. Problems arise, however, from the imperative to compete and to be seen to be competitive, and from the speeds at which recognized economic activity takes place. The broader demands of Finland as a national innovation system take inadequate account, as does social theory, of the needs of nurture and reproduction. A more appropriate social theory needs to develop an understanding of these things as part of making a living, and to articulate this with the powerful but loosely defined discourses of economics.

This essay considers environmental futures through documenting and analyzing aspects of turn-of-the-millennium life in Finland. Pondering environmental futures as part of the study of social and cultural life is still a minor pursuit. For cultural studies to go beyond critiques of environmentalism to engage with environmentalist critics, an agenda advocated by Phaedra Pezzullo in this volume, it must take nature seriously and help connect it to identities and to socio-economic choices. This essay draws inspiration from scholars such as David Harvey (1996), Barbara Adam (1998) and Teresa Brennan (2000, 2003), all social theorists who have made a point of taking nature seriously as they seek to understand culture.

I look at how identity formation is entangled in material transformations that transcend Finland's boundaries and colonize future lives. Yet I am uncomfortable with the fashion for language that accommodates these conceptual border crossings and invokes space as flows and celebrates culture as the shaper of nature. Instead, my story highlights the extent to which natural forces remain fundamental to nourishing human life. The problem is not simply that they have been forgotten, they are under sustained attack from globalization as it currently operates.

Economic globalization is a concern for my ethnographic interlocutors as well as for research, but it is also a poorly defined concept. That is no doubt where much of its rhetorical power lies. I should make it clear that I use globalization primarily to refer to global capitalism today, the dominant framework for organizing politics as well as commerce.

To make sense of identity formation, a key theme of cultural studies and a major strand in this essay, it is necessary also to consider modernity, another powerful concept. I use it to refer to an idea as well to the techno-political (Mitchell 2002) framework that has helped make that idea material: in both manufacturing and agriculture modernity has promoted efficiency; projects easily identifiable as modern have mapped and shaped territories as well as treated human work as a commodity. Modernity has fuelled concerns over identity, but it also functions as an identity so that to be Finnish is, among other things, to be modern (Berglund 2003). For Teresa Brennan (2000), to be modern is also to risk creating more death than life.

In the spirit of Brennan's radical critique, I suggest that the confidence, even the hubris, of those who build self-consciously on globalization, on modernity (late, post, or other) and on capitalism is not shared by everyone and it should be forcefully tackled by social theory and cultural studies.

The problem and its setting

Since 1996 when I started doing intermittent fieldwork in Finland[1] I have heard the phrases 'we're living in a market economy now' and, 'it's globalization, what can we do?' over and over again. Particularly in the more remote areas people have talked to me about how to make the best of new circumstances. World events have altered the financial situation, but people's experiences of community, identity and place have changed too. My interlocutors seem to have been pleased to talk about them with a curious and broadly sympathetic outsider, a London-based but Finnish-born anthropologist.

In Kainuu province, the nodes and intersections of the network that make up the space of flows are so sparse as to make the region rather small in the terms of the information society even though its area is large, 24,452 km^2. With an average population density of 3.6 inhabitants/km^2 (in 2002) and declining, it is one of Europe's most sparsely populated regions. Forestry and nature still form the mainstays of its economy but it also produces people who migrate to growth clusters like Oulu or Helsinki. Consumer desires and the hegemony of the global economy are as keenly felt in Kainuu as elsewhere, but the possibility of forgetting about geography and imagining that the world can be constructed at will, is not available as it appears to be in centers of power.

At the periphery, lack of choice and a feeling of being squeezed into a poorly fitting mold, can feel as normal as the laws of nature, merely the latest in a series of top-down measures imposed since time immemorial. But the current sense of there being no alternatives clashes starkly with the emphasis on openness that characterizes rhetoric at national level. Finland is, after all, routinely represented as a bold, new information society, where anything is possible if everyone does their bit and if the (virtual) capital is available (Berglund 2003). Looked at from a different angle, in Finland as elsewhere, flesh and blood seems to be losing out to robotics, environmental sustainability to economic competitiveness.

From the point of view of social theory, addressing the denial of nature by harking back to an overconfident, boundary-imposing modernity is neither possible nor desirable. Late twentieth century critical social thought opened up new possibilities by ceasing to treat modernity as synonymous with neutrality. It was historicized and a more curious stance towards cultural difference flourished. Crucially, the role of cultural forces in constructing nature was finally brought to the fore (Glacken 1967, also Escobar 1999). Tenacious misunderstandings about science were dispelled and the violence perpetrated in its name was admitted into history (Nandy 1988). As the mystique of science was unveiled, boundary transgressions and both/and descriptions began to be celebrated. An iconic and influential example is the feminist and cyborg-inspired work of Donna Haraway (e.g. 1997), informed by a 'searing sense that all is not well with women, as well as with millions of nonwomen' (1997, p. 269).

Struggles are taking place everywhere over the boundaries of land and the limitations of living bodies, many stuck between exploitation and redundancy. They remind us of limits, but for self-described critics of the world's social order it has become rather unfashionable to be talking about limits to anything, certainly not nature. The argument has also made by Kate Soper. There are, she writes, very good reasons to resist the currently dominant 'culturality of nature' thesis and the proliferation of cyborgs, hybrids and networks in what she calls 'fuzzy constructionist thinking' (2003, p. 99). Its promise of 'pleasurable or liberating opportunities for individual self-realisation let alone ... a platform for a collective post-capitalist utopian agenda' is contestable (2003, p. 107). One reason is that politics and commerce are also keen on the human capacity to keep pushing limits. Put another way, mainstream cultural studies is not that different from mainstream policy-making or business.

In relation to geography, the drive to overcome limits is neatly captured in the notion that in the globalized era it is organized as a space of flows. The idea was initially developed by Manuel Castells (1996). For him, space is the materialization of social relations, and today it is best conceptualized as a flow that escapes the control of specific societies. His contribution articulates a discernible shift in spatial practices, and captures both the organization of economic activity as networks and hubs of innovation and the instant mobility of financial capital. Further according to Castells, in the space of flows elites are cosmopolitan and people [sic] are local (Castells 1996, p. 415). This has also become manifest in the pressures on citizens to be mobile as well as innovative.[2] Cosmopolitanism is 'in'.

Ulrich Beck, another pioneer of environmentally sensitive social thought, has considered cosmopolitanism from the point of view of sociology. He defines cosmopolitan as being rooted both in the cosmos or nature and the polis or the city/state (2003, p. 16). His efforts are directed at going beyond a methodological nationalism where social thought builds upon the image of a sovereign nation state. In a post-colonial world without pure nations to define the limits of society, the 'only way forward is into a cosmopolitan world beyond both nationalism and imperialism' (2003, p. 27). According to Beck, if modernity once meant a correspondence of languages, territories and allegiances (a view that can itself only be taken as a crude heuristic) contemporary reality is one of overflowing across national borders.

Zygmunt Bauman identifies fluidity as a key problem too, when he writes of the increased 'risks and anxieties of living together, and apart, in our liquid modern world' (Bauman, 2003, p. xii). Richard Sennett (1998) sees the impacts of a spatially disembedding economic system as corroding character. Marc Augé (1999) sees the alienating placelessness and lack of connection involved in contemporary life as afflicting everyone.

If these empirical observations contrast current fluidity with former fixity, theory must contribute to rather than hamper public deliberation of the difficult experiences this brings. However, as a replacement for methodologically nationalist sociology and for the dualistic framework that separates nature and society/culture, networks and flows, just like hybrids, glide over the substantive costs of economic globalization as we know it. Yet we can no longer equate matter and nature, or wish away economic relations that reward immaterial production (information as a commodity) and shallow commitment to specific location.

My perspective on the hyper-flexible information society is eclectic. It grows out of and is accountable to forms of knowledge encountered in 'the field' and in academia (see Strathern 1999, p. 6). The result is a text that travels back and forth between concerns that emerge from Kainuu and social science writings on nature, space and place. I prefer academic discourses to stay in touch with non-academic concerns firstly because if environmental threats are a challenge to everyone, professional thinkers in particular should rise to it. Secondly, although academia prides itself on questioning routinized habits of mind so do many, many others. Finally, in the information society, everybody tries to be transgressive and innovative. A warning should be heard here, for these characteristics, like flexibility, are routinely contrasted to the backward features of earlier forms of modernity, increasingly conceptualized as ossified, fixed and hierarchical, lacking in innovation. There is continuity here; early moderns too saw their predecessors and their un-modern contemporaries as passive and backward. Rural populations and women in particular came to be associated with slowness and naturalness and described as passive and irrationally unwilling to change. Such views still inform the regional and rural policy promoted by the European Union (EU) (Rosenqvist 2002, Äikäs 2004). Other ways of thinking are possible as well as necessary.

The subsequent text is organized into four parts, all informed by the tension between the space of flows and social reproduction. I start by looking at the imperatives of movement and competition as factors in the construction of local identity. I then consider the mixing of proximate nature and local culture as part of social reproduction. The nurture and regenerative work involved in making a living from forestry and on the ways these imperatives are being developed within the new context of the information society are the focus of the penultimate section. Finally I suggest that the social theory of globalization remains vacuous if it does not address the question of how global society is to make a living.

Competition and regional branding

Driving to a meeting in May 2002 through seemingly endless forests, I heard a voice on national radio intone 'towns and municipalities are in ever more intense competition against each other. It's no fun being the loser'. The presenter questioned the wisdom of a political and economic system that encouraged everyone to compete against everyone else. Yet improved competitiveness in the global economy is presented as the only way forward (*Osaaminen* ... 2004, Berglund 2003). Finnish newspapers, promotional publications, shop windows and billboards proclaim that Finland is already a successful information society. So does academic discourse (Castells & Himanen 2001).

Before it became an icon of high-tech, Finland lived from the forest. But the forest is no longer a reliable or taken-for-granted economic good.[3] This means that Kainuu, where over 90% of the produce of the forest is exported in some form, is ever more dependent on an ever less dependable external market.

Not only does information technology outstrip forestry in its capacity to bring in profits, forestry in Finland is challenged by climate. Slow-growing northern forests are less interesting to investors than fast-growing plantation forests in the south. Globally the forest industries are in a drawn-out transition that is altering relations between companies, local communities and state institutions (Marchak 1995, Lehtinen *et al.* 2004).

On becoming a member of the EU in 1995 Finland agreed to adapt rural policy to directions already established by the core countries whose socio-spatial environments, however, were vastly different to Finland's. As elsewhere (O'Riordan & Church 2001), municipalities now compete for inward investment. This requires that they project as positive an image of themselves as possible. While I was in the field the small town where I did much of my fieldwork said this on its website:

> Prizes for being Finland's most creative municipality, for developing a successful image and for municipal development all testify to the open-minded, lively and bold activities of Sotkamo Municipality. ... Here you'll find an excellent environment both for living and for conducting business amidst beautiful unspoilt nature.

According to geographer Anssi Paasi (2003) there has been a boost in the production of 'landscapes of publicity' in EU-Finland. Paasi argues that literary and mass media discourses personalize regions and create new coordinates for social and territorial inclusion. But Finnish localities offer similar virtues to many other localities: the newest in high-tech, eco-efficiency, cleanliness and strong local heritage too, both natural and cultural (cf. O'Riordan & Church 2001, p. 12).

Like so many municipalities around the world Kainuu has made use of a corporate slogan: 'Kainuu, renown for its nature' though a more idiomatic translation of the original Finnish might be 'Kainuu, wealthy by nature'. As I write in 2005 the slogan is less visible than it was at the turn of the decade and there is even debate about the virtue of highlighting nature at all.[4] The landscape itself, however, draws attention to nature, and the region's geology and ecology are considered indispensable to understanding its human history (Virtanen 2004). Its natural resources have been commercialized as tourism, as 'adventure' or authentic 'experiences' as shooting rapids, fishing, hunting and even skidoo safaris are sold alongside regional foods and vernacular tradition. The claim to richness is not straightforward and unemployment is high as dominant livelihoods in farming and forestry have yet to be replaced.[5] Nevertheless, the slogan undoubtedly naturalizes the link between the people and their forested environment.

At this point some clarification is necessary. Over half of Finland's forest land is privately owned even though a national forest administration oversees its care (Forests in Finland 2005). This broad base of ownership of what used to be called green gold is still in place, but mechanization has been reducing opportunities for paid employment since the 1950s, as people never tired of telling me. This also means that, contrary to conservationist views, Kainuu's forests are not wilderness. The elements are in place, however, for images of the region to continue to be developed around the tropes of forest folk.[6]

Forest peripheries like Kainuu have not tended to resist neo-liberal economic development, but they have become flash points for clashing imperatives (Lehtinen et al. 2004). Flexibility of production, neo-liberalism, environmentalism and aboriginalism (Hayter 2004) jostle uneasily with each other in the competition to define what forests are and how we should relate to them. Around Finland, including Kainuu, conflicts over specific forests have flared up regularly, drawing attention to the construction and the politics of nature (Berglund 2000, Lehtinen 2002).

Yet there is a sentiment that Kainuu's forests belong to the people of Kainuu, not to multi-national industrialists or Helsinki-based bureaucrats or even environmentalists who speak on behalf of an abstracted nature. The converse sentiment attached to it, is that Kainuu people belong to the forests. I have heard the view expressed through references to the forest as a source of livelihood, a place of comfort, a general source of life force or natural creativity and the context of everyday life. The forests are thought about as a healing place. With a mixture of enthusiasm and hesitation (which I interpreted as a concern to avoid appearing overly romantic) one school teacher elaborated on an argument I have often heard in Kainuu, that difficult children tend to behave better in those situations where they are allowed into the forest, as they sometimes are as part of biology or other school projects. Finally, if academic proof were needed, the regional government's own research on what Finns call people's nature relationship provides it (Mäntymaa 1998).

Historically such nature relationships have, however, fostered territorial identities associated with exclusionary and even violent politics (Anderson & Berglund 2003). It is thus no wonder that territorial identities, particularly in their modern, administratively policed form, have been a focus of intense scholarly deconstruction (e.g. Paasi 2003). Forests in particular carry a weight of symbolism at least in European and North American experiences (Lehtinen 1990, Schama 1995), which demands vigilance. Whether as paradise, as national wilderness, or indeed as the scary chaos that lies beyond the city walls, forests have often been drawn on as naturally unchanging and thus powerful symbols of continuity and they can be pressed into service as the opposite or the other of civic society as well as cosmopolitanism.

Landscape and Memory, Simon Schama's (1995) analysis of the Western preoccupation with natural landscapes, leaves us in no doubt about the political potency of natural landscapes like forests. For example, no German government ever concerned itself more with the fate of Germany's forests than the Third Reich (Schama 1995, p. 119). In German nationalist imagination, if 'the rootless Jew was the purveyor of the corrupted, citified society, the forester was his antithesis – the embodiment of ethnic authenticity, rooted like his trees in the ancient earth of the Fatherland' (1995, p. 114).

Historical research like Schama's has demonstrated not only that cultural norms and social action have been fundamental in shaping the natural world and our experiences of it, but that social exclusion of the most violent kind has be legitimated through essentializing the links between natural landscapes and people. Injecting history or temporality into accounts of landscapes is a powerful way of resisting such essentialism. It also foregrounds nature as environment, the surroundings for human life. This eventually raises the question not of 'where but how we live' (Adam 1998, p. 31).

Regional, cultural identity, in other words, emerges out of much more than imagery and representation. It is what is done, how life is lived. This is very striking in the context of environmental catastrophe where loss nature entails losing culture and agency also (Kirsch 2001) but the argument holds more generally. How life can be lived, how nature and culture are fixed, is the focus of the next section.

Experimenting with nature is ordinary

In 1996 a small biotechnology laboratory was set up in the town of Sotkamo to help reorient the forestry and agriculture-centered economy towards knowledge-based industries. Attached to Oulu University 90 km away, from the start its remit was technology transfer and the commercialization of local resources, notably berries, herbs and dairy products.

The rationale for high-technology was inextricably tied to nature. Using the vast forests and developing local food production are central goals of regional policy (Kainuun Liitto 2002). As both interviewees and media accounts put it, the challenge was a spatial one: how to move the local richness of Kainuu somewhere else and exchange it for money. High tech could help.

The director of the laboratory told me that biotechnology will enable less wasteful utilization of natural products. In conversations, a meta-narrative of the laboratory's work quickly emerged, according to which the task was to find in the surrounding nature, with the help of up-to-date techniques the beneficial properties of raw materials like clover, berries, reindeer and cow's milk and even pine tar could be systematically isolated and rendered into products such as cosmetics and food.

Sotkamo, though small and unassuming, does not conjure up a sense of poverty. It has also been voted the most innovative town in the province. Two landmarks provide clues to why. An indoor ski-tunnel was built in the mid-1990s to extend the winter-sports season. The first of its kind in the world and a commercial success, it was often invoked by locals as a reminder of what is possible. In the expansive sports village close by, an artificial tropical paradise has been built. Both are, in a straightforward way, artificial. The one enables skiing on snow even when outside temperatures reach $+30°C$ and the other makes possible splashing in water when outside temperatures reach $-30°C$. Both seem aimed at defying nature. Yet my interviewees saw these things as indications of what one could do by experimenting with knowledge already acquired. 'It's crazy, but it shows how much can be done', summed up the attitude of many. People in it talked about the laboratory in much the same way.

The technology used by the laboratory is not at the cutting edge. However, its application to the resources available in Kainuu is innovative and, to an extent, it has been commercially successful. Developing high-tech food and testing the safety of 'organic', 'natural' or 'local' products were all part of the same, broad objective, to use technology to get the most out of nature. Particularly in the case of genetics, the general feeling seemed to be that if untoward things were to come out of biotechnology it would happen because of unscrupulous individuals or extreme greed, neither of which were considered likely to take place here. Furthermore, as I was told, 'you can't put anything into nature that isn't already there'.

In the context of Kainuu's long history of forest-dependence the idea that nature and culture are in some kind of conflict in the application of technology began to sound absurd even to me. The key issue was livelihood. That requires a sustained engagement with the surroundings, a point often made in conversation but also in the copious literature on forestry (e.g. Jokinen & Holma 2001). The temporality and sociality of landscape may have to be highlighted in academic discourse (Adam 1998, Ingold 2000), but to the inhabitants of the margins it is an unremarkable fact of life.

Fitting into the hegemonic space of flows has, however, required effort and it has raised awareness of the time and effort embodied in place. Almost everyone I spoke to made the point that they were pleased to have found a job in their field so close to home, the majority of the workers being from, or married into, the region. Market forces beyond their control compel them to be creative and enterprising, even crazy. There is, as I was told so often, no real alternative to taking more risks and to adapting to capital- and technology-intensive production.

Are not experiments with nature, crazy or otherwise, part of defending place by inhabiting it? Since the early twentieth century and arguably before, insiders and outsiders have experimented with new forestry techniques, arrangements of ownership and commercialization and with novel uses of the forests (Virtanen 2004). None have been able to overlook the resistances of natural processes, nor have experiments been embarked upon without concern for danger. Similarly in the laboratory, constant deliberate calculations about the costs of taking and not taking risks must be made.

I am not suggesting these calculations are transparent or free of power relations, merely that the globalized economy renders them necessary. Further, techno-hype notwithstanding, the values and considerations that inform them both emerge out of and constitute place. Place is also the context for nurture and social reproduction, as the next section illustrates.

Nurture and the global economy

The massive recession of the early 1990s was arguably as great a catastrophe for Finland as the depression of the 1930s had been. In its wake came the new rise whose icon was Nokia corporation. The penetration of information technologies into everyday life was treated as a naturally Finnish achievement, suggesting that Finland has finally made its mark and is now hurtling toward an even greater future. Ethnographically speaking, everyday life in Finland is routed through a dense network of information and communications technologies that tend not to be resisted. However, getting out of the recession also meant cutting welfare provision. Labor was also expected to work longer and harder (Kiander 2001, Siltala 2004). The nation needs more and more well-educated youth, but there are also fears that globalization is causing a brain drain. The risk of losing young people, trained with Finnish taxpayers' money, to overseas companies animates discussion at all administrative levels.

Fifteen years from the onset of the recession, the state still subsidizes infrastructure, education and research and development, and envisions Finland as a pioneer information society (Himanen 2004). With some regional variation, the same tune dominates across the country. It is exemplified in this extract from an interview with a high-ranking regional official:

> I'd like for people to see Kainuu's future as a long-term thing. In the short run we really can't expect much in the way of a radical improvement, but I've seen enough of the world to be able to say that a region like this, with such a robust natural environment, we've got renewable natural resources, there's a varied, healthy and interesting natural landscape and clean air and so on. And really, after all these natural resources form the basis of production. And then also people are capable and their education and training is improving all the time. So, surely with these ... basic elements we can put the structures in place that will give us enough volume in the economic sense so that this region will be able to succeed in the future too'. (Interview 12 December 2002)

Overall, adding value to improve competitiveness was her answer to the challenge. However, not everyone is happy or willing to go along with the market-led way of adapting. Among white-collar workers there is increasing resistance to what one commentator termed 'hyper-capitalism's experiment with the human body' (Siltala 2004). How much of the work involved in creating new generations of successful entrepreneurs will be carried by 'the economy' and how much of it will go on in its shadows is now up for debate.

The fact that 'the economy' has overlooked tasks such as nurture is not news to feminists. But the conflict between the short-termism of economic calculation and the long time it takes to produce labor for the informational economy is becoming a central problem in contemporary capitalism too (Jessop 2003). In the areas of childcare and care of the elderly and even in sectors like the arts and environmental protection, exchanges that do not involve money are relatively common. Adam captures this willingness to work for no pay, and at slower speeds than the money economy in her phrase 'moonlighting for the environment' (1998, p. 94). She treats it as a promising development from the point of view of sustainability.

Individuals, families and communities must negotiate the tensions between the biological temporalities of people and the technological speeds of the economy. One woman from the biotechnology laboratory noted that her husband was not a farmer. He was, she said with considerable sarcasm, a business-oriented countryside entrepreneur. They had both grown up on farms, so it had seemed natural if not inevitable that they – he primarily – make their living by farming and forestry. Rather than labor-intensive dairy production, however, they have beef cattle, a new departure in their experience. Despite landing a job that matched her training in genetics, even for her, entry into the EU had been frightening, demanding great emotional energies. But things were getting better by 2001 when I first met her.

Many of her colleagues expressed a close identification with the state, and a sense of duty towards it, typical in the context of Finland's historically consensual style of government. This woman, however, saw her relationship to the state as more antagonistic. 'Me? Owe something to the state?' she exclaimed when I broached the subject. For four years, she said, she had been at home bringing up the next generation, underpaid. If anything, the state owed her.

Adam (1998) develops her idea of moonlighting to demonstrate that people are not blind followers of economic self-interest. Despite capitalism's amnesia about time and nurture, working in the shadows also serves the needs of the money economy. From the perspective of the economy, for the state to be asked to contribute towards child care simply demonstrates what Brennan has dubbed the 'prohibitive cost of life' (2003, p. 87) now is being translated worldwide into an assault on women and their dependents.

Whereas in the shadows of the economy, mothers and nature regenerate life, the official economy encourages waste and loss of energy (Brennan 2000). The discourses of the information economy and the space of flows systematically obscure the need for nurture. Yet by now the overwhelming evidence is that in its wake come exhaustion, suffering and violence. These are most evident in the margins (Martinez-Alier 2002), but they appear throughout world society, we only need look for it (Adam 1998, Brennan 2003, Siltala 2004).

The option to follow capital into growth centers has already taken many women out of Kainuu. One researcher and social activist I interviewed had chosen to remain an inhabitant of the 'backwoods' where there are more square kilometers than people. She told me that in these municipalities as many as half the women are unemployed or involved in state-subsidized, short-term work. Her own work for the Kainuu Rural Advisory Centre in the mid-1990s concentrated on improving economic opportunities for local women. When I talked to her she emphasized the hugeness of the challenges.

Although she is connected to geographically dispersed networks, her ideas center around sustaining life in this place. The information society is routed through her projects technologically, but also in the emphasis that she too puts on know-how. Like in the biotechnology laboratory, though, the know-how she talks about is embedded in the forests. Hand-made crafts and berry- and mushroom-based delicacies aimed at the tourist market jostle here alongside ideas to develop the region's facilities for caring for the elderly and infirm. A key word for her is care, of people and of forests. Might there, she pondered, be a parallel between Kainuu as old-growth forests and Kainuu as a haven for old-growth people.

Sakari Virtanen, historian, retired PR-officer and tireless champion of forests, used a different verbal image: old folks as toxic waste. He personifies efforts to live off the forests both sustainably and viably and thus to reproduce life in this place. A man of action as well as words, he helped initiate and organize an annual educational project that focuses on all aspects of the forest in a bid to engage young people with 'nature, economics, society and the human spirit' as he put it.

Since 1997 the Kainuu Schools' Forest Week has been organized in a different municipality each year. Schools focus on the theme of forest incorporating it into all aspects of the curriculum; mathematics classes by measuring and assessing its growth and sales, history lessons by looking at past traditions, language classes through forest-related vocabulary, and so on. I was able to observe it in 2001 and in 2005 I interviewed several of the people involved. By then it was running in conjunction with a sister event, an international forest week for young people, involving various European forest-dependent regions, such as Spain's Galicia, Russian Karelia and Värmland in Sweden. These regions experience similar challenges relating to the conflicting demands that post-industrial audiences and consumers make of forested regions. Exchanging ideas about how to 'sell' forest-dependent regions as something other than backward resource colonies is as important as exchanging know-how about sustainable forest management and tourism.

Households still treat forest as savings in the bank, to be managed with future generations in mind — boreal forests here can take up to 100 years to regenerate. In Kainuu state owned forests are 40% of the province's managed forests and continue to secure work and raw materials above all for the United Paper Mills plant in the regional capital, Kajaani. This explains why state property in forests is so vehemently protected from the protectors, environmentalists who would turn them into expanses of old-growth unavailable for human use. Raising the issue of forest-use as a regional economic question was a way of recapturing some of the control over the economics of forests, to where they are part of the context of everyday life.

Hands-on knowledge about the multiple meanings and uses of forests offered the children both fun and a collective sense of responsibility. I was told the trip for a class of 12-year olds I attended was quite typical. They were accompanied by two teachers, a representative each from the Regional Forestry Centre (a public institution), the Forest Management Association (for private owners) and the Forest and Park Service (the national body that oversees forests) as well as a journalist, a researcher from a regional research centre, two teachers visiting from across the Russian border, and Sakari Virtanen whose key role in the project I mentioned already.

With the help of maps the forest experts talked of different kinds of forests. Different colors, for example, indicated the types of ownership: private, communal, state and company. We visited a private farm and one of its woodlots, drove through a variety of forest types and were given practical demonstrations of management techniques and tools. From the children's comments, it was clear that some were familiar with what was being shown, even savvy about the proverbially endless form-filling that forest- and farm-ownership involves. At one point we were listening to a forester explain what he does. Surrounding us on the forest floor were old chain saws arranged as in a museum. A little further away was a now obsolete truck for transporting logs but also a state-of-the art harvester with its computerized control panel and, so we were told, comfortable cabin. The children participated with varying degrees of enthusiasm and the adults whispered among themselves: would this generation, brought up on the modern conveniences and labor- and time-saving devices available, ever follow in their forefathers' footsteps and get into forestry?

The other children I was able to observe were some years older. They were a group of six students picked to go to Spain, creating a power-point presentation of Kainuu's forestry. Among other things they worked on generating a map that placed their village in international context. They enjoyed the technical tasks involved in working with computers, but they were also obviously looking forward to the actual trip. The face-to-face contact that their involvement promised was considered by all to be an added extra, a privilege that could not be substituted by virtual tours of forests elsewhere.

The forest week amounts to a chance to study the environment at home in all its natural, cultural and economic dimensions. In the minds of the teachers and organizers with whom I spoke was the growing need, as they saw it, to impress upon the students the value of engaging with nature as environment. They need to be taught in the abstract, if they do not learn it in practice, that the environment they take for granted is the result of culture and nature interacting, and that forests need attention too, even if political rhetoric draws their attention elsewhere.

The process also feeds the need to generate positive imagery about home. It incorporates aspects of a nostalgia for a less risky past and possibly a claim to a natural entitlement to whatever resources Kainuu might deliver. However, it also rehearses the point I made earlier, that combining nature and culture/technology is taken-for-granted. And finally, the schools' forest weeks' emphasis on regeneration and temporalities is paralleled by an emphasis on the dual nature of locality. As the teenagers working on their power-point realized, to globalize is to localize.

Place-making increasingly builds on successful information gathering and networking, as exemplified here in the collaboration between different forest-dependent regions, and the efforts made to publicize them (including the students' presentation). Global communications are thus ever more crucial to defending place-based practices, local cultures and ecologies, a point argued strongly by Arturo Escobar (2001, p. 167). Subaltern claims to rights and resources may increasingly depend on an appeal to local nature together with local culture (Kirsch 2001) but far from place-based activism leading to some intransigent defense of 'tradition', in the current predicament it is more likely to be a 'creative engagement with modernity and transnationalism' (2001, p. 168).

Kainuu's population is relatively advantaged in the global scheme of things. Yet the preoccupation with care, of people and nature, and the strong pull of place, is a way of drawing out of the shadows some of the creative and regenerative work that economic and political orthodoxy prefers to ignore and intellectual currents assume to be outmoded.

Reassessing the slogan

Even in as wealthy a part of the world as Finland, unreflexively celebrating mobility and flux is as problematic as denying the body. The costs of a capitalism disconnected from the requirements of regeneration, nurture and concern for livelihood, are borne somewhere, some time. To some extent they are being carried by regions like Kainuu, whose unemployed and disheartened have not made it into my interviews, let alone this text.

While capitalism creates unending waste yet demands that citizens be active consumers, the ecological distribution conflicts that this increasingly creates have given new life to local identities. I suggested earlier that aestheticizing identities and natural landscapes by reducing them to imagery serves capitalist interests (see also Duncan & Duncan 2001). It is equally important, however, that post-cyborg theorists focus on identities and landscapes or environments as the locations where nurture and regeneration happen. This requires going beyond the space of flows into the shadows of non-monetary exchange. As Adam points out, here, in the moonlighting world of domestic and voluntary work, the assumptions of greed and individualism on which economics is built, cease to operate (1998, p. 95). However, moonlighting is not going to resolve the contradictions of capitalism. These can only be expected to get starker as the cost of making money grow is pushed onto more and more vulnerable people and depleted nature.

Modernity in the form of a globalization that ignores nurture and reproduction is exhausting (Brennan 2000). That there is a spatial dimension to how this exhaustion is organized is clear from the violent forms of identity politics strangling societies everywhere.

In an article about memory and territory, Edward Said reminds us that, 'the study of history, which of course is the underpinning of memory ... is to some considerable extent a nationalist effort premised on the need to construct a desirable loyalty to and insider's understanding of one's country, tradition, and faith' (2000, p. 176). These are exactly the kinds of processes I have been describing, but they should be complemented by an appreciation, if not an exhaustive analysis, of the economics by which people make a living. In the Finnish case this is not difficult, since the list of loyalties expected of insiders includes the economy. Until recently it was a Finnish citizen's duty to support the forest industries. Now we are to show our allegiance by contributing to Finland as an information society (Kantola 2003).

People hint that forest-Finland was more legitimate a socio-economic system than the information society (see also Donner-Amnell 2004). It would be unhelpful, if predictable, to explain away this belief by arguing that it just goes to show how unreasonably unwilling people are to change. It would be more useful and more honest to examine how social arrangements provide economically, and to ask how they understand the intertwining of nature and culture and the identities that flow from this mix.

Let me revisit the slogan 'Wealthy by Nature' which may have appeared disingenuous and grossly overoptimistic. Places and regions are currently locked into mutually destructive competition, and the prognosis for Kainuu is hardly rosy. However, the possibility – at any scale – of growth, or of planning for future prosperity, depends on acknowledging the forces of nature and respecting the work of nurture.

Notes

1. Since the initial eight months in Helsinki in 1996, I have travelled to Kainuu, the focus of this paper, several times a year, for periods of under a week to a month. I have met and interviewed regional administrators and scientists above all. Thanks to all the people who have shared their thoughts and extended their hospitality. Acknowledgements – BA, W-G.
2. Internationalization is government policy (*Osaaminen* ... 2003).
3. Dependence on the export of forest products was never comfortable, but its benefits were widely distributed and the forest administration enjoyed legitimacy (Berglund 2000, Donner-Amnell 2004).
4. Councillor Merja Ylonen lodged a request that the Regional Council drop this phrase from its publications.
5. Over 20 percent across the region in 2000, by 2005 differences between municipalities had grown, with unemployment in some as low as 14 percent, as high as 22 percent in others. For evidence of these trends, see the province's own website, available at: http://www.kainuu.fi.
6. A research project commissioned by the regional government indicated that Kainuu's inhabitants see themselves as close to nature and are concerned with the 'health and vitality of the forests, the beauty of the landscape and the opportunity to pick wild berries and mushrooms' (Mäntymaa 1998, p. 4).

References

Adam, B. (1998) *Timescapes of Modernity: The Environment and Invisible Hazards*, London, Routledge.

Äikäs, T. A. (2004) 'Kaupunkien ja seutujen imagot aluetasojen välisessä kilpailussa', *Terra*, vol. 116, no. 1, pp. 3–16.

Anderson, D. G. & Berglund, E. (eds) (2003) *Ethnographies of Conservation: Environmentalism and the Distribution of Privilege*, Oxford, Berghahn Books.

Augé, M. (1999) *An Anthropology for Contemporaneous Worlds*, trans. A. Jacobs, Palo Alto, CA, Stanford University Press.

Bauman, Z. (2003) *Liquid Love: On the Frailty of Human Bonds*, Cambridge, Polity Press.

Beck, U. (2003) 'Rooted cosmopolitanism: emerging from a rivalry of distinctions', in *Global America?: The Cultural Consensus of Globalization*, eds U. Beck, N. Sznaider & R. Winter, Liverpool, Liverpool University Press.

Berglund, E. (2000) 'Forestry expertise and national narratives: some consequences for old-growth conflicts in Finland', *Worldviews*, vol. 4.

Berglund, E. (2003) 'Finland as information society: an anthropological critique', *Suomen Antropologi*, vol. 4, no. 28, pp. 2–16.
Brennan, T. (2000) *Exhausting Modernity: Grounds for a New Economy*, London, Routledge.
Brennan, T. (2003) *Globalization and its Terrors*, London, Routledge.
Castells, M. (1996) *The Rise of the Network Society*, Malden, MA, Blackwell.
Castells, M. & Himanen, P. (2001) *Suomen Yhteiskuntamalli*, SITRA and WSOY, Helsinki (also published in English).
Donner-Amnell, J. (2004) 'To be or not to be Nordic: how internationalization has affected the character of the forest industry and forest utilization in the Nordic countries', in *Politics of Forests: Northern Forest-industrial Regimes in the Age of Globalization*, eds A. A. Lehtinen, J. Donner-Amnell & B. Sæther, Aldershot, Ashgate, pp. 179–204.
Duncan, J. S. & Duncan, N. G. (2001) 'The aestheticization of the politics of landscape preservation', *Annals of the Association of American Geographers*, vol. 91, no. 2, pp. 387–409.
Escobar, A. (1999) 'Steps to an antiessentialist political ecology', *Current Anthropology*, vol. 40, no. 1, pp. 1–30.
Escobar, A. (2001) 'Culture sits in places: reflections on globalism and subaltern strategies of localization', *Political Geography*, vol. 20, pp. 139–174.
Forests in Finland (2005) [online] Available at: http://www.mmm.fi/english/forestry/forests/ (accessed August 2005).
Glacken, C. J. (1967) *Traces on the Rhodian Shore: Nature and Culture in Western Thought from Ancient Times to the End of the Eighteenth Century*, Berkeley, CA, University of California Press.
Harvey, D. (1996) *Justice, Nature and the Geography of Difference*, Cambridge, MA, Blackwell.
Hayter, R. (2004) 'Requiem for a "local" champion: globalization, British Columbia's forest economy and MacMillan Bloedel', in *Politics of Forests: Northern Forest-industrial Regimes in the Age of Globalization*, eds A. A. Lehtinen., J. Donner-Amnell & B. Sæther, Aldershot, Ashgate.
Himanen, P. (2004) 'Välittävä, kannustava ja luova Suomi: Katsaus tietoyhteiskunnan syviin haasteisiin', *Eduskunnan Kanslian Julkaisu*, vol. 4.
Ingold, T. (2000) *The Perception of the Environment: Essays on Livelihood, Dwelling and Skill*, London, Routledge.
Jessop, B. (2003) 'The state and the contradictions of the knowledge-driven economy', Department of Sociology, Lancaster University, [online] Available at: http://www.comp.lancs.ac.uk/sociology/papers/Jessop-State-and-Contradictions.pdf
Jokinen, A. & Holma, K. (2001) 'Temporalities and routines in the control of private forestry in Finland', in *Social Sustainability of Forestry in Northern Europe: Research and Education, Final Report of the Nordic Research Programme on Social Sustainability of Forestry*, ed. Marjatta Hytönen, TemaNord 575, Copenhagen, Nordic Council of Ministers, pp. 341–358.

Kainuun Liitto (2002) *Kainuun Maakuntasuunnitelma 2020, III luonnos 9.12.2002*, Kainuun Liitto (Regional Council of Kainuu), Kajaani

Kantola, A. (2003) 'Loyalties in flux: the changing politics of citizenship', *European Journal of Cultural Studies*, vol. 69, no. 2, pp. 203–217.

Kiander, J. (2001) Laman opetukset. Suomen 1990-luvun kriisin syyt ja seuraukset. VATT julkaisuja 27:5, Helsinki.

Kirsch, S. (2001) 'Lost worlds: environmental disaster, "culture loss" and the law', *Current Anthropology*, vol. 42, no. 2, pp. 167–198.

Lehtinen, A. A. (1990) 'Metsäluontomme kulttuurihistoriasta – yhteiskuntakehityksen heijasteita suomalaisessa metsämaisemassa', *Terra*, vol. 102, no. 4, pp. 284–293.

Lehtinen, A. A. (2002) 'Globalisation and the Finnish forest sector: on the internationalization of forest-industrial operations', *Fennia*, vol. 180, no. 1–2, pp. 237–250.

Lehtinen, A. A., Donner-Amnell, J. & Sæther, B. (eds) (2004) *Politics of Forests: Northern Forest-industrial Regimes in the Age of Globalization*, Aldershot, Ashgate.

Marchak, M. P. (1995) *Logging the Globe*, Montreal, McGill-Queen's University Press.

Martinez-Alier, J. (2002) *The Environmentalism of the Poor: A Study of Ecological Conflicts and Valuation*, Cheltenham, Edward Elgar.

Mäntymaa, E. (1998) Kainuulaisten metsäasenteet 1997. Oulun Yliopisto, Kajaanin Kehittämiskeskus (Research and Development Centre of Kajaani), Tutkimusraportti 5.

Mitchell, T. (2002) *Rule of Experts: Egypt, Techno-politics, Modernity*, Berkeley, CA, University of California Press.

Nandy, A. (ed.) (1988) *Science, Hegemony and Violence: Requiem for Modernity*, Delhi, Oxford University Press.

O'Riordan, T. & Church, C. (2001) 'Synthesis and context', in *Globalism, Localism and Identity: Fresh Perspectives on the Transition to Sustainability*, ed. T. O'Riordan, London, Earthscan.

'Osaaminen, innovaatiot ja kansainvälistyminen' (2003) Valtion tiede ja teknologianeuvoston julkaisuja, [online] Available at: http://www.minedu.fi/tiede_ ja_teknologianeuvosto/julkaisut/katsaus_2003.html (accessed December 2003); English summary available at: http://www.minedu.fi/tiede_ja_ teknologianeuvosto/eng/publications/Review_2003.html (accessed August 2005).

Paasi, A. (2003) 'Finnish landscape as social practice: mapping, identity and scale', in *Nordscapes: Thinking Landscapes and Regional Identity on the Northern Edge of Europe*, eds M. T. Jones & K. Olwig, Minneapolis, MN, University of Minnesota Press.

Ponnikas, J. (1998) Pohjois-Suomen aluepoliittiset ohjelmat ja ympäristökysymys, Working Papers 17, Research and Development Centre of Kajaani, Kajaani.

Rainisto, S. (2004) Paikkojakin pitää markkinoida, Helsinging Sanomat vieraksynä, 26 March.

Rosenqvist, O. (2002) 'Aluekeskuspolitiikka ja muut yhdentävän maaseutupolitiikan esteet Suomessa', *Terra*, vol. 114, no. 2, pp. 59–67.
Said, E. (2000) 'Invention, memory, and place', *Critical Inquiry*, vol. 26, pp. 175–192.
Schama, S. (1995) *Landscape and Memory*, New York, Vintage Books.
Soper, K. (2003) 'Humans, animals, machines', *New Formations*, Spring, pp. 99–109.
Strathern, M. (1999) *Property, Substance and Effect*, London, Athlone Press.
Virtanen, S. (2004) Siniset Metsät, Vihreä Kulta: Kainuun Metsätalouden Historia, Oulujoen Uittoyhdistys.

Jody Berland

CAT AND MOUSE

Iconographics of Nature and Desire

> *The popularity of digital cat photographs circulating through the Internet and across North American visual culture provides an occasion for a critical exploration of human—cat relations in contemporary culture. The representation of animals in traditional and digital photography is discussed in relation to the technologies of visual culture, human—animal relations, the companion animals debate, the social history of cats, and species interactions in urban culture. The highly ambiguous physical and symbolic status of cats and the proliferation of human—cat networks in urban and electronic space are part of an emergent 'post-human' landscape in which the mutual dependency of diverse animals is more important (if no less volatile) than the unique qualities of distinct species.*

In recent years, public criticism of cruelty and malpractice in agribusiness and the fast food industry has enhanced the social visibility of animals and the dilemmas surrounding our relations with them. The linking of corporate malfeasance with cruelty to animals is being countered by an emergent dialogue between conventionally separate discourses in science studies, feminism, animal rights activism, new social movements, and cultural theory. Critics concur that the status of animals cannot be addressed separate from their representation, and argue that the human—animal distinctions we inherit from the history of this representation must be transformed to enable better modes of interaction between species. At the same time, some of the most profound critical theorizations of this shift are marked by hierarchy, sexism and superstition. That is evident in which animals they talk about and in how they talk about them.

Nowhere is this more salient than with the subject of cats. Cats are widely celebrated in contemporary cinema, marketing, kitsch, feminist iconography, common domestic paraphernalia, children's culture and literature of every genre. A dazzling array of poets, novelists and artists has crafted homage to their cats.[1] It is rare now to find substantive fissures between popular culture and contemporary theory. Yet, if cats inhabit a wildly disparate range of life conditions, ranging from cultivated domestic aristocracy to homelessness and torture, they evoke an equally diverse range of affective responses in humans, some of whom deplore the intimacy of cat–human relations. This fissure between theories and practices is one of many features that make the study of cats irresistible.

Among a portion of e-connected persons of my acquaintance, pictures of cats are the new currency. This is not altogether surprising, since cat images have been (along with pornography) the most prolific visual content to feed the new medium of the world wide web. I have countless photographs and urls in my inbox. Their background is a generalized domestic suburban landscape, free of humans; as with pornography and wildlife documentaries (Chris 2006, p. 36), *Homo photographicus* has removed himself from the visual field. Regardless of their orientation to gender, race, vegetarianism or digital art, my correspondents are entranced with these cat photos. This is not hard to understand. These cats are not endangered, vulnerable or distressed; they appear to be at the centre of the universe, yet young, furry and innocent. The photographs foreground the luxuriously comfortable sensuality of these cats and their bodacious interaction with the worlds they inhabit. They look tactile and touchable, in contrast to the digital graphic interface on which they appear (see figure 1).[2]

What does it mean to describe these images as a currency? These snapshots are portable items or tokens exchanged between people within specific mediated environments. Their value is not founded in their physical substance or direct usefulness but in symbolic values whose weights and meanings are defined by the social context and organization of their circulation. Materialized as objects, these symbolic values can be exchanged for others – ideas, friendship, community, and commerce. The circulation of cat images seems to offer communion with a group of like-minded people, a cat-nation if you like, with implicit but unstated codes and beliefs. Their meanings can fluctuate in response to changing contexts and values. Indeed history assures us that this is the case, for nothing is more unstable than the identity of cats.

In disseminating cat images, my network of correspondents is constituting a hybrid animal-Internet locale. The cat totem unites people under its sign and invites them to admire and imitate the cat's outstanding characteristics, as depicted therein: sensuality, softness, cuteness, a strong sense of personal space, and a wily capacity to pretend indifference. As viewers we are not required to relive the history of agriculture, witchcraft, children's literature or animal torture, or to summon our energies to protect these animals from harm. Indeed, these photographs expel such traces from the visual field, inviting their viewers to feel as innocent and forgetful as a kitten. Of course no one is expected to actually inhabit this subject position. These cat images are not totemic in a conventional sense – they do not postulate a one-to-one

FIGURE 1   Gotmouse.jpg. Received by email, source unknown.

exchange of qualities between animal and person – but mobile, free-floating, suggestive, and sporadic. As iconoclastic digital images they openly defy realist expectations, just as cats themselves, according to folklore, like to defy human expectations. These pictures are created for exchange, not information; in this respect they mimic everyday encounters between neighbours or strangers who through their pets find a pathway into talk. Perhaps this is why cats have been a medium of human communication far longer than they have been a totem of exchange between image-savvy Internet users.

Images of animals circulating in this manner are simultaneously letters between friends, icons of a nascent epistemology, comfortably empty signifiers, links with childhood or childlike feeling, reiterations of gender/animal taxonomies, extensions of hominess and neighbourliness into the random paths of cyberspace, and symptoms of anxiety about the future of the natural world. These meanings tease one another in the visual culture of animals the way a cat teases a mouse, with the same playfulness and perhaps even the same deadly stakes.

Cats have been known to humans for so many centuries that it is fair to say that the two species co-evolved in connection with one another. The histories of agriculture, gender, class, religion, and urbanization are punctuated with the presence of cats; each bears the marks of radical transformations in attitudes toward these animals. It would be a mistake to assume consensus on what cats 'mean' or how a photograph of a cat is instructing us to act. Still, the prolific dissemination of cat images in contemporary culture tells us something about human–animal relations and the role of images in constituting or challenging these relations. I am interested in why cats are now so visible, and why they appear in the forms they take, as cute cyberphotos, cartoons and cinematic extras, calendars and kitsch. Notwithstanding the predominant sweetness of the imagery, its proliferation also provokes negative energy or even phobia (projected in more than one instance against this project) that reflects deep ambiguities toward the cat and its place in contemporary culture. No animal in history has been so routinely murdered, tortured or massacred as the domestic cat.[3] At the same time, no other animal image is today as persistently and prolifically circulated across the terrain of commercial culture. This essay explores this tension by unravelling the symbolic function of the images, which operate both as tokens of exchange referring us to our animal natures and as visual tactics de-naturalizing the meaning of the animal itself.

This approach was not my first response to the images accumulating in my inbox. I might like and understand some cats better than some people, but I had not considered registering this affinity in a professional context. I grasped intuitively, without knowing the history of such prohibition, that it was fine to talk about cats within the family or neighbourhood but not in any larger social or intellectual context. Confining this interest to the physical spaces actually traversed by cats obeyed a silent injunction, through which 'a constellation of power is inscribed in its own – its proper-place'. De Certeau defines such control strategies as '[a]ctions which, thanks to the establishment of a place of power (the property of a proper), elaborate theoretical places (systems and totalizing discourses) capable of articulating an ensemble of physical places in which forces are distributed' (1984, p. 169). For de Certeau, the relationship between power and space combines property, discourse, and place, each of which seeks mastery by means of the others (1984, p. 38). Tactics for countering such strategies are thus therapeutics for deteriorating social relations. Reproducing cat images might be an invitation to explore interspecies sensuality and compassion, for instance. But such tactics cannot avoid these ensembles of physical and discursive power. With the prohibition I just described, a scholar can accrue legitimacy and esteem by talking about whales, wolves, horses or lobsters, but not cats. The intensity of negative response to this project echoes a prejudice deeply rooted in the history of species relations in the West, through which the proximity between women and cats, in particular, has produced ostracism, contempt, and the murder of hundreds of thousands of both species. This negative energy is only partially discharged through the more contemporary association between children and cats. These images also raise the question of how far photographic mediations can contest or intervene in the constitution of enhanced sensuality and connection (as they so strongly imply), especially when they represent a species famous for communicating in its own terms.

There is a connection between de Certeau's injunction to analyse space–power relations in terms of property, discourse and place, and the classification of animals. Edmund Leach documented 'astonishing parallelity between the popular categorizations of space, kinship classification and the differentiated treatment of domestic, farm and wild animals' (Bauman 1998, p. 28). Leach's research on parallels between kinship systems, animal categories and domestic/distant spaces provides a solid anthropological antidote to the currently more influential scholastic antipathies to domestic animals reviewed later in this essay. Cats can be understood to be traversed by three binary inscriptions: human enterprise versus nature and wilderness, companionate animals or 'familiars' versus wild and edible animals, and domestic (feminine and familial) space versus public space. The cat's cultural identification with the first of these terms threatens 'proper' animal attribution while identification with it threatens a subtle self-diminishing in social and professional stature.[4] The subtly entrenched nature of this gendered taboo was part of what attracted me to the subject. 'You aren't talking about CATS,' my loved one said. 'Whatever you do, don't say CATS. You will be known as the CAT-LADY'. Friends laughed knowingly at this and signed messages 'CAT LADY'. Colleagues sharpened their focus and looked at me appraisingly: you are doing what with cats, they asked? Some claimed it was impossible to take the subject seriously. The electronic proliferation of photogenic cats together with the lively antipathy of these responses was enough to send me scurrying for the books.

To take these cat images seriously, this essay makes three main moves. First, I revisit post-humanist animal theory in light of companionate culture. Then, I map a history of cats to foreground their roles as liminal creatures in culture. Finally, I attempt to read across a series of representative cat images circulated on the Internet to re-assess our theoretical approaches to animals in representation and to comment on some of their implications.

Thinking through becoming-animals

Since post-humanism has become the reigning conjugation of contemporary art and philosophy, the status of the human species in relation to non-human animals and cyborgs has been an important subject of speculation and debate. The question of animals is reorganizing the ways we address questions of identity, representation, language and power that have occupied the attention of theorists and artists over the last quarter century or so. What constitutes meaning when the subjects are non-human, and what constitutes communication when the language is non-verbal? This question (to which we return) is crucial to the following one. To what extent has Western culture defined the human species by what it is not, by othering and diminishing other animals, and to what extent has this historical process effected closure on inter-species relations and permitted the appalling state of abuse in which many animals live today?

The increasingly popular representation of cats draws on the enhanced visibility of animals in contemporary thought and culture, yet remains separate from it in vocabulary and disposition. The cats proliferating on coffee mugs, greeting cards, calendars, handbags, cartoons, websites, and personal emails are not exactly 'animals' in so far as they do not occupy wild space in these depictions and are therefore not wild. This rhetorical ambiguity draws our attention to the degree to which we are encouraged to draw a singular connection between animals and the spaces they inhabit: pigs, farms; horses, fields; wolves, forests. The depiction of animals that have crossed such boundaries – horses in slaughterhouses, wolves in farms – is accompanied by unease, even panic, arguably arising from the disruption of boundaries as much as the perceived cruel treatment of animals. Cats are famous for their fascination with doors and their capacity to cross spatial boundaries of every kind. In, out. In, out. That is their nature. But that is not nature enough. Cats do not evoke powerful 'otherness' for humans hungry for connection with the natural sublime. Where the discourse on animals has become abstract and universalizing – to the extent that Jacques Derrida famously exclaimed his dislike of that terrible word, 'the animal' – the culture shared by cats and humans is intimate and particular. It continues between acquiescent agents over long periods of time. Jacques Derrida himself wrote that his own cat's eyes 'provide his own *I*'s first mirror' and confessed that this glimpse opened the door to a fundamental compassion for animals and a transformation of his understanding of both philosophy and self-knowledge (Baker 2003, p. 86).

Indeed it is precisely the particularity of companionate culture – the fact that, as Gilles Deleuze and Felix Guattari (1988) put it, one can talk about 'my cat, my dog' (p. 240) – that so disgusts these thinkers. Where is the boundary between 'my' and 'other'? Our language encourages us to affirm such boundaries, so that we refer to 'my' neighbour, 'my' student, 'my' partner, 'my' world. For Deleuze and Guattari, however, the possessive pronoun attached to animals evokes something pathological.[5] As Steve Baker comments, 'postmodern practice cannot quite come to term with its fear of pets' (2003, p. 166). They prefer more complicated and abstract relations with pack animals (even if, in secret, at least one of them did cohabit with a cat). These critics cannot imagine the idea of cross-species intimacy because that relation defies the more virile antagonism between human and animal natures (imaginaries) that underlies their work. They are not interested in companion animals but something more exotic, more distant from everyday urban and suburban culture, like coyotes (a tradition initiated by Joseph Beuys), wolves and lobsters (a favourite reference for Deleuze and Guattari), sharks (featured in the work of artists Olly and Suzi and reproduced on the cover of *Postmodern*

Animal), insects (sometimes in mutated form), or bears (live or stuffed). 'Anyone who likes dogs and cats,' Deleuze and Guattari (1988) state firmly at the centre of this commotion, 'is a fool' (p. 240). For them, marshalling the 'animal' is to summon those species farthest from us and, to their way of thinking, least vulnerable to our way of life. One could say this extends the phenomenological impulse so far into thought that it reverses itself (to borrow a favourite trope from Marshall McLuhan), offering a narrative of animal being that is too coherent to be real. They imagine untouched spaces where wildness dwells and evoke an analogous wolf-like wild space within the human soul. In summoning these species to represent the idea of difference-in-becoming, they erase actual and potential animal subjects.

This philosophical problem is accompanied by a political problem, for the security of this wild space is increasingly dubious. While these authors rarely address the subject(s) of zoos, one could argue that it is the animals 'protected' and spectacularized in zoos or aquariums that comprise the imaginary population of the post-humanist bestiary. Just as these animals are reduced to subjects of the imperious gaze, as Berger (1980) so poignantly writes, so they are reduced to 'things to think with' in post-humanist philosophy. The idea of the impossible encounter continues to interrupt the image, but now deliberately so. Animal bodies are summoned to stand in for general animalness, not so much opposed to human nature as indifferent to it (Baker 2003). Nature is constituted discursively and spatially as escape from the mundane confines of human practice. In other words, this is still a human-centred discourse. It offers a provocative challenge to conventional animal representation but it backfires when it confronts the world of living animals with their material bodies and depleting environments. Whether or not a distancing from the actuality of human–animal lives is what one should expect from philosophy, its usefulness for my work is largely symptomatic.

This animosity towards pets reinforces the dominant taxonomy of animals through which humans across cultures have created separate categories for non-human species, including wild animals, edible animals, working animals, and companionate animals. The companion animal category invites ambivalence because it threatens to reveal the arbitrariness of all these categories. 'Wild' animals symbolize through their difference, the otherness of their animality, while 'domestic' animals express the abjection of this symbolic power. Not only are pets intimate with our home spaces and habits, they are an important part of constituting these spaces and habits. For Deleuze and Guattari (1987), becoming-animal must be understood as 'an absolute de-territorialization of the man' (pp. 35–36). This sheds light on the underlying contradiction of the iconographic cat. Cats (one of our most proximate animals) are both an escape from an industrialized civilization into animal nature, and an escape from the terrors of wilderness into domestic comfort. Some part of us still wants to insist on absolute distinctions between these realms.

The animosity toward pets in this literature goes beyond categorical critique and into the plane of highly charged polemic. The keeping of pets, especially cats, is posed as a symptom and source of human neurosis located specifically in the domestic sphere. Such critique is not a new phenomenon. The attack on pet keeping has been posed on several grounds. First, some claim that to domesticate an animal is to enslave it to human needs (although cats arguably helped humans to domesticate as much as the reverse). By training animals to depend on humans for food and survival, we transform them from free beings into enslaved beings. The slavery motif implies that if we were not intent on being masters, our slaves (animals) would be free. This idea is widely debated in critiques of master–slave relations and mercilessly attacked by Donna Haraway in her research on companion species. The ahistorical attack on pet keeping implies an autonomous biological essence able to sustain diverse species, an idea that defies zoological knowledge. 'There cannot be just one companion species,' Haraway (2003) observes; 'there have to be at least two to make one. It is in the syntax; it is in the flesh' (p. 12).

Second, critics contend that the keeping of pets is necessarily linked to wealth and decadence; if we were not able to waste and squander our resources in a conspicuous manner, we would not keep pets. Without entering into the details of this argument, it has been soundly trounced by anthropologist James Serpell (1986), whose research demonstrates an extensive geography and history of tribal pet-keeping in complicated and often impoverished multi-species environments.

Third, critics claim that the practice of inter-species domestic kinship systems represents a deluded attempt to replicate reactionary family relations and kinship systems, and to reinforce Oedipal personalities. The love of cats or dogs, as distinct from admiration for wolves and lions, prevents the emancipation that follows from writing their lives and their art wildly and interchangeably. In contrast to the first critique, it is humans who need emancipation here; animals are the vehicle of human emancipation rather than the victim of human empowerment. But the prospect of emancipation offered in this 'post-human' vision is a strangely disembodied one, more akin to the absinthe-inspired surrealism of early modernism than to the critique of bio-power so important in contemporary theory and activism. It pursues the freeing of animal natures without regard for the animals.[6]

There is also a problem with the definition of kinship in this critique. The love of pets is a recognizably distinct emotion. 'To regard a dog as a furry child, even metaphorically, demeans dogs and children,' Haraway insists (2003, p. 37). In many cases pets are embraced precisely because the relationship is not familial in a conventional sense. Surveys of American pet owners show that millions of pet owners feel closer to their pet than to their best friends, their children, and their spouses. And they spend accordingly! One could conclude from this finding that pet kinship preserves reactionary familial relations that would otherwise dissolve into more autonomous units (an argument also made about television). This is an interesting issue with respect to cats, for single women are the largest portion of the North American cat-owning population. In some accounts, cats accompany women in the formation of new kinship systems and perpetuate, as Clea Simon (2002) points out, both deep interspecies solidarity and a longstanding suspicion of the woman–cat relationship with its perceived capacity to displace marriage, husbands, and normal property relations.

Engaging cats critically, in sum, offers more than just a sequel to Haraway's discussion of dogs in her work on companion species, and more than an emotive gloss on personal relations with a species which perhaps more than any other accepts all the projections we can impose upon it. This endeavour requires us to take seriously the specific historical–political relations evoked by this species and to interrogate reflexively the bio-politics involved in our interactions with them.

Cats in history

In the popular genealogies of cats now filling the bookstores and documentary channels, the earliest cats were wild animals. Later cats were worshipped as gods in Egypt and then massacred as representatives of Satan in the middle ages. As a result of popular mobilizations against cruelty to animals throughout modern Europe, they became household pets (Jay, 2000). This narrative of transformation is as popular to cat lovers as Christmas and Easter are to Christians, and follows a somewhat similar trajectory. Contemporary cats may live as domestic pets, these histories remind us, but never be fully domesticated. The persistent 'de-naturalization' of cats in popular iconography paradoxically fuels this repetitive retelling of the history of cats as a powerful and subjugated species. Cats' persistently ambiguous status may account for the terror aroused by them in ancient and modern mythology and for the concentrated belittlement of cats today, when the domestic cat exemplifies both the threatening amorality of the non-human and the innocence of children and small furry animals. Their representation builds on this history and works in continuous tension between these meanings.

It is important to contextualize the symbolic work of animals in the context of their social history. With the growth of industrialism in England and across Europe, city life made it impossible – unhygienic and illegal – to keep many species of animals as domestic pets. The pet became a non-working animal while other animals worked like slaves in the streets and undergrounds of the city. As working and farm animals were forcibly ejected from the domestic sphere, machines replaced both people and animals. The cat switched from being a hybrid worker-spirit-demon to being a pet as a consequence of changes in the social landscape that redefined the roles of animals as violently as those of people. The popular embrace of dogs and cats as domestic pets was part of this rationalization process (Tester 1991). Human and animal bodies and their meanings were reorganized together by the discursive regime of industrial capitalism. Once nature seemed comfortably under control, pets were safe for middle- and upper-class households to love and to embrace. The sense of complacency engendered by this perceived taming of nature helps account for the rage of critical theorists who attack them. There is no doubt that cats occupy a special place as targets of such rage. There have been numerous bestseller books inciting hatred for cats as well as those advocating love for them. As Rogers remarks, 'there are no *I Hate Dogs* on the lists' (1998, p. 163). And surely no scholars of other animals have so often been required to respond to hostile questions about why their research subject matters.

By the early twentieth century, cats, like pianos, were part of the ideology and practice of domestic life in many countries. If their lives were initially symbiotic with human life because of their hunting abilities, such attributes are rarely visualized today. Perhaps the public recollection of cats' capacity to decimate large rodent and bird populations would undermine the symbolic regime connecting cats with childhood that emerged in the Victorian era and has so dominated children's culture in the last century. It would also cut into the billions of dollars spent each year on feeding our pets. In this context the pointed recollection of cats' hunting capacities is a step toward re-animalizing their representation, thus departing from the de-naturing of cats that has become 'naturalized' in our culture (see figure 2).

In Western culture the term nature arises through contrast to some entity opposed to it: nature versus civilization, nature versus man in the imperial project, nature versus nurture in the biogenetics war, nature versus capitalism and technology in ecological thought. It is remarkable how tenacious the polarization between nature and its other has been in our culture and how complex and difficult the attempts to overcome it.[7] Such human–animal distinctions have been fundamental to Western culture. Humans have language; animals do not. Humans can reflect on their actions, and are moral beings; animals are not. Humans have hands; animals do not. Humans can pretend; animals cannot. Whoever proposed this last distinction must have not known a cat, for cats are great pretenders. They pretend to bite, pretend to chase, and pretend to sleep, and they know as well as we do that they are pretending. Similarly, primates have hands, and animals have language.

'If a lion could talk,' Ludwig Wittgenstein (1958) famously said, 'we would not understand him'' (p. 223). In other words, animals require us to prise apart our understanding of the link between language and communication, if only to re-connect them in a species-specific context. Animals communicate with body language, territory, scent, sound and other registers.

FIGURE 2 Lola, the author's cat, with catnip mouse. Photo by Bob Hanke.

Of course Wittgenstein is using the lion to make a point about language in much the same way that Deleuze and Guattari talk about wolves or lobsters to make a point about subjectivity. What we can conclude from this is simply that any cultural or political history of the animal is equally a history of human representations, and animal representations today must be understood in light of the history they are helping to write. But this is not the whole story about animals.

For thousands of years cats have inhabited the dual role of hunter and human companion. Their multi-tasking has made them mediators between the world of animals and the world of humans. In the iconography of various cultures they represent mediators between the dead and the living, earthly and supernatural, night and day, God and the devil. In ancient and matriarchal cultures cats are powerful entities. The perception of cats' link to the supernatural made them the subject of early Christian prohibition and mass executions. Cats were killed off in large-scale massacres in the eleventh century, because the Pope believed they were representatives of Satan, and again in the eighteenth century, because the spectacle of cat killing entertained the workers. Between these dates, cats were executed by the thousands together with the often impoverished women who kept them as 'familiars'. The massacre of cats in the eleventh and twelfth century contributed to the spread of the plague by allowing the population of rats and mice to explode and spread across the cities of Europe. The eighteenth century massacres point

FIGURE 3 Satanic cats dressed as witches. Available online: http://www.literary-cat.cwc.net/Witchcraft_3.htm

to transformations in the uses and understandings of animals at the dawn of the industrial era. Urban scholars mocked the rural yokels who continued to believe that animals had feelings. This contempt was part of the symbolic reclassification of humans and animals with profound effects on the history of humans, animals, and the land (see figure 3).

If the disenchantment of the universe had far-reaching effects, cats suffered particularly brutal consequences. In France, cats were ritually murdered in annual sacrifices first recorded in 1344 and last performed as late as 1905 (Kete 1994, p. 119). French scientists of the nineteenth century defined cats as wild animals and voluptuous seducers, whose wildness has as much to do with their perceived 'rapacious feminine sexuality' as their skills at hunting (Kete 1994). Like the prostitute, the cat was discrete but not respectable, neither bourgeois nor working class but rather a bohemian figure flaunted by artists and intellectuals who enjoyed the 'independent, almost heartless' character of the cat. The cat defined the way one should behave, intellectual cat lovers suggested (Kete 1994, p. 125). They had independence, integrity, egotism and a poetic sensibility, enough that they hid the traces of their savagery and their sex.

It took the concentrated efforts of naturalists, animal protection societies, artists, writers and illustrators to rehabilitate the cat as an animal deserving of compassion and rescue. Cat books, illustrations, and exhibitions, culminating in a show at the Crystal Palace in 1871, turned popular sentiment in favour of cats and spawned an outpouring of compassion for them. Cats and children were brought together in narrative and imagery through a re-feminized ideology of natural innocence. Cats were so thoroughly rescued by Victorian culture that by the end of the nineteenth century their image evoked a decorative claustrophobia that had little to do with cats themselves. The massacres stopped, but even today, if an animal is randomly tortured, it is likely to be a cat. Humane societies across North America still refuse to release black cats near Halloween, to protect them from this end.[8]

The mass production of cat images has contributed both to their visibility and to their increasing abstraction as animals through symbolic, commercial and/or decorative strategies. The language of this imagery is often hyperbolically gendered. It is not clear whether the special connection between women and cats has been a cause of cat mistreatment or arose in sympathetic response to it, or more likely a combination of the two. Women and cats appear across periods and genres as a twosome denoting intimacy, sensuality and watchfulness inflected with a wide range of dispositions: maternal, sentimental, magical, seductive, and malevolent. It is only by appearing as (masculine) cool cats that the feline species seems capable of safe independent agency.

Animal taxonomy endows categorical distinctions with moral, aesthetic and political significance. The post-modern animal is less post-modern than its advocates believe, I would suggest, for its categories resemble the social and mental architecture of exterior and interior space in the modern period. The contempt for domestic pets echoes the modernist antipathy to doors, textures, and domestic interiors. Preferring purity and function, the modernist aesthetic required the overturn of sentiment, tactility and other qualities associated with the feminine. This was a logical reaction against Victorian culture with its values of enclosure, cuteness and intimacy (Sparks 1995, p. 108). It is also a misunderstanding of cats. It is a commonplace of cat knowledge that cats do not respect doors, or rather that they are obsessed with them and insist on going in and out a hundred times a day. They need to inspect and reconstitute their territories. Feline tenacity and delight in multi-spatialism were semiotically eradicated by representational regimes of the late nineteenth and much of the twentieth century. It is not clear what these digital snapshots do to counteract such mythification. Notwithstanding the hyper-domestication of the cyber-cat, live cats inhabit not just interiors but also the yards beyond our doorways, the walls over which they escape, the alleys extending the space

FIGURE 4   Received by email, source unknown.

down the block. Cats actually transverse a larger scale of exploration than we think, according to Desmond Morris (2002) and my neighbours, moving knowledgeably between domains, local geographies, and work assignments with ease (see figure 4).

Henri Lefebvre (1991) writes of space:

> Visible boundaries, such as walls or enclosures in general, give rise for their part to an appearance of separation between spaces where in fact what exists is an ambiguous continuity. The space of a room, bedroom, house or garden may be cut off in a sense from social space by barriers and walls, by all the signs of private property, yet still remain fundamentally part of that space. Nor can such spaces be considered empty 'mediums' [sic], in the sense of containers distinct from their contents. (p. 87)

This passage resembles the thought-practice of a cat. Just as wolves and lions survive in the wild, cats survive in the 'hood'. Thus the iconography of urban Cool Cats whose images celebrate the bravery and wiliness needed to negotiate the metropolis at night. Cats wander, and please themselves, and cannot be trained or herded. These cool cats reconcile urban life with animal behaviour, and offer a different image of urban wildlife. They symbolically cruise their urban wilderness hunting for game while beguiling their female companions in the human population. This is a long way from the sweet iconographic world of digital kitties, whose cuteness evades the hunting question altogether. This question is taking on new significance because of the threatening impact of feline overgrowth on the populations of small animals. No one is more aware of cat overpopulation than local human networks that feed them and pay for their neutering; it is ironic that such people should be blamed for the overpopulation of cats. 'It is not clear,' Rogers muses, 'why cats alone should be condemned for a predatory drive that they share with dogs, nor why it is more villainous to kill birds than other small animals' (1998, p. 161). Obviously cats hunt; that is why they were domesticated in the first place. How much does human hostility toward them derive from their cruelty to (smaller) animals, how much from their longstanding association with women, and how much from their sometimes ostentatious comfort and independence from human will? What power–space relations are at stake in this debate?

If urbanization has fuelled cat overpopulation, homelessness, and starvation, it has also contributed symbolically and materially to cat survival. Toronto neighbourhoods are dotted with cat rescue networks that spay and neuter homeless cats and find homes for them. They work by word of mouth, email, and local vets, and like the cats themselves, by patterns of urban proximity. There are no comparable networks for dogs, whose owners rescue them from shelters in far higher proportions. These off-line cat–human networks are echoed in the on-line networks of cat images sent from one inbox to another. Rather than having to stand in for whatever fantasy of the animal we humans need in order to Other ourselves from it, these human–cat networks represent the interconnectedness of all animality, including our own, in the urban wilderness. The circulation of Internet images acquires clearer meaning in the context of emergent interspecies interconnectedness forced upon all of us by the vicissitudes of urban life.

Studies in iconography

To the extent that they are horizontal, costumed, or flirtatious, the cats in the emailed images that provoked my writing of this essay confirm their association with traditional perceptions of women and children. Their tone is playful, familiar, and innocent. Yet their visual aesthetic is hygienic, impersonal, and slightly ironic, that is to say, digital. By expressing a self-conscious knowledge of photographic codes, they distance and yet reinforce the efficacy of these same codes. In disposition they stand somewhere between pink flamingos, with their archly decorative suburban flare, and babies, with their direct innocent gaze. They suggest that cat images require no decoration, for cats are decorative all by themselves and, therefore, if you add a ruffle or prop to the image of a cat – poof! You have kitsch. Semiotically, these photographs distance us from the subject they seemingly embrace, which makes them peculiarly appropriate for electronic messaging. Posed in various settings and enduring the occasional costume, the cats are mocked for the distance they have traversed from their animal natures. But such distance is exaggerated by the photographic act. In displacing the cat from its natural habitus and disposition, while expressing a sense of anxiety about this displacement, the photographer makes a fetish of the feline body (see figure 5).

The de-naturalized animal photograph simultaneously evokes and distances the sense of animal self. Why this ambivalence? Sarah Kember (1998) describes photography as:

> A mechanism of knowledge and power which allows the subject to compensate for a perceived loss, absence or threat in the object world and for the feelings of anxiety, fear or despair which are thereby provoked. This may include a loss of power over the object, the absence of a loved one or the threat of difference. A photograph is a small, tangible object, a trophy or token which defies the passing of time and insists on the presence of that which it depicts. It offers up a scene or event to perpetual scrutiny and immortalizes the subject's perspective. (p. 6)

FIGURE 5   Partied out. Received by email, source unknown.

In this account, the animal picture compensates for the sense of loss we experience in connection with our animal selves. Critics differ about the photograph's ability to heal the distance such loss implies. John Berger notes in his landmark essay 'Why Look at Animals' (1980), 'The zoo to which people go to meet animals, to observe them, to see them, is, in fact, a monument to the impossibility of such encounters' (p. 19). For Berger, the act of looking is at the core of this impossibility, for the photographic gaze depends upon and reinforces a cumulative impoverishment of the sympathetic imagination. In writing of the longing evoked by the photograph, however, Roland Barthes claims that we can know the impossibility of the real in representation but we can nevertheless feel its presence (Kember 1998, p. 31). The link between the photograph and what it represents maintains wordless intelligibility even in its absence, and he resolves to 'make myself the measure of photographic "knowledge"' (Barthes 1980, p. 4). In his analysis of the photographic punctum, the inescapable chasm between the representational and the real gives rise to moments of genuine feeling and recognition. For Barthes, photographs were never interchangeable with their referent, or perceived to stand in for the real. The ambiguous relation with their subject is part of their poignant affect, a sense of remembrance and loss, as Barthes discovers by looking at a photograph of his mother as a child. In this light, photographing animals makes explicit the act of representation conjoined momentarily with a sense of the real, and thus (though we do not want to make this connection too mechanical) a simultaneous experiencing of the cognitive self and the animal self.

But the digital kitties romping through the Internet enact a studied indifference to this moment of affective investment. If they strongly evoke cuddling, the studied failure of these pictures to fulfil the sensuous connection between 'pet' as noun and 'pet' as verb contributes to their signification. Their photographic performance represents both the desire for and impossibility of intimate connection with them. Kevin Robins (1996) describes image technologies as modernism's defence mechanism against 'the fear of being touched by the unknown' (p. 12). In this context, the mutual complicity of zoos and photographs can be understood as a logical element of modern imaging culture, justifying Berger's criticism of the photographs taken in that context. In contrast to these imprisoned wild animals, the digital cats are simultaneously closer to and more autonomous from our gaze. Being both more proximate to and co-dependent with us (as a species) and more autonomous from one another (as individual members of the species) than wild animals like wolves, their place in post-humanist animal classification can be seen as directly opposite to them. Cats represent sensuality, independence and a complete lack of conscience and remorse. Like their photographers, these digital kitties enact a complex performance around the ideal of authentic connection. They seem to participate knowingly in their own fetishization.

Kember (1998) notes that: 'Fetishism is always an inadequate and unstable means of control because it is a compensatory mechanism. The fear which stimulates it remains embedded within it, and the fetish object (in this case the photograph) is always marked by the absence behind the presence and the fear behind the desire (to eradicate it)' (p. 66). The compensatory nature of the photograph and the compensatory nature of the cat, both powerful and unstable affective connections, seem to join seamlessly and irresistibly in the digital photographs disseminated through the Internet.

The rhetorical disconnection of these Internet cat images from animal embodiment frees them to leave the urban-animal-domestic spaces of everyday life and to travel through cyberspace, leaving behind while referencing cat-bodies and the conventional circumscribed cat-space of running from the upholstered chair to the front sidewalk or the neighbour's back lawn. Just as such images evoke both intimacy and fear, they also challenge our perceptions of feeling 'at home'. *Home* is the product of people working on pets and pets working on people, forming a 'family unit' comprised of multiple species, and marking territories through daily practices. For many in North America, this collective presence communicates home and seems increasingly indispensable to the specificity and meaning of home; the more unstable that meaning, the more important the work of the cat. Electronic cat images simultaneously reference and abandon these contexts, helping to constitute new kinds of landscapes that surround us and flow into and through the Internet.

Spatially and symbolically, the 'human' has been defined by specific (if culturally relative) relations to the non-human. The formation of home as private domestic space contributed significantly to the development of the modern human subject. The adoption of domestic animals seemed to enhance, rather than to destabilize, the unique moral and cognitive qualities through which humans distinguished themselves from other animals. Humans assumed a special place in the universe by denying their bestial nature; the keeping of pets was a good illustration of human compassion. Those described as resembling beasts (such as the aboriginal, the enslaved, the lusty, and the mentally ill) were not human, that is to say, not deserving of compassion, dignity or rights. The term 'post-humanist' communicates the recognition that speciesism was fundamental to the formation of Western subjectivity and has wrought its own forms of violence on history. The ascendancy of speciesism has been rightfully critiqued as related to the categories and practices of racism that shame the history of humanism in the world. If European Empire was founded on a cultural taxonomy of unacknowledged racism and colonialism, as Edward Said (1993) so powerfully demonstrates, Western world history was founded on categorical moral distinctions between human beings and non-human animals that have orchestrated differences between human cultures. The dominant question posed by animals and animal being throughout the

West, reaching its peak with the ascendancy of industrialization, was not how to understand animals, but how to dominate and use them.

While the representation of cats has been shaped by this tradition, such representation also has an interesting history of contesting it. We have already seen traces of this ambiguity in the contrast between digital cat photos and the conventional animal photographs assessed in Berger's essay. But this ambiguity can speak only if we contest some of the animal thematics in contemporary philosophy. A prolific commentator on animal representation and post-humanism, Baker (2003) argues that since modernism evacuated animals from the visual field, that they can be revisited only through an aesthetic strategy that refrains from social commentary and moral judgment. This normative claim derives from an interpretation of Deleuze and Guattari's 'becoming-animal' and its association with making art. As Deleuze and Guattari put it in *A Thousand Plateaus*, 'artists "become-animal" at the same time as the animal becomes what they willed' (1998, p. 305). This emphasis on the malleability of the animal subject (which is neither subject nor form) reinforces the assumption that meaning is produced by and within the human subject. Deleuze and Guattari write, 'how to operate other-than-in-identity' — and of how to operate as an artist — has to do with speeds. To 'make your body a beam of light moving at ever-increasing speed,' they write, is something which 'requires all the resources of art, and art of the highest kind' — the kind of art, that is to say, through which 'you become animal'' (quoted in Baker 2003, p. 137).

The animals evoked in these texts are metaphors (notwithstanding the authors' objection to metaphor) having little or nothing to do with real animals or their interaction with humans. As Baker notes, 'Admirable and imaginative as such creative practices may be, they fail wholly to address the problem they create for artists whose concern is to represent animals' (2003, p. 137). Despite his commitment to 'becoming animal,' Baker (2001) concludes, 'Animals, for Deleuze and Guattari, seem to operate more as a device for writing — albeit a device which initiated its own forms of political practice — than as living beings whose conditions of life were of direct concern to the writers.' He points to their 'revealing remark' that Franz Kafka's novel *The Trial*, in contrast to some of his earlier works, 'liberates itself from all animal concern to the benefit of a much higher concern' (Baker 2001, p. 95). In that respect, animals play a purely metaphoric function; our connection with them can only be asserted through a reaffirmation of their difference and distinction from us. As with the genre of nature films, however, such depiction minimizes conflict between natural environment and human society, animals and persons, and so 'seems to invite viewers to forget that their view of nature is mediated, even as the very act of nature spectatorship underscores its distance and unfamiliarity' (Chris 2006, p. 71).

Many artists featured in *The Postmodern Animal* seek to make the lack of fit between human and animal evident, and to make this disjunction productive of liberating thought. Their work corresponds with critical animal studies in that they seek to trouble normalizing distinctions between humans and other animals (e.g. Doniger, 1999; Wolfe, 2003). Many of them intentionally refuse to let the representation of the animal be subsumed by human terms, even if such terms include empathy, compassion, or protest (Baker 2003).

Wherever you stand in these debates, there is a politics at work in the encounter between human and animal — not just about morality and feeling, but also the constitution of space and time within which the encounter is staged. These authors' interest in 'the speed of light' echoes the Futurist manifestos and, closer to home, defies widespread criticism of the condensed rhythms of nature documentaries by Disney and *National Geographic*, in which hunting and aggression are sped up and foregrounded by editing (Wilson 1991, McKibben 1992). Like the producers of such documentaries, these writers presuppose a state of wildness that can only be authenticated in vast natural territories that are catastrophically shrinking. Both prefer virility and speed to empathy and proximity. No doubt you, like Olly and Suzi, would wish your encounters with wolves, spiders and sharks to be cautious and swift. Even Beuys, who spent a week with his coyote, maintained that their 'roles were exchanged immediately' (Baker 2003, p. 44) so presumably the remainder of the week was a performance of redundancy. In contrast, cats invite a more leisurely acquaintance. It is mundane, it is sensual, and it can last for years. Cats may like you one day and taunt you the next; they may enter or leave at any time; cohabiting cats and humans feel each others' comings and goings and rely on each others' presence without words. It is not (but also not not) the 'quality' of the cat or the human either that is at stake in this encounter, but (in connection to these) the qualitative interaction of several species in constructing the spaces of everyday life.

At stake in the study of these proliferating feline images on the Internet is our social and symbolic relationship with the natural and the urban world. The circulation of images of non-human others is closely related to the organization of social interaction and power within human cultures. A commonplace truth about cats is that they are never completely tamed; they retain traces of the wild, residues of independence and guiltlessness no matter how domestic they become. There may be some projection in the readiness with which traditional Western perceptions of women and children retrieve and remind us of this knowledge. If something as sensuous and domestic as a cat retains aspects of its species nature, then obviously those of us associated with cats have not lost ours. But is this a good thing? Given the ambivalence with which we approach our own species, the conjunction of sentiment and violence evoked by cat representation makes sense. As domesticated animals, cats allow us to feel good about ourselves but only if our feelings and practices really are good

FIGURE 6 Tuppence.jpg. See: http://www.infinitecat.com, downloaded 2005.

natured. We can romanticize and distance ourselves from wolves and lobsters, even as their spaces of inhabitation rot and shrink, but cats are part of our everyday urban ecology; they directly mirror and incorporate our understanding or lack of it. Just as representations of angels oscillate between the transcendental and the corporeal, so cats oscillate between human and the animal, inside and outside, wild and tame, just as we hope we might.[9] Just as hearing angels requires a cosmological conception of heavenly space, so 'reading' cats depends on reflexively understanding the embodied languages of animal space and the combined sentiment and violence with which humans seek to share or enter it. The cats being messaged across cyberspace call upon us to revisit the obdurate differences we have constructed between ourselves and those connections through which we make our histories (see figure 6).

Acknowledgement

The author thanks Phaedra Pezzullo for her adept editorial input on this project.

Notes

1. Notable examples of authors honouring cats include Michel de Montaigne, Samuel Johnson, Charles Beaudelaire, Pierre Loti, Rudyard Kipling, Edward Allen Poe, Mark Twain, T.S. Eliot, Edward Lear, Sidonie-Gabrielle Colette, Tennessee Williams, Gary Snyder, Haruki Murakami, Jack Kerouac, and Timothy Findlay; in the visual arts, a short-list includes Leonardo da Vinci, William Hogarth, Gustave Courbet, Paul Gallico, Andy Warhol, and Walt Disney.
2. Popular websites currently available include: http://www.themoggy.com/olympics.htm; http://www.stuffonmycat.com/; http://www.petoffice.co.jp/catprin/honten/index.htm; http://www.i-love-cats.com/; http://cats.about.com/; http://catsinsinks.com/
3. While raising and killing animals such as chickens and pigs in contemporary agribusiness undoubtedly involves an element of torture, the ostensible aim is to produce food. In Western cultures, wherein cats are not served as food, the purpose of torturing a cat is intransitively the torture. Rogers (1998) notes that while many animals 'suffered ... in cold-blooded scientific investitations and ... were unprotected by the moral teachings of the Church, [cats] were more liable to be victims of sadistic popular customs'. Before the eighteenth century, they were 'an obvious object for random sadism'; even after cats were household pets, 'tormenting cats was still seen as acceptable fun' (pp. 153–154).
4. This obviously does not apply to male writers and philosophers (see note 1).
5. Levi-Strauss, Wood, Lyotard and Derrida all evoke the cat's special value to (and in) their writing. Cats stop, Lyotard suggests, 'at thresholds that we do not see, where they sniff some "present beyond"' (cited in Baker 2003, p. 184).
6. Similarly, pre-modern Roman Catholic churchmen frowned upon pet owning and on the practice of giving 'Christian' names to pets (Shell 1986, p. 135).
7. As Haraway (2003) emphasizes, 'Dogs are not an alibi for other themes; dogs are fleshly material-semiotic presences in the body of technoscience. Dogs are not surrogates for theory; they are not here just to think with. They are here to live with [and] partners in the crime of human evolution' (p. 5).
8. For a directory of black cat superstitions and legends, see: http://www.austinlostpets.com/kidskorner/2October/InfoBlackCat.htm.
9. Michel Serres, Regis Debray, and Margaret Wertheim, all philosophers of science, have written about information flow in terms of cyber-angels and the messages they bear.

References

Baker, S. (2003) *The Postmodern Animal*, London, Reaktion Books.

Baker, S. (2001) *Picturing the Beast: Animals, Identity, and Representation*, Urbana, IL, University of Illinois Press.
Barthes, R. (1980) *Camera Lucida*, London, Flamingo.
Bauman, Z. (1998) *Globalization: The Human Consequences*, New York, Columbia University Press.
Berger, J. (1980) *About Looking*, New York, Pantheon Books.
Certeau, M. de (1984) The *Practice of Everyday Life*, trans. S. Rendall, Berkeley, CA, University of California Press.
Chris, C. (2006) *Watching Wildlife*, Minneapolis, MN, University of Minnesota Press.
Deleuze, G. & Guattari, F. (1987) *Kafka: Toward a Minor Literature*, trans. D. Polan, Minneapolis, MN, University of Minnesota Press.
Deleuze, G. & Guattari, F. (1998) *A Thousand Plateaus: Capitalism and Schizophrenia*, trans. B. Massumi, London, Athlone Press.
Doniger, W. (1999) 'Reflection', in *The Lives of Animals*, ed. J. M. Cooetzee, Princeton, NJ, Princeton University Press.
Haraway, D. (2003) *The Companion Species Manifesto: Dogs, People, and Significant Otherness*, Chicago, IL, Prickly Paradigm Press.
Jay, R. (2000) *The Kingdom of the Cat*, London, Firefly Books.
Kember, S. (1998) *Virtual Anxiety: Photography, New Technologies and Subjectivity*, Manchester, Manchester University Press.
Kete, K. (1994) *The Beast in the Boudoir: Petkeeping in Nineteenth-century Paris*, Berkeley, CA, University of California Press.
Lefebvre, H. (1991) *The Production of Space*, trans. D. Nicholson-Smith, Oxford, Blackwell.
May, J. & Marten, M. (1983) *The Book of Beasts*, New York, Viking Press.
McKibben, B. (1992) *The Age of Missing Information*, New York, Plume.
Morris, D. (2002) *Catwatching: The Essential Guide to Cat Behaviour*, London, Ebury Press.
Robins, K. (1996) *Into the Image: Culture and Politics in the Field of Vision*, New York, Routledge.
Rogers, K. M. (1998) *The Cat and the Human Imagination: Feline Images from Bast to Garfield*, Ann Arbor, MI, The University of Michigan Press.
Said, E. (1993) *Culture and Imperialism*, New York, Vintage Books.
Serpell, J. (1986) *In the Company of Animals*, Oxford, Blackwell.
Shell, M. (1986) 'The family pet', *Representations*, vol. 15, pp. 121–153.
Simon, C. (2002) *The Feline Mystique: On the Mysterious Connection between Women and Cats*, New York, St Martin's Press.
Sparks, P. (1995) *As Long as Its Pink: The Sexual Politics of Taste*, London, Pandora.
Tester, K. (1991) *Animals and Society: The Humanity of Animal Rights*, London, Routledge.
Whiteside, K. (2002) *Divided Natures: French Contributions to Political Ecology*, Cambridge, MA, MIT Press.

Wilson, A. (1991) *The Culture of Nature: North American Landscape from Disney to the Exxon Valdez*, Toronto, Between the Lines.

Wittgenstein, L. (1958) *Philosophical Investigations*, 3rd edn, New York, Prentice Hall.

Wolfe, C. (2003) *Animal Rites: American Culture, the Discourse of Species, and Posthumanist Theory*, foreword by W. J. T. Mitchell, Chicago, IL, University of Chicago Press.

Catriona Mortimer-Sandilands

QUEERING ECOCULTURAL STUDIES

> *This paper begins with Slack and Whitt's ('Ethics and cultural studies' in* Cultural Studies, *eds L. Grossberg et al., Routledge, New York, 1992) crucial imperative to cultural studies: that we need to (re)develop its normative commitment, and that ecological relations are the site from which to do so. Although their argument eventually relies on a problematic understanding of nature as an integrative totality 'beyond' culture, this paper maintains that it is nevertheless important to follow their lead and consider ecological relations in their articulation with, and implication in, other relations of power in late capitalism. 'Queer' ecocultural studies, given its considerable skepticism with 'normative' natures as well as its emphasis on sex/nature articulations, would have us focus precisely on challenging the intersections of power, beginning with heteronormativity, and ecological relations. For an example of queer ecocultural studies, the paper then reads Jane Rule's novel* The Young in One Another's Arms *(Pandora Press, London, 1977), a sophisticated example of 'queer nature writing' with its focus on the intertwined becomings of a queer family and a wounded landscape. Following from Rule's narrative, the paper argues that a critical practice of queer ecocultural studies demands that we read 'for' nature, for the implication of culture in ecosystemic relations, and that we also insist on understanding these more-than-human implications as part of, and not beyond, complex articulations of power.*

Introduction: from ecocultural studies to queer natures

In their important 1992 essay 'Ethics and Cultural Studies,' Jennifer Daryl Slack and Laurie Ann Whitt raise an important challenge for cultural studies: 'Given the growing appreciation of the nature, scope, and implications of ecological interdependence, cultural studies must respond to the political and ethical challenges which that recognition poses' (p. 571). Specifically, they argue that the normative commitments characterizing the (Marxist-humanist) history of cultural studies require both expansion and transformation in order to approach an 'ecocultural alternative,' a practice of cultural studies to adequately address and challenge the ways in which ecological relations are imbricated in the cultural fabric of late capitalism. They begin by tracing the emergence of a more 'holistic' perspective in cultural studies, pointing to the increasing importance of ideas of articulation and interdependence that have resulted from cultural studies' convergences (and divergences) with feminism, anti-racism, structuralism, and post-modernism. Yet, as a way of maintaining its ethical commitments and possibilities beyond 'the mesmerization with the play of surfaces' (p. 584) that may result from an over-enthusiastic embrace of ideas of difference and popular cultural resistance, Slack and Whitt also argue that cultural studies requires an ethical concept of totality. Indeed, they argue that the 'totality' to which their ecocultural alternative must speak is one that necessarily pushes our understandings of articulation and inter-dependence beyond the limited anthropocentric realm with which cultural studies has historically been concerned.

Following environmental philosophers such as Arne Naess and Baird Callicott, Slack and Whitt are particularly interested in the idea of totality as *ecosystem*, which they understand as 'an ecological description of the natural environment based on the priority of integrated, differentiated wholes over their component parts, of relations over discrete, individual objects that are related' (1992, p. 585). At one level, their conception of the ecosystem, and particularly its emphasis on ecological unity as a *non-determined*, *non-essential* and *non-static* totality,[1] offers a generative and significant account of contingency that can nudge cultural studies beyond both structuralism and atomism. Read literally and metaphorically, the ecosystem works, for Slack and Whitt, as an expanded understanding of materiality.[2] At another level, they write, 'what an ecoculturalist theoretical perspective suggests for cultural studies is an appreciation of the significance and of the sense in which human beings, and the social and political formations in which we are immersed, are *implicated* — in the etymological sense of being enfolded, involved, or engaged — in the environment' (Slack & Whitt 1992, p. 588). This second use of the ecosystem underscores the specifically ethical imperative of an ecocultural studies to understand the involvement of cultural in ecological process, and vice versa. In my interpretation, we are compelled to give preference to this second move by reading culture *for* nature. Here, I mean that cultural studies offers a unique promise that moves an ecocultural project *into* nature, not just in the sense of understanding the politics of nature representation, nor of merely recognizing the involvement of a particular cultural phenomenon (often involving commodification) in processes of environmental change (often involving degradation). Rather, an ecocultural studies has the ability to make *appreciable*, in the multiple modalities of that word, the ecological relations in which cultural ones are always already involved.[3]

Where Slack and Whitt's imperative runs into some trouble, however, is in its argument that ecosystemic thinking, because grounded in a totality that rests *outside* of cultural contingency, provides a normative answer to what they characterize as the 'moral snares of postmodernism' (Zylinska 2001, p. 179). There are two significant problems with this argument. In the first place, Slack and Whitt posit the biotic as a realm 'beyond discourse' (1992, p. 585), and emphasize that the ecological totality in which we are located thus also positions our ontological interconnectedness 'outside' cultural relations. While I certainly agree, for reasons that I have discussed at length elsewhere (e.g. Sandilands, 1999), that there is an element of nature that resists its discursive appearance, and while I imagine that Slack and Whitt were simply pointing out that nature can not be reduced to culture or discourse, their argument toward an ethics of ecosystemic totality leans on a naturalization of the idea of the ecosystem as a realm that is, somehow, exterior to the cultural relations with which it interacts and, increasingly, by which it is constituted (to whit: there is no longer a living cell on the planet that does not contain traces of the synthetic pesticide DDT). Andrew Ross has warned explicitly against the lurking (and sometimes overt) authoritarianism inherent in relying on the idea of a normalizing nature outside culture, specifically 'against the tendency, surfacing again, and often in the name of environmentalism, to wield biological authority as a model for social well-being' (1994, p. 5, see also Evernden, 1992). Although I doubt that Slack and Whitt, given their previous argument about articulation, would consider doing so, ignoring the bio-politics internal to the idea of the ecosystem itself is very dangerous, as 'there are too many ventriloquists about who will speak [in the name of the planet] for us to feel entirely comfortable with that' (Ross 1994, p. 14). Not only is the biotic *not* outside the social, but it is a dangerous fiction to theorize an ecological ethics as if it were; a task of ecocultural studies may be to recognize the involvement of ecological processes in cultural relations, but a second task must be to interrogate the cultural relations in and through which such processes are interpreted and organized.

Second, as Joanna Zylinska emphasizes, 'Slack and Whitt rely on a very narrow, almost caricatured version of "postmodernism" as a state of moral confusion' (2001, p. 179). As I read it, in their essay, the relativism of the post-modern eventually serves as a foil *against* which to present the extra-social solidity of the biotic. This retreat from uncertainty and contingency to the (illusory) safety of the biotic actually contradicts Slack and Whitt's own argument about the centrality of the concept of articulation to the ethical promise of cultural studies (they emphasize articulation to the point at which it meets the biotic, but not beyond). As they write, 'cultural studies cannot adequately ground its interventionist strategy by appealing to a single principle (class, gender, or race), [and must] shift [its] concern to the articulating principles that connect gender, race, and class, principles in which relations of subordination and domination are entailed' (1992, p. 579). Slack and Whitt do not, in their particular appeal to the ecosystem, emphasize the continued importance of these questions of articulation to ecocultural studies: articulation was not a partial step on the way to ecocentric holism but must remain an active analytic focus, and that is the specific value of the tradition of cultural studies to ecological inquiry. So it strikes me that a key value of an ecocultural approach to ecological politics lies in the observation that making nature *appreciable* is never only making *nature* appreciable, precisely because ecological relations are always already implicated in and by cultural processes. At the same time as ecology undergirds and permeates the social world, ideas and practices of nature — including the idea of the ecosystem and the scientific processes and institutions through which the idea has taken shape — are always already made socially present in the midst of cultural relations of power. In this light, an ecocultural study that insists on 'social nature' (Castree & Braun 2001) is attuned not just to a critical practice of reading for nature, but to one of reading for the ways in which ecological relations, at specific intersections, constitute and are constituted by precisely those relations of power with which cultural studies historically has been concerned.

What I advocate, then, is an ecocultural studies that makes nature appreciable in cultural practices and that also always reads 'nature' as a porously-bounded realm of relations intertwined with (but not reducible to) others. More specifically — and here I finally come to the 'queer' part — I advocate a critical practice of ecocultural analysis that challenges, as part of an analysis focused on the contingency and articulation of power relations, the ways in which natural and ecological relations have been read and organized to normalize and naturalize power, and likewise the ways in which cultural relations have incorporated and shaped other-than-human actors and processes in the unfolding and re/production of power. To 'queer nature,' in this view, is to actively intervene in ideas and practices of nature (ecological and otherwise) in order to disturb its naturalizing and normalizing effects. A specifically ecocultural rendition of this queering, however, insists not only on denaturalizing power — e.g. calling into question the sexual, class, racial and gender effects of 'nature' practices from genetics to gardens to GIS (geographic information system) (see Moore *et al.* 2003) — but also on considering the ecological contexts and outcomes of the deployment and arrangement of power as part of the process.

There is, however, a more precise meaning to the idea of 'queer nature' that I invoke here that rests on the specific interrogation of heteronormativity and homophobia highlighted by recent queer theory, as it is from such particular interrogations that an intersectional understanding of articulation appears. Queer theory has amply highlighted the fact that 'queer' is not merely an identity-based preposition, but rather a mode of examining and challenging specific relations of power in intersection with others, equally specific; it is a place to begin, and in its consciously situated particularity offers a view outward. At one level, of course, the idea of queer nature highlights the fact that other-than-human nature is filled with sexually diverse interactions, which clearly exposes the fallacy of any idea of an evolutionarily or ecologically-sanctioned nature-telos of ideal, gender dimorphic, reproductive sexuality against which all other forms can be measured and found deviant or pathological: Bruce Bagemihl (1999) has, in fact, compiled an extraordinary weight of biological evidence to the contrary.[4] In conjunction with this observation, but with a more careful eye to the historically contingent intersections between discourses of nature and of sex, queer nature also suggests an active practice of interrogating the heteronormative and homophobic relations through which ideas and institutions of nature – medical and biological science, zoological display, park and garden design, camping facilities, urban planning, natural history, population policy, environmental politics – have been organized to shape both homosexual and heterosexual practices, historically and in the present (Mortimer-Sandilands 2005). In response to this proliferation of heteronormative natures, gay men, lesbians, bisexuals, and transgendered persons have themselves deployed a variety of discourses of nature as part of a strategy of resistance; a choice to 'naturalize' the queer through animal, genetic, literary, and even environmental arguments has particular significance in a context that connects, for example, minority rights with ideas of innate, naturalized difference.

These last questions have, perhaps ironically, underscored the instability of nature as a site in and through which naturalization proceeds, not to mention the politically-charged quality (along class, race, and gender lines) of any and all articulations of sexual with ecological argument. Indeed, queer theory, with its ongoing political distrust of normalizing strategies and its emphasis on anti-essentialism and performativity [cogently reconsidered in Butler's (2004) study], has been deeply skeptical of most invocations of nature, whether they facilitate reproductive heterosexuality, lesbian feminism or, indeed, same-sex marriage. Thus, when I advocate a queer nature, I do not do so to place g/l/b/t concerns within the sphere of the ecological (they are already there), nor do I do so to focus attention singularly on the politics of heteronormativity within and across environmental discourse. Instead, I emphasize a queer ecocultural studies that includes both the eco-ethical act of making nature appreciable and the deliberate skepticism, born from the complex traditions comprising a queer theoretical and political project, with the normative implications that this appreciation cannot help but produce. In this sense, I echo Judith Halberstam's recent claim to 'queer space,' in which queerness is not so much a question of sexual identity as it is a practice of space – and, here, nature – developed, 'at least in part, in opposition to the institutions of family, heterosexuality, and reproduction ... according to other logics of location, movement, and identification' (2005, p. 1). To be as clear as possible: far from recapitulating an identity politics, queering ecocultural studies begins, in both its insistence on the centrality of sex and its skepticism with normative invocations of nature, from a specific interrogation of heteronormativity and heterosexuality, but necessarily develops an articulated view of culture, power, and nature in which the reverberations of 'queer' are heard in multiple milieux, across multiple forms of cultural/natural implication.

Jane Rule: queering ecotopia

My ally in this project is Jane Rule, on whose novel *The Young in One Another's Arms* (1977) I would like to focus on in order to highlight the possibilities of a queer ecocultural project in a specific context. Although, as Marilyn Schuster has noted (1999, pp. 3–4), Rule has been virtually ignored by academic critics (queer and otherwise), her novels, multiply reprinted and adapted to film,[5] have been very important to several generations of queers and lesbians. Schuster argues that part of the reason for this skewed response – critically ignored, privately cherished – is that, by dint of both geographic and political distance from the urban US north-east, Rule's 'texts were not informed in and by those [political lesbian] communities and tend to go against the grain of 1970s separatism and triumphalism' (Schuster 1999, p. 40). In addition, and in direct contrast to both 1950s lesbian pulp and 1970s lesbian feminist works, Rule's fiction does not focus on the publicly visible institutions of gay and lesbian culture but rather both represents and reaches 'a less public but no less important network of lesbian lives' (p. 40). Rule's characters are not all lesbian, and their struggles are not all overtly political; this stance got her into trouble with some lesbian feminists such as Karla Jay who, in her review of Rule's *Contract With the World* (1982), accused the 'politically incorrect' work of being a 'heterosexually dominated novel' and dissuaded lesbian readers from buying it (quoted in Schuster, 1999, p. 234).

Rule's emphasis on the intimate complexities of lesbian and queer identities, families, and communities – always plural – was not, however, born from a lack of awareness of lesbian feminism; neither was her focus on their intricacies and private details a refusal of politics. Quite the contrary: Rule and her partner, Helen Sonthoff, were key figures in the Vancouver, B.C. feminist community in the early 1970s (Rule was originally from California but chose Canadian citizenship); in addition, Rule began, in 1976, to write for *The Body Politic*, a controversial Toronto gay liberationist magazine that was in the midst of fighting obscenity charges.[6] Indeed, in her fiction, perhaps especially beginning in the 1970s, Rule actively chose to write in a way that emphasized the multiple and contradictory ways in which power relations are expressed in everyday life, resulting in neither clear-cut identities nor permanent positions. In Rule's fiction, being a lesbian is as much an ongoing and layered process of negotiation with power as it is a public act of empowerment. In addition, not all of the 'queering' of sexuality is homosexual. Both historically and intimately, sexuality is organized in articulation with race, class, and gender; it is also embodied and lived, taking shape in fleshy particularity rather than idealized universality. Indeed, Rule's fiction also frequently plays with point of view, disrupting the singularity and authority of third-person narrative – and also the potentially confessional tone of the first-person – as part of her emphasis on the *implication* of sexuality in lived experience, the ways in which a life lived against the grain might simultaneously change the world and satisfy the self. I would argue, in fact, that Rule was 'queer' before her time; in her fiction, sexual identity is certainly part of, but is never all of, 'queer friendships, queer networks, and the existence of these relations in space' (Halberstam 2005, p. 1).

Perhaps not surprisingly given this lead-in, I would like to argue that Rule's novels and essays also include a strong awareness of the particularities of place and nature in these articulations of queer bodies and practices, and particularly, that her critical ideas on identities, families, and communities are embedded in ecological desires, and vice versa. Rule is, here, clear that her views of place and nature are implicated in her sexual politics; as Schuster writes, 'Rule doesn't pretend to be unmarked by the places she lives, but to have understood her relation to them differently' (1999, p. 188). Not a nature writer in any narrow definition, Rule nonetheless offers a strong advocacy for a heightened perception of nature that blends an awareness of the difficulties of forging a home-place for queer individuals and communities, with a strong interest in the biotic communities in which such home-places take particular shape and meaning. These perceptions and interests contribute to a writing of nature that is profoundly informed by a non-normative, queer sensibility of 'identity, embodiment, and activity in space and time' (Halberstam 2005, p. 6); that sensibility, in turn, informs both our understanding of nature and our apprehension of queer bodies and practices.

Although 'queering' families and modes of belonging in general is a central focus of Rule's writing,[7] I would suggest that this line of inquiry also nominates Rule as an exemplary queer ecocultural critic. For Rule, important dimensions of human relations to nature are revealed and produced by the narrative (or actual) insertion of queer lives, bodies, and communities into a place; at the same time, the biophysical materialities of that place exert a huge influence on the nature of queer practices and identities.

In this light, I suggest that Rule's novel *The Young in One Another's Arms* should be read as a work of queer nature writing, and in particular, as a work that both challenges heteronormative articulations of family, community, and urban/rural space with nature and refuses, queerly, to replace one destructive certainty with another, ecotopian one. To understand its significance in this regard, it is important to understand the novel in the political and social context of its 1977 publication. In the first place, Rule was writing as an expatriate US-American living in Vancouver in the middle of the Vietnam

War, and in the midst of widespread public recognition of pollution, overconsumption, and other environmental problems. In the second place, urban Vancouver was, in this period, in the midst of a controversial process of (re)development, which involved the large-scale destruction of both residential and industrial neighborhoods to pave the way for urban transportation corridors to the suburbs, and for modern, high-density apartment buildings to house the city's increasingly single, white-collar workforce (see Kennedy 1974, Vancouver Urban Research Group 1972). Although I should note that these same apartment buildings, with their de-privileging of single family homes and other hetero-spaces, facilitated the emergence of a very successful gay male enclave in the city's West End (Bouthillette 1997), it remains the case that urban Vancouver in the 1970s was under intense pressure to modernize, and that this modernization was faced with highly-politicized challenges that were located simultaneously in local, national, and international concerns, including ecological ones.

Both in the US and in Canada, the political and economic unrest of urban centers like Vancouver, combined with the profound mistrust of many marginalized and other people with state institutions and mainstream political processes at all levels (including urban planning) prompted many to seek out alternatives in less-obviously authoritarian and polluted places. Utopian back-to-the-land movements were thus in the midst of a visible resurgence, and rural natures were, in the context of anti-establishment and countercultural politics, figured as places where individuals could escape from the rising tide of capitalist consumerism and, through spirit-building hard work in the company of like-minded others, build community and achieve a rustic spiritual and physical wholeness. Although, by and large, rural landscapes have been, in the twentieth century, figured as sites of a strongly conservative, heterosexual morality – it is important to note that this is not, in fact, historically the case (see Phillips et al. 2000) – lesbians were quick to participate in this movement. Most prominently, in the mid-1970s heyday of lesbian feminist separatism, thousands of women moved to 'lesbian lands' all over North America; as a 1976 collaborative memoir from one Oregon separatist collective put it, they 'sought a life on the land, to "live near the healing beauty of nature," and to have, in a sanctuary carved outside of urban patriarchy, "a safe space to live, to work, to help create the women's culture [they] dreamed of"' (Sandilands 2000, p. 137). As I have noted earlier, and as David Shuttleton's (2000) work indicates in particular, this 'lesbian pastoral' is part of a long history of sexualized resistances to, and appropriations of nature discourse. Attempting to becoming 'natural' is an authenticating political strategy for a lesbian identity commonly understood as unnatural; lesbians in the 1970s constructed a story of leaving apparently unnatural patriarchal and heterosexist cities to find, in 'the healing beauty of nature,' their authentic erotic and emotional identities.

As with many things, Jane Rule forcefully writes against the grain on this issue. Although *The Young in One Another's Arms* centers on a story of intentional movement from urban to rural, her anti-essentialist resistances to ideas of ecotopia, lesbian and otherwise, are informative. A public and outspoken advocate on both feminist and gay and lesbian issues, even in the 1970s she disliked lesbian separatism 'because it, like all forms of bigotry, judges people by gender and class rather than as individuals' (Rule 1986, p. 96). She also consciously refused a politics based on utopian feminist narratives, stating that they 'are escape literature, not maps of the future which, if it arrives, will be as real as the present' (p. 97). This stance does not indicate a rejection of ideas of community, of conscious ecological implication, or of rural Galiano as a site that is *different* from urban Vancouver in its particular articulation of livelihood with environment. Rather, for Rule, no space (or identity) is sacred, and any movement into a communal landscape must be made with the complexities of its present, not the glories of its past or future – nor idealistic comparisons with a degraded, anti-environmental urbanity – in mind. Not surprisingly, her views on nature are equally anti-pastoral; an essay that explores vegetarianism, for example, contains a healthy distrust of romantic idealizations of nature (1986, p. 240). In their place, Rule emphasizes the vital importance of *mindfulness*, a pragmatic and earthbound but deeply respectful sensitivity to the complexities of human attachments to nature that she apparently cultivated early in her life. Loss and contingency are central to her formulation; appreciation involves both mourning and choice. As she writes,

> Back there in my rural childhood, I had not only a fishing rod and a rifle, I had a hatchet, too. I cleared brush, cut down small trees, chopped wood. I was present at the felling of a two-thousand-year-old redwood tree, whose impact shook the earth I stood on. It was a death more simply shocking to me than any other I've ever witnessed. The house I lived in then was made of redwood. The house I live in now is cedar. (1986, p. 242)

Stacy Alaimo has written very insightfully on the effects of Rule's deliberate anti-pastoralism on one of her fictional depictions of nature and sexuality. Alaimo notes that Rule's first published novel, *Desert of the Heart* (1964), rejects a celebratory idea of lesbian connection to nature, and instead plays with a complex tension between an idea of nature as discursive constraint on lesbian sexuality, and an idea of nature as a physical space that can both incite and represent lesbian desire. Briefly, the novel's protagonist, Evelyn, is in Reno to get a divorce that will free her from the landscape of marriage, a place in which Evelyn feels alien, an 'unnaturalized' citizen. While in Reno, Evelyn meets Ann, a young woman with whom she eventually has a passionate sexual relationship. As Alaimo notes, Ann is a role model for Evelyn in flaunting natural convention; she 'revels in her freedom from nature' (1999, p. 167) and has taken up a job at a casino; 'at the center of this desert industry, symbol of it, she wanted to take her place, for there was no nature' (Rule, 1964, p. 94). Here, Ann – and lesbian desire – are figured as unnatural; at the same time, however, it is in the natural environment of the desert, specifically, a still and barren desert lake, that Evelyn comes to recognize her erotic attraction to Ann, an attraction that is both parallel and tied to her eventual appreciation of the desert itself. Evelyn is struck with Ann's sexuality in its *relationship* to this landscape; as she wades out into the lake, her body is eroticized by the desert, and vice versa. Thus, as Alaimo concludes, 'the fact that nature is experienced via the body of Ann, the face of Evelyn, and Evelyn's 'being with Ann' suggests ... that their desire actually drives the embrace of the desert as a 'natural' but queer place' (1999, p. 169).

Turning back to ecotopia, then, it seems clear that we must read Rule's choice to use such a narrative in The Young in One Another's Arms as something other than a celebration of the pastoral virtues of natural simplicity, or even the political virtues of lesbian authenticity. What we have in this novel is, rather, an extension of the body-nature-landscape dynamic Rule initiates in *Desert of the Heart* (1964). Against contemporary pastoral discourses of full and fertile nature in which lesbians and others might find wholeness and authenticity, Rule writes about wounded people coming to 'belong' in a rural nature by physically experiencing and embracing *its and their fragility*, and by thus mindfully and daily recognizing the contingencies and tensions of their web of attachments, including their implications on other-than-human communities. Queer nature, in this reading, requires displacing an idea of nature that essentializes and normalizes particular bodies, families, and sexualities in a pastoral mode, and slipping in instead an articulated daily and bodily awareness of the multiple and contingent losses and wounds that bind us to nature, and to each other.

The Young in One Another's Arms: Vancouver

In the opening paragraph of The Young in One Another's Arms (Rule 1977), we are introduced first to the protagonist's *body*:

> In the darkened street, Ruth Wheeler might have been mistaken for a boy of middle growth, spare bodied, light on her feet. She nearly always wore trousers, and the empty right sleeve of her windbreaker could seem a boy's quirk of style. But if she stepped under a streetlight, looked up and sharply beyond that illuminated space, her face redefined the first impression, the color of false pearl, dark eyes of remarkable size but limited by aging lids,

anchored by taut lines in her temples: the face of a seventy-year-old woman. Ruth Wheeler was, in fact, just over fifty. (p. 1)

Here, Rule introduces two of the key dynamics of the novel. First, Ruth Wheeler is, like all of the other characters in some way or another, badly wounded. Although we frequently forget her missing arm in the midst of her conspicuous competence, Ruth bears visibly in her marked body all of the physical and emotional traumas of her 50 years. Indeed, the accident of her mutilation is a corporeal testimony to all of the other accidents that have scarred her spirit: a beloved father 'crushed under a redwood tree' in her childhood, a daughter 'falling like a sparrow out of the sky' in a fatal car crash (p. 2), a failed marriage to a bully of a husband. Second, Ruth's life is profoundly illuminated by, and embedded in, the landscapes through which she walks, in this case a dim street in downtown, 1970s Vancouver. This particular, downwardly mobile street is badly-lit because all the houses on it have been expropriated for imminent demolition 'to make way,' as Rule describes, 'for a new approach to the bridge' (p. 3). The doomed homes include Ruth's own, a boarding house she was able to buy with the insurance money from the loss of her arm and daughter: 'What you lose,' says Ruth, 'is what you survive with' (p. 3). Like Ruth, the landscape is wounded; still, it illuminates her, and its transformation locates, embodies and propels her story and her survival.

Immediately after Rule introduces us to Ruth and her city, we meet the characters who inhabit her about-to-be-demolished boarding house. In order, there is: Gladys, a headstrong, politically-and sexually-charged object of desire for almost everyone else in the house; Mavis, a closeted lesbian completing her PhD on Dickens and searching for traces of its moral certainty in her world; Willard, a developmentally delayed shoe salesman whose wellbeing relies on obsessively-followed schedules and routines; Joanie, a young and rather thoughtless secretary dreaming of husband and suburbia and working her way earnestly through the bearers of its possibility; Tom, an early Vietnam draft resister from Iowa, now a Canadian landed immigrant working as a short order cook; Stew, a musician and acid-head who has dropped out of his middle-class Vancouver family; and Arthur, the most recently-arrived of the deserters and resisters who rely regularly on Ruth's unquestioning welcome. Later in the story, Rule introduces Boyd Wonder, a gay African American draft resister who is also wanted on fraud charges; calling himself 'Boy,' he regularly changes names, part of a larger practice of taking on and parodying the racist and homophobic stereotypes that confront him daily, defensively becoming the caricature that the world expects (and, in the process, avoiding detection by the state). Most importantly, however, there is Clara, the mother of Ruth's estranged husband; Ruth loves her mother-in-law deeply and, although their relationship is not sexual, it is emotionally the most loving and intimate throughout much of the story, certainly more powerful than the bond of the marriage.

The house and its occupants are imminently threatened by urban redevelopment. As Schuster insists, however, the novel 'is much more than the stories of Ruth Wheeler's semipublic house with its odd lot of temporary residents caught in the way of progress' (1999, p. 207). Crucially, the novel interlaces two stories, one about the transformation of nature and landscape, and the other about the transformation of bodies and communities; both of these stories centre on the dynamics of power and resistance, and in their articulation develop exactly the queer ecocultural sensibility that I am advocating in this paper. As Schuster notes, on top of the visible mechanisms of power apparent throughout the novel in the form of state repression, each of the characters bears in her or his body 'capillary' forms of power through which their everyday lives are organized: 'The defenses that each major character assumes to compensate for the wounds and losses sustained before the narrative begins all express the ways in which power has reached into their bodies' (1999, p. 208). The novel thus contains an important narrative of corporeal conflict. There are large-scale bodily repressions, such as when the police come, clearly acting on behalf of the US government and with the complicity of the Canadian state, to deport Arthur over the border and into the waiting punitive hands of the US military. But there are also smaller, everyday traces of corporeal power. Although the novel never tells us unequivocally, it is almost certainly Stew who, angered by a developing sexual relationship between Arthur and Gladys, has tipped off the police to Arthur's presence in the house. Stew, here, bears an unbearable wound of betrayal over Gladys and Arthur's pleasure; in response, however, his body cannot bear the guilt of his own betrayal, and he overdoses, later to recover and become, rather significantly, a law student.

What I think is crucial in the novel is that the characters' bodies and identities are both embedded in and reflect the physical places of their daily lives as the *environment* is subject to political and social power. The fragility of the boarding house in the face of the looming homogeneity of urban highway and high-rise locates each character in a daily physical reality that echoes the movement of the changing city. The members of the boarding house family live through, participate in, and bear in their bodies the wounds that are, in the process, marked on the place itself. The power relations that leave their traces in Mavis' self-protective posture, Stew's addiction, Clara's decreasing physical mobility, and even Ruth's missing arm, do not just reflect personal troubles, or even issues from the world theatre such as Vietnam or economic recession. Rather, the environment carries and engenders the systemic traumas of urban modernity; as the characters live daily these traumas of place, their bodies are wounded with relations of dislocation, loss, death. Ruth's daughter has died in a *car* accident; Ruth's father was killed when a tree fell on him, its roots weakened by *road* development; the house is to be razed to make way for a new *approach to the bridge*. In this novel, urban environments connecting and disconnecting people with and from the land both bear and engender the physical and emotional wounds borne by the characters.

Perhaps the clearest example of this traumatic body–landscape relation involves Willard. More than any of the other characters, Willard's life is bound to the repetition of a particular life routine in a particular place. He goes to the movies on Monday, to Chinatown for cards on Wednesday, to the beer parlor on Friday with a regularity that is his only way of coping with a bewilderingly complex urban reality. He is Ruth's longest boarder, and, as Willard is simply incapable of thinking about the change himself, Ruth assumes he will come with her when she is forced at last to make the move from the boarding house. In the shiny new West End high rise that she has picked for herself, Clara and Willard, Ruth reasons that he would still be able to have his all-important routine. But she underestimates how tied Willard is to the *places* of his life, how deeply his unchanging spatial routine has carved itself into his body. When the boarding house disperses – Ruth and Willard to high rise, Clara (in fact) to seniors' home, Joanie to her own apartment, Stew to parents and law school, and the rest to a farmhouse out toward the Fraser Valley – Willard, who cannot speak of such things, displays his fear in his body, 'a threatening looseness in his face' (1977, p. 108). Significantly not on the day they move out but later, on the day that the *house* is to be torn down, Willard barricades himself inside the house with a gun. In his panic, he shoots Tom in the arm and, just as Ruth is getting him to put the gun down, the police blast away Willard's marked and fearful face. In this scene, Willard cannot cope with the demolition of the place that has anchored most of his adult life; his routine, deprived of its carefully negotiated landscape, is not the same, and his body cannot adjust. The destruction of the house kills him; like Arthur's deportation, however, Willard's death is composed of both horrific police-state repressions and the small and unbearable wounds written on his body in its relationship to landscape.

Rule has thus written, in this account of what she has elsewhere called 'urban sadness' (Schuster 1999, p. 210), a powerful statement about effects of such landscape transformations on human bodies and being. In the boarding house, despite the fact that there was not a single biological kinship relation, there was a family; drawn together by accident, it cohered nonetheless, clearly queer in several respects. In the new, clean landscape of the West End, there are beautiful views of a distant and aesthetically commoditized 'nature' from tall buildings designed for singles and couples, but there is no space for this kind of queer family, such decidedly un-pristine bodies and relationships, and there is also no space for the dirtier realities of the other-than-human world (in the novel, what is most apparent is the absence of a garden in which to bury the bones of dead birds). They are crushed from outside, or they explode from within, but they cannot survive unless they take in the new spatial and political relations of urban modernity. The homogeneously commoditized space of the city is, here, powerfully akin to the repressive mechanisms of the state; each ensures corporeal conformity, and if seduction into its normative requirements does not work, as it did with Joanie and Stew, then brute force does.

The Young in One Another's Arms: Galiano

It would have been very easy for Rule to move from this violent, urban body-landscape story into a pastoral tale of freedom from repression, personal healing through bioregionally-appropriate labor, and eventual self-actualization in the accepting, *gemeinschaft* arms of rural mother nature. Of course, she does nothing of the sort. Yes, Ruth's queer family – or what remains of it, in the bodies of Mavis, Tom, now-pregnant Gladys, Boy, Clara, Coon Dog, and Puss the white cat – moves to Galiano Island and opens a café. Yes, they stay, Gladys and Tom's baby Ruthie providing a sense of second-chance resurrection with which to end the story on a relatively optimistic note. And yes, they become attuned to the subtle and sustaining particularities of the other-than-human world of Galiano, to develop hitherto-unknown relationships with native evergreen trees, birds, weather, and quiet. But Galiano is no ecotopia. The repressive mechanisms of the state follow them to the island in the form of police helicopters searching for Boy, who has been forced to leave upon being discovered by one of his casual sex partners who also happens to be a police officer. There is death, illness, poverty and destructive drug use on Galiano. The wounds of the characters' pasts also do not fully heal: an incendiary love-triangle among Tom, Gladys and Mavis erupts when Gladys' second twin baby, the boy, dies at birth and Tom, unable to distinguish mourning from jealousy, sexually assaults Mavis. Mavis, in response, injures him quite badly with her still constant companion, the brandy bottle. In typical Rule fashion, the resolutions are not neat, 'nature' is not an idyllic sanctuary, power does not go away, and this queer family does not get to ride off into a multicultural, polysexual sunset. 'There is,' as Ruth says to herself toward the end of the story, still '*no place our violent mistakes can't reach. We plant time bombs in our own flesh*' (1977, p. 192, italics in original).

As I suggested earlier, however, the characters *are* able to claim a fragile refuge in the landscape that is Galiano. They do so, in fact, by recognizing the island's scars and wounds alongside its pleasures as they discover it on an everyday basis. For example, when Ruth arrives on the island with the others to look at the café, the island, and the possibility of a future there, she sees in the rocks and trees the shadows of her past: 'Ruth wasn't sure why this tiny island reminded her of the redwood landscape of her childhood. In miniature it seemed done to scale, Douglas firs tall enough to dwarf the hills, here called mountains' (1977, p. 140). Later, we see that this return has had a healing effect: 'Often now [Ruth] could be several hours alone, her childhood with her in the soles of her feet on the earth again. She had nearly stopped smoking for the pleasure of the fragrance of the woods, field grasses in the hot sun, berries' (p. 160). Ruth thus viscerally recognizes the softer, smaller landscape. Still, it is not a return 'home'; Mavis corrects her, for example, when she calls an arbutus tree by the US-American name 'madrone.' Nor is the landscape childlike or innocent; on visiting a graveyard, Boy, Mavis and Gladys comment on a Japanese grave, noting that the old plot is 'probably the only piece of land we didn't expropriate during the war' (p. 141).[8] But it is *because*, not in spite of these scars of history that Ruth is aware of a possibility of peace in this place. She thinks to herself, for example, how much Clara would like not only the eagles up on Mount Galiano, but *'the graveyard, or perhaps I'm the only one it matters to, a place finally to bury my dead'* (p. 141, italics in original). Galiano becomes a place in which living is possible precisely in the recognition of the island's ecosocial location *in* history, *in* power, and against it at the same time.

Indeed, it is largely through relationships around Clara that the family comes to know and understand the natural world around them; often happier with birds than with people, chair-bound Clara spends hours watching the particular flora and fauna of the family's new home. This daily observation is completed, however, in the family ritual of evening conversation that they brought with them from their boarding-house days, from the relations of survival they learned in the city. 'They all carried fragments of their days back to Clara, and as she taught them needle and cone shape to name the trees, they taught her the names of island children, of old-timers and newcomers. Gladys described and imitated so well that Clara could, when Boy or Mavis took her for an occasional ride, identify people along the road' (1977, p. 160). Here, we see the family make sense of its new landscape in the midst of a relationship bound to and enabled by the characters' different physical histories in the world. In *Desert of the Heart* (1964), Ann's body is the medium that crystallizes Evelyn's understanding of her sexuality and appreciation of the desert landscape. In like manner, on Galiano *Clara's* corporeally unique ability to speak from its dependent stillness about the intricacies of the other-than-human world crystallizes the relationship by which the rest of the family can appreciate and belong in this crucial part of the island landscape. For all of them, however, belonging is symbiotic, and exists because, not in spite of their wounds and losses: Only through the intimate relationships of this queer, chosen family is refuge possible in this queer, chosen nature.

What we have, then, on Rule's Galiano is a complex, more-than-human community that is every bit as permeated by power as the city of Vancouver, but nonetheless contains the possibility of a different kind of belonging, a fragile and mindful recognition of interdependence and implication. For Rule, the ability to flourish in a place does not arise from abstract ecological principles that promise authenticity (nature is, as Clara says repeatedly, 'a bad bible' anyway). Rather, it emerges from the embodied and situated everyday life of existence in a place, involving attention to the complexities and tensions of both human and more-than-human and relationships. Indeed, for Rule our bodies' wounds, the places where we have been marked by power and violence, open us to the possibility of connection both to each other and to nature. Crucially, for Rule, that is a question of choice. Rather than aspire to an impossible fantasy of fullness that is as totalizing and ultimately destructive as the worst homogenizing violences of the city, we can *choose* to live in other landscapes, and in one another's arms, aware of the traumas that bind us all in our imperfections. As Ruth tells us, 'Always as a child her fantasy had been of something washed ashore or onto a high rock, but she had not drifted here, like a log storm-broken from a boom, marooned and placid. She had chosen this place with the stubborn intention of taking root' (1977, p. 199).

Conclusions

A reading of *The Young in One Another's Arms* (1977) reveals important insights on questions of human communities' implication in more-than-human natures, and it does so from what I see as a specifically queer ecocultural perspective, one that begins in a challenge to homophobic, heterosexualized relations of nature and then expands outward into broader bio-political intersections. Although the novel is certainly not the same type of text of lesbian desire as *Desert of the Heart* (1964), it is apparent that it is partly the family's bodily and relational queerness that, in excess of and challenge to heteronormative familial and spatial realities, helps develop the lasting emotional links that keep it together on Galiano. Mavis' sexual relationship with Gladys is as important a family bond as Gladys' eventual marriage to Tom: in fact, it may even be stronger (it certainly continues, marriage or no). Certainly also, Ruth and Clara's relationship is a central part of the family's survival; their quiet, contented companionship is the loving relationship around which all the others circulate, a queer family foundation. And the spaces inhabited by this queer family are also excessive, challenging: they literally could not 'fit' in the neat apartments of the West End, either physically or, especially for Willard, psychologically. This queer family lies at the centre of Rule's commitment to a non-romantic, anti-heteronormative, anti-essentialist understanding of community and belonging: one must make a choice to live together, and work from and across imperfection to stay together as necessary. As with her own experience of the community of Galiano Island, this queer family illustrates Rule's sense that, in communities, the one thing we know is that 'we don't want to burn it down.'

From this perspective that values and validates the experience of a queer community tied together despite — and because of — its wounds, Rule also develops unique insight on communities' relations to the natural environments in which they are embedded. The family's move from an increasingly commodified 1970s urban Vancouver to the more spatially accommodating Galiano Island is not an exercise in fictional escape or romantic contrast; not only do the power relations organizing bodies and families extend well into the Gulf Islands, but the wounds that continue to scar social relations also extend into even the most apparently bucolic *places*. Thus, Rule reveals that power organizes more-than-human nature in complex and visceral ways and that the quest for a natural refuge or biotic certainty, as if either were 'away' from power (or beyond discourse), is as fictive as the quest for a perfectly unscarred body. Not only that: Rule's beautifully imperfect Galiano, revealed to us in the layers of conversation between Clara and the others, shows how a respectful relation can emerge in the fragile interactions between a queer family and the more-than-human communities in which it is embedded. Reading *The Young in One Another's Arms* for a queer nature, then, shows that we can see ourselves belonging in a wounded nature, not by imagining the environment (or ourselves) as whole and pristine but in embracing the fragility of our location and finding community in precisely our shared incompleteness, our articulations in and through nature. This relation is at the heart of a queer ecocultural politics. Queer, here, is a mode of specific cultural interrogation that illuminates both sexual and ecological relations as part of a larger web of biopolitical threads.

Returning to the larger project of ecocultural studies outlined at the outset of this paper, I would like to reiterate that the novel both illustrates and propels a queer ecocultural 'alternative.' At the same time as a critical practice of ecocultural analysis demands that we read 'for' nature, for the implication of culture in ecosystemic relations, queer theory, far from being reductionist, insists on understanding these more-than-human implications as inseparable from complex articulations of power, including but not limited to heteronormativity. As Halberstam writes, 'what has made queerness compelling as a mode of self-description in the past decade or so has to do with the way it has the potential to open up new life narratives and alternative relations to time and space' (2005, pp. 1–2). As Rule illustrates, queer nature thus suggests a practice of reading and inhabiting more-than-human worlds that has a similar potential of opening spaces anew to a diversity of bodily practices, a richness of forms of implication in biotic communities, without relying on utopian temporal, spatial, or ecological desires 'beyond' the messiness of the present.[9]

I feel compelled, however, to end this paper with another example, this time an account that locates the possibility of queer nature squarely in *urban* environments, and not only in the rural Galiano (now itself heavily permeated with suburban desires) in which Rule chose to locate her queer ecological possibility. Indeed, I would like to argue that one can and must locate and produce queer ecocultural views in those spaces most obviously organized by capitalist modernity, including the urban Vancouver that has resulted from the authoritarian and capillary relations of power so forcefully depicted by Rule in *The Young in One Another's Arms* (1977). As I mentioned earlier, precisely the high rises that could not sustain Willard came to facilitate an entirely different sort of queer spatial possibility, in the form of the gay male community of Vancouver's West End [as Bouthillette (1997) notes, lesbian communities in Vancouver have inhabited different spaces and have inhabited them differently, partly for the socio-economic, familial, and sexual reasons portrayed in Rule's novel]. The West End is, in the early twenty-first century, a distinctly and visibly gay cultural space that includes 'commercial, residential, institutional, and fleeting and relatively permanent meeting places' (Bouthillette 1997, pp. 223–224), not least because of its general affluence. Although hostile to certain kinds of queer natures, the redevelopment of Vancouver's West End clearly facilitated others; thus, the place also suggests a site in and from which to consider queer ecocultural possibilities.

The existence of this 'gay ghetto,' however much it might challenge a particular articulation of heteronormativity, space, and capital, clearly does not in itself indicate an ecocultural awareness (indeed, one might argue exactly the opposite; some highly-visible versions of queer culture have been roundly criticized for their advocacy of an un-ecological hyper-consumerism, see Gosine 2001). For queer urban planner Gordon Brent Ingram, however, such spaces, in so far as they actively include landscapes coded as 'natural' – such as the (in)famous Vancouver gay/nude Wreck Beach[10] – indicate crucial sites in which queer and ecological politics interact, forcing, from an ecocultural perspective, an understanding of the implication of the one in the other. At Wreck, public gay sex collides audibly and visibly with other ideas of urban nature recreation that are coded as heterosexual. At the same time, although (south) Wreck's atmosphere and activities fall generally outside the inner circle of gay consumer culture (and although sex is a relatively 'low-impact' recreational pursuit), there is nothing inherently ecological about an afternoon of cruising on the beach or in the forest; these activities have to be thought differently, which is what Ingram adds to our understanding. As Ingram describes, 'Wreck is as much an arterial and expressway for a range of male homoerotic groups and an experimental station, with its share of toxic residues, as it is a rich and intact forest and shore ecosystem' (2001, p. 202). Still, queer modes of inhabitation that explicitly deny and defy the presumed heterosexuality of natural space, and ecological modes that challenge anthropocentric hubris, coincide here. At Wreck, in the face of multiple-use pressures, 'both 'nature' and 'natural homosexuality' are harmed by continual ecological degradation' (p. 204).

While it is clear that a gay community's advocacy of public sex does not guarantee an utopian nature any more than the preservation of 'wildlands' necessarily facilitates an utopian gay sexual culture, Ingram's practice of queer ecocultural studies fosters a clearer understanding of the ways both are implicated in the history, present, and future of the place. Here, as with Rule, we have a clear example of a queer ecocultural practice that begins with a direct challenge to heteronormative constructions of and practices in nature, and then opens the landscape to a variety of intersecting challenges to the normative relations that permeate human cultures in the more-than-human world. Queer is both specific and general, here: Ingram's reading of Wreck Beach insists that sexuality and ecology be read together, but that they also intersect with class, race, gender, and aboriginal concerns, and so I would argue that a queer ecocultural studies would emphasize the intersections of power as much as the specific sexuality of the place. In addition, it bears repeating that the ecosystem does not authorize or normalize any particular activity at Wreck, but clearly shapes the kinds of interactions that are possible in the place (think terrain, visibility, texture, safety, privacy, shelter, elevation, density, sound) even as it is also shaped, for good or ill, by these interactions. One thus cannot understand the dynamics of the social/natural place of Wreck without considering both the specific organization of sex *and* the multiple ways in which power organizes and is organized by particular landscapes, particular ecological relations, particular natures. To make nature appreciable, here, involves its revelation and production as a tangible, material, and experiential element in a complex, articulatory web of relations. Beginning with the queer foregrounds in this critical production.

Notes

1. Slack and Whitt (1992) outline an ecosystemic understanding that assumes neither an evolutionary teleology in which the meaning of the individual organism is determined by its reproductive/adaptive success, nor a functional contingency in which the meaning of a given organism is cast in relation to the overall integrity of the ecosystem. Much of cultural studies' allergy to ecology is, I think, triggered by the related spectres of biological determinism and functionalism, and the fact that Slack and Whitt have opened up the question of organismic-cultural meaning to a more complex array of possibilities is a very important contribution.
2. Even in the early 1990s, many thinkers were concerned with the collision between 'the linguistic turn' of social theory – perhaps especially cultural studies? – and questions of 'nature' in environmental thought and politics. Although the 'nature wars' of the late 1990s – in which environmental historian William Cronon was lambasted by for his argument that wilderness is a historically and socially constructed set of social relationships to nature, not 'nature' itself (1995) – were not terribly productive, several authors

took the thorny problem of materiality seriously. In particular, the works of writers in the field of feminist science studies, for example as recently collected in Alaimo and Hekman (2007), have led the way in this conversation in their insistence on the 'artifactuality' (Haraway's term) of the biotic (to whit: all nature is constructed, but that doesn't mean that humans are the only ones doing the constructing). What cultural studies adds, I think, is a more careful understanding of what 'construction' is all about.

3   In this idea of 'making nature appreciable,' I am indebted to Raymond Williams' *The Country and the City* (1973).

4   Noting again Ross' justifiable suspicion of 'using' nature to authorize the social, I relate Bagemihl's biological evidence more as a challenge to the assumed heterosexuality of 'normal' nature than as proof of the 'naturalness' of any form of sexuality. In fact, as Simon LeVay documents, animal research has a long and sordid history of 'proving' the naturalness/bestiality of homosexuality (1996, p. 195). Bagemihl's use of animal behavior to 'naturalize' homosexuality says as much about ideas of nature-as-authority as it does about the desirability of any particular kind of sexual activity.

5   Rule is perhaps best known for the 1985 film *Desert Hearts*, an adaptation of her 1964 novel *Desert of the Heart*.

6   *The Young in One Another's Arms* (1977) was one of the books detained by Canada Customs as obscene, an ironic counterpoint to Jay's criticism of Rule's work as too mainstream.

7   Rule and Sonthoff moved from Vancouver to Galiano Island in the 1970s, living there full-time by 1976. Galiano Island is one of the Southern Gulf Islands of British Columbia, in the Strait of Georgia between the mainland and Vancouver Island. During the 1970s, Galiano was home to an interesting mixture of farmers, retirees, and hippies; following Vancouver and Victoria, it has become progressively gentrified in the intervening years. On the centrality of the themes of home and community to Rule's mid- to late-career writing, see Schuster (1999).

8   In fact, Galiano was the site of a quite considerable Japanese fishing community, and there remain visible remnants of these lives in the form of several charcoal pits. Their lands were, like that of all Japanese-Canadians living on the West Coast, expropriated during World War II. This violence was not, of course, the only one to shape Galiano's history; the Coast Salish People, whose physical presence is also still part of the visible landscape of the island—for example, in a large midden at Montague Harbour – were decimated by disease.

9   It is precisely in the long-term transformation of these communities from an utopian to a 'queer ecological' orientation that they have found the possibility of flourishing (although, good lesbian feminists still, they don't much care for the term 'queer') (Sandilands 2000).

10 Wreck Beach is not physically part of the West End, but certainly – as Fire Island is to Manhattan – it is part of the spatial sensibility of the West End gay male community.

References

Alaimo, S. (2000) *Undomesticated Ground: Recasting Nature as Feminist Space*, Ithaca, NY, Cornell University Press.
Alaimo, S. & Hekman, S. (eds) (2007) *Material Feminisms*, Bloomington, Indiana University Press.
Bagemihl, B. (1999) *Biological Exuberance: Animal Homosexuality and Natural Diversity*, New York, St Martin's Press.
Bouthillette, A.-M. (1997) 'Queer and gendered housing: a tale of two neighbourhoods in Vancouver,' in *Queers in Space: Communities, Public Places, Sites of Resistance*, eds G. B. Ingram, A.-M. Bouthillette & Y. Retter, Seattle, WA, Bay Press, pp. 213–232.
Butler, J. (2004) *Undoing Gender*, New York, Routledge.
Castree, N. & Braun, B. (eds) (2001) *Social Nature: Theory, Practice, Politics*, Oxford, Blackwell.
Cronon, W. (1995) "The Trouble with Wilderness: Or, Getting Back to the Wrong Nature," in *Uncommon Ground: Toward Reinventing Nature*, ed. Wm. Cronon, New York, W.W. Norton, pp. 69–90.
Evernden, N. (1992) *The Social Creation of Nature*, Baltimore, MD, Johns Hopkins.
Foucault, M. (1978) *The History of Sexuality: Volume I, An Introduction*, Vintage Books, New York.
Glotfelty, C. & Fromm, H. (eds) (1996) *The Ecocriticism Reader: Landmarks in Literary Ecology*, Athens, GA, University of Georgia Press.
Gosine, A. (2001) 'Pink greens: ecoqueers organize in Toronto', *Alternatives*, vol. 27, no. 3, pp. 35–36.
Halberstam, J. (2005) *In a Queer Time and Place: Transgender Bodies, Subcultural Lives*, New York, New York University Press.
Ingram, G. B. (2001) 'Redesigning Wreck: beach meets forest as location of male homoerotic culture and placemaking in Pacific Canada', in *In a Queer Country: Gay and Lesbian Studies in the Canadian Context*, ed. T. Goldie, Vancouver, Arsenal Pulp Press, pp. 188–208.
Kennedy, W. (1974) *Vancouver Tomorrow: A Search for Greatness*, Vancouver, B.C., Mitchell Press.
LeVay, S. (1996) *Queer Science: The Use and Abuse of Research into Homosexuality*, Cambridge, MA, MIT Press.
Moore, D. S., Kosek, J. & Pandian, A. (eds) (2003) *Race, Nature, and the Politics of Difference*, Durham, NC, Duke University Press.
Mortimer-Sandilands, C. (2005) 'Unnatural passions: notes toward a queer ecology', *Invisible Culture*, Issue 9, [online] Available at: http://www.rochester.edu/in_visible_culture/Issue_9/sandilands.html.

Phillips, R., Watt, D. & Shuttleton, D. (eds) (2000) *De-centring Sexualities: Politics and Representation Beyond the Metropolis*, London, Routledge.
Ross, A. (1994) *The Chicago Gangster Theory of Life: Nature's Debt to Society*, London, Verso.
Rule, J. (1964) *Desert of the Heart*, Toronto, Macmillan.
Rule, J. (1975) *Lesbian Images*, Toronto, Doubleday.
Rule, J. (1977) *The Young in One Another's Arms*, London, Pandora Press.
Rule, J. (1981) *Outlander*, Tallahassee, FL, The Naiad Press.
Rule, J. (1986) *A Hot-eyed Moderate*, Toronto, Lester and Orpen Dennys.
Sandilands, C. (1999) *The Good-natured Feminist: Ecofeminism and the Quest for Democracy*, Minneapolis, MN, University of Minnesota Press.
Sandilands, C. (2000) 'Lesbian separatist communities and the experience of nature: toward a queer ecology', *Organization and Environment*, vol. 15, no. 2, pp. 131–163.
Schuster, M. (1999) *Passionate Communities: Reading Lesbian Resistance in Jane Rule's Fiction*, New York, New York University Press.
Shuttleton, D. (2000) 'The queer politics of gay pastoral', in *De-Centring Sexualities: Politics and Representation Beyond the Metropolis*, eds R. Phillips, D. West & D. Shuttleton, London, Routledge, pp. 125–146.
Slack, J. D. & Whitt, L. A. (1992) 'Ethics and cultural studies', in *Cultural Studies*, eds L. Grossberg, C. Nelson & P. Treichler, New York, Routledge, pp. 571–592.
Vancouver Urban Research Group (1972) *Forever Deceiving You: The Politics of Vancouver Development*, Vancouver, Vancouver Urban Research Group.
Williams, R. (1973) *The Country and the City*, New York, Oxford University Press.
Wolfe, S. J. & Penelope, J. (eds) (1993) *Sexual Practice, Textual Theory: Lesbian Cultural Criticism*, Cambridge, MA, Blackwell.
Zylinska, J. (2001) 'An ethical manifesto for cultural studies ... perhaps', *Strategies*, vol. 14, no. 2, pp. 175–188.

Jennifer Daryl Slack

RESISTING ECOCULTURAL STUDIES

> *Ecoculturalism ought to have transformed cultural studies over a decade ago. Yet it has not. I examine the troubled articulation of cultural studies and the 'eco,' focusing on what I perceive to be cultural studies' resistance to, and difficulties with, ecoculturalism. In the end, I seek to make good on the transformative potential of the 'eco' by advocating a seemingly counterintuitive move: that ecoculturalism be jettisoned in favor of a revitalized commitment to cultural studies.*

Ecoculturalism ought to have transformed cultural studies. However, despite the efforts of cultural theorists to introduce questions involving environment, ecology, biology, and nature (efforts which for the sake of simplification I refer to here as ecoculturalism),[1] the potential for transformation has not been realized.[2] More than 10 years after *Cultural Studies* published its first special issue on cultural studies and the environment (1994), this second special issue evidences a continued peripheral status of ecocultural issues: they are 'special,' not transformative; they have not contributed sufficiently to a new and better practice of cultural studies.

This article explains why and how ecoculturaliam ought to have transformed cultural studies, explores why it has not been transformative, and proposes how it might be made to be so. I organize this task around a consideration of what I perceive to be cultural studies' resistance to, and difficulties with, ecoculturalism. For the turbulence of articulating cultural studies and the 'eco' – the term I use here to designate the range of issues relevant to ecoculturalism – exposes both the failure and promise of cultural studies to transform thought and practice. In the end, I urge that we learn from both the failures and the potential, and I advocate what at this point may seem counterintuitive, but which I trust will make sense eventually: that we jettison ecoculturalism, in favor of a revitalized commitment to cultural studies.

Resisting ecoculturalism

Five discouraging forces articulate to render ecoculturalism peripheral to cultural studies (at best) and profoundly difficult for cultural studies (at worst): (1) the eco is marginalized by the weight of the history of cultural studies as the study of popular culture; (2) it is simply too much to ask of a cultural study to consider everything; (3) the eco makes painfully salient the problem of handling that which cannot be reduced to the discursive; (4) the language of the eco requires a fair amount of inelegant stuttering; (5) ecoculturalism perpetuates a misleading limitation of what it evokes: the assemblage of culture. Each of these concerns raises progressively more complex difficulties; yet, each also reveals increasingly more potent reasons to consider the transformative potential of ecoculturalism.

The eco is marginal to popular culture

The earliest manifestations of cultural studies articulate deep commitments to the everyday expressions of working-class life. Recognizing, dignifying, and honoring that life was very much the project of Richard Hoggart (1970) in his 1957 book, *The Uses of Literacy*. Hoggart resisted both the high culture assessment of the working class as uncultured, and the vulgar Marxist assessment of the working class as pitiful, debased victims of the upper class. Rather, the everyday lives of working-class people constituted a creative and unique culture that was fully the expressive equivalent of high culture. The historical moment made salient in *The Uses of Literacy* is the effects of modern mass media entertainment on traditional working-class culture. Thus much of Hoggart's study is devoted to exploring the daily experience of the working class as expressed in speech, attitudes, clothing, and home as the culture changed creatively in the encounter with new mass media: newspapers, books, radio, music, advertisements, television, and so on. How culture is lived – lived experience – becomes, for the most part, conflated with the encounter with media. Trained as a literary theorist, Hoggart (1969) proposed reading the media as one would read a classic work of literature, but with a new cultural studies orientation, asking what are the values, feelings, and beliefs revealed by these media and what is it they embody, reflect, or resist?

Hoggart's work sets up the question that continues to give shape to cultural studies even today: What is the role of popular media in relations of class and power? From its origins, then, the project is theoretical, empirical, and political: What is the nature of (working class) culture? What is the character of actual (working class) cultures? What is the nature of power in relation to media and class? And what can be done to change those relations?

Theoretically, Raymond Williams and Stuart Hall wrestled with Marxism to develop a concept of culture equipped to make sense of working-class life in unequal relations of power (Hall 1992). Williams (1961) contributed a pivotal claim that culture has three aspects: the lived culture, the recorded culture, and the selective tradition (which connects the lived culture with other/past cultures) (p. 66). As with Hoggart, the expressions of the culture that figure in his analysis are speech, education, the popular press, dramatic forms, and literature. In other words, what counts as lived experience is predominantly that which can be accessed through popular media. Further cementing the equation that cultural studies entails the study of popular culture are Hall's analyses of class, race, and media (for example, Hall 1973, 1980a), Hall's theoretical exploration of the 'popular' (1981), widely circulated work coming out of the Center for Contemporary Cultural Studies at Birmingham (for example, Hall & Jefferson 1976; Dick Hebdige's popular book *Style* (1979)) and Lawrence Grossberg's work on popular music in the US [much of it republished in Grossberg 1997].

This is not all that was going on in cultural studies for sure, but this is the (part of the) story that becomes potent reality—that cultural studies entails the study of popular culture: of music, news, television, film, and literature. A notable early exception is Raymond Williams' 1974 *Television: Technology and Cultural Form* (1992), which advances a critical argument about technology in terms of television's technological form rather than its content. However, Williams's argument does little to change the thrust of cultural studies' commitment to the study of popular culture; even *Television* is in large part about the content of popular television.

It truly can be said that feminism transformed cultural studies, marked by the moment of Angela McRobbie's critique of the subcultural literature (1981), and Hall's work on the articulating role of race (1980b). Culture, it became clear, could not be reduced to class, just as it could not be reduced (as the vulgar Marxists would have it) to the economic. Culture could only be understood as articulating class, gender, race, and, later, ethnicity. Consequently, the study of power and popular culture became linked to an understanding of culture as the multiple articulations of relations of identity. Cultural studies has in large part come to be *about* making links between popular culture and class, gender, race, ethnicity, identity, representation, difference, contingency and power.

The *de facto* impact of understanding cultural studies as consisting of the study of popular culture is that it is not *about* technology, the environment, biology, ecology, nature, or the body. Unless, that is, the study is organized around popular media presentations of these eco matters. Recent examples of this include Kim Sawchuk's analysis of images of the inner body in popular culture and art (for example, 2001) and Nigel Thrift's (2004) analysis of the way that computer software produces new hybrid, 'electric' animals. But even such excellent work, which expands the boundaries of cultural studies, does not transform the project. It merely considers the eco as expressed in new and varied popular media. To examine the eco in any other way places a cultural theorist still farther outside the mainstream. This proclivity to work through popular cultural representation constitutes a *de facto* resistance to the eco as fundamentally transforming cultural studies.

You can't include everything

In the 1980s, Lawrence Grossberg defined the project of cultural studies thus:

> Cultural studies is concerned with describing and intervening in the ways discourses are produced within, inserted into and operate in the relations between people's everyday lives and the structures of the social formation so as to reproduce, resist and transform the existing structures of power. That is, if people make history but in conditions not of their own making, cultural studies explores the ways this is enacted within cultural practices and the place of these practices within specific historical formations. (1988, p. 22)

If those discourses, relations, and practices are constituted of multiple and contingent articulations of difference — of gender, race, class, ethnicity, identity, and representation — as cultural studies claims, then the task of describing, let alone intervening, is enormous. As Grossberg acknowledged:

> Apart from the more explicitly theoretically and politically driven questions of what sense one makes of contemporary popular culture and how, it is difficult to know where to begin to describe the terrain itself, to locate its significant exemplars and to identity its most powerful vectors. (1988, p. 19)

When culture is understood as a complex and ongoing articulation of forces, relations, discourses, and practices that constitute the context of an artifact of popular culture, then the task of analyzing the artifact is to contextualize it, that is, to explore the moving forces, relations, discourses, and practices that constitute it. This is a daunting task; no cultural theorist can ever hope to get it all. At best one can hope to get at what seems most significant at a particular movement given a particular project. Besides, cultural theorists must also be willing to acknowledge that what seems most significant will change; projects must change as the terrain changes and as new knowledge requires. No single study can do justice to the task when you are after a moving target. As I once wrote:

> To trace both synchronically and diachronically all the constitutive articulations that can account for any changing identity [or artifact], to critique that configuration, and to offer rearticulations is more than any

> researcher can hope to accomplish in a lifetime. This is a serious problem in cultural studies, and I am not merely posturing by raising it. It is a problem that is unlikely to be resolved but will be struggled over as we seek to identify and critique the 'most important' articulations, given our different projects. (Slack 1989, p. 340)

Enter into this problematic moment the assertions that technology matters, or the body matters, or the eco matters. At the very least, these are structures and/or conditions (with discursive components) that 'operate in the relations between people's everyday lives and the structures of the social formation so as to reproduce, resist and transform the existing structures of power' (Grossberg 1988, p. 22). How is it possible to contextualize a televison program without including the technological form through which it is delivered? Or the material organization of environmental matter that constitutes it? Or the creation and organization of audience bodies? Bracketing such matters as outside a particular project is only possible if those vectors are determined by the project to be (relatively) insignificant, or if they are simply not 'seen.'

Even if the significance of the material is recognized, any reasonable cultural theorist might respond, 'How can we consider everything? We have to make choices. Besides, to consider technology, the body, or the eco is outside the traditional purview of cultural studies.' Any college course on cultural studies will likely emphasize class, gender, race, ethnicity, identity, representation, difference, contingency, and power. It will far less likely include technology, the body, or the eco. If it does, those topics will likely be covered near the end of the class, as examples of how one might apply cultural studies, not of how cultural studies has evolved.

But I would have it otherwise. Technology, the body, and the eco are every bit as fundamental to the context of popular culture as gender, race, class, and ethnicity. How could one contextualize a television program without also considering the earthly elements out of which the television and its delivery system are manufactured? The generation of power that enables its creation and distribution? The organization of skills and bodies? The circulation of money? While political economists insist on the political economic aspects of production, cultural theorists ought to go beyond that by insisting on the articulating vectors of technology, the body, and the eco to contextualize the artifact or practice in all stages of circulation: production, distribution, and reception. Whereas feminism forced cultural studies to rethink the necessity of fundamentally human cultural articulating vectors — gender, race, class, ethnicity — the eco ought to insist on the fundamental other-than-human articulating vectors: technology, environment, ecology, biology, and nature. The eco can only be ignored by falling back on a disturbing anthropocentrism, as evidenced by the emphasis on 'discourse,' particularly the discourse of popular culture.

The problem of the discursive

Cultural studies is hobbled by its commitment to the anthropocentric concepts of discourse and apparatus. Cultural theorists enrich the vernacular sense of discourse as that which is communicated in speech or writing with Foucault's definition of discourse as statements or practices that systematically form the objects of which they speak. As explained by Stuart Hall,

> By 'discourse', Foucault meant 'a group of statements which provide a language for talking about — a way of representing the knowledge about — a particular topic at a particular historical moment. . . . Discourse is about the production of knowledge through language. But . . . since all social practices entail *meaning*, and meanings shape and influence what we do — our conduct — all practices have a discursive aspect.' (Hall 1997, p. 44)

Discourse speaks — in some form. It does not speak 'of' objects, but figures them. Discourse bestows meaning to the ways that individuals act in particular times and places; it is the process of languaging life. Cultural studies foregrounds this human activity in which even the other-than-human is reined in by, given shape by, and spoken though discourse. In an analysis of everyday life, the goal is likely to be, as Barry Sandywell aspires, to locate 'the grammar of "everyday life"' (2004, p. 161).

Focus now on the human centeredness of Grossberg's definition of cultural studies cited in the previous section: 'Cultural studies is concerned with describing and intervening in the ways discourses are produced within, inserted into and operate in the relations between people's everyday lives and the structure of the social formation . . .' The relationships among discourse, everyday life and social (i.e. human made) structures are at issue; and the way to access them is though the grammatical structures of everyday life — that is, discursive 'texts,' be those literature, music, television, or other popular media texts.

Even if the object of analysis is extended beyond discourse to the 'apparatus' (which can be seen as an equivalent to understanding culture in terms of articulation), the tendency is to rely on an anthropocentric conception of apparatus. The debt to Foucault can again be witnessed in the influence of his definition of apparatus, or *dispositif*:

> a thoroughly heterogeneous ensemble consisting of discourses, institutions, architectural forms, regulatory decisions, laws, administrative measures, scientific statements, philosophical, moral and philanthropic propositions — in short, the said as much as the unsaid. Such are the elements of the apparatus. The apparatus itself is the system of relations that can be established between these elements. (Foucault 1980, p. 194)

This apparatus remains decidedly human centered: humans assemble institutions, fashion buildings, make decisions and laws, apply administrative measures, and craft statements and propositions. There is nothing explicitly articulated here outside the human. Thus, to the degree that articulating vectors resembles Foucault's apparatus, the cultural apparatus is understood to be essentially anthropocentric.

Perhaps, a cultural theorist might argue, there is nothing wrong with being anthropocentric: 'This is "cultural" studies after all, not eco studies. Cultural studies is unique precisely in that it elevates the role of human culture, specifically the discursive "aspect" of culture.' Even nature is cultural, as argued by Alexander Wilson in his book *The Culture of Nature* (1992).

In response to this superficially reasonable position, I garner evidence from ongoing attempts of cultural theorists who seek to acknowledge an increasing multiplicity of factors that matter, beginning with the challenge against reducing culture to economics and class. At this point the argument gets more difficult, in part because, as the factors multiply, the theoretical language is increasingly challenged to perform in ways it was not designed to perform.

There have long been attempts in cultural theory to grapple with the tendency toward reduction. Earlier I pointed out that cultural studies struggled against reducing the working class to a definition preferred by either the elite upper class or by the vulgar Marxists. In doing so, cultural studies boldly resisted the reduction of class to economic determinants. Further, especially after recognizing the articulating significance of race and gender, cultural studies resisted the reduction of culture to class determinants. Indeed, the problem of reductionism has consistently occupied theoretical and practical analysis in cultural studies. Hall's brilliant analysis of Marx's *Eighteenth Brumaire* (Hall 1977) – in which he demonstrates that not even Marx reduced politics to economic class – offers the quintessential cultural studies warning against reduction.

Hall's arguments drew on the work of Louis Althusser (largely in the 1970s) and offered cultural studies further theoretical grounds for resisting reduction. In particular, Althusser's concept of relative autonomy was instructive. Briefly, Althusser posited three levels to the social structure: the economic, the political, and the ideological.[3] Together these constitute a complex whole, a 'structure articulated in dominance' (Althusser 1970, p. 202), in which each level exhibits its own logic of development and in which one level or the other will exercise more effectivity than another at any particular time. A change in one level is not necessarily caused by a change in another; a change in one level will not necessarily cause a change in another. Yet, with every change, the whole is changed. The semi-autonomous levels in relation constitute the ensemble, or totality. The significance of this contribution can not be overestimated. Hall once characterized Althusser's impact as both theoretical and personal:

the ensemble of relations which make up a whole society ... [is] essentially a complex structure, not a simple one .... Another general advance which Althusser offers is that he enabled me to live in and with *difference*. Althusser's break with a monistic conception of marxism demanded the theorization of difference — the recognition that there are different social contradictions with different origins; that the contradictions which drive the historical process forward do not always appear in the same place, and will not always have the same historical effects. We have to think about the articulation between different contradictions; about the different specificities and temporal durations through which they operate, about the different modalities through which they function. (Hall 1985, pp. 91–92)

While it is no longer *au currant* to read or cite Althusser, revisiting relative autonomy offers further support for imagining something other than an anthropocentric cultural studies; it suggests a way of thinking that forbids reducing everything to discourse but without diminishing the fundamental importance of the discursive. While it may be the case that we can only know the world in and through discourse and that the archaeology of the world as we know it is discursive, this does not mean that the world is essentially discursive. The other-than-human can best be understood as having its own origins, as having the potential to function though its own modalities, as being, in short, semi-autonomous. Semi-autonomy insists that we acknowledge the 'different modalities' though which different vectors function.

Those of us who study technology have had to wrestle with this idea in order to begin to understand the role of technology in culture. In 1985 I argued for cultural studies to develop the concept of a 'technological apparatus,' which would acknowledge the role of the material 'thing' or mechanism in cultural relations: in relation to economics, politics, and ideology (Slack 1985). As Latour (1988, 1996) puts it, technology exercises agency too; once created, technology 'impinges' back on humans to affect them. To say that does not imply that technology exists outside the discursive, just that it cannot be reduced to the discursive. The physical organization of matter matters, regardless of the human centered processes that bring it into being. The materials out of which any technology is constructed — acknowledged, named, organized, and used by humans — do not owe their existence to discourse any more than politics owes its existence to economics. They are related, yes. They affect each other, yes. But not in the sense that one determines the other. One cannot be reduced to the other.

This acknowledgment of the material, of the 'technological other,' requires that we rethink apparatus, so that other-than-human otherness can be acknowledged. Drawing on the work of Gilles Deleuze and Félix Guattari (1987), Greg Wise and I offer the term 'technological assemblage' — in lieu of apparatus — to suggest a non-anthropocentric apparatus. We argue that *'an assemblage is a particular constellation of articulations that selects, draws together, stakes out and envelops a territory that exhibits some tenacity and effectivity'* (Slack & Wise 2005, p. 129). Assemblage, thought this way, is made up of all kinds of bodies: the bodies of machines and structures, earthly bodies, human bodies, governmental bodies, economic bodies, geographical bodies, bodies of knowledge, and so on. To characterize culture as the intermingling of modalities, we use the term 'technological culture' rather than the binary-evoking 'culture and technology.' Of course, the discursive figures. An archaeology of knowledge is constituted by creating and designating these bodies as bodies. As bodies, they do not exist outside discourse. Yet none can be contained by discourse. None can be reduced to discourse.

Of course, the eco is still more difficult to fathom than technology using the theoretical language readily available. To use the term culture is to bring into the room the nature/culture split. To use the term environment is to bring into the room the long held belief that it refers to that which surrounds humans (Slack 2005, p. 106). To use the term ecology or biology is to invite the specter of positivistic science and the specter of essentialism that accompanies it. All the terms of the eco — environment, ecology, biology, and nature — suggest an absolute binary distinction between all that is human and all that is not. The binary is tenacious. Yet, to combat the binary with an equally simplified reduction engineered through the discursive is equally unacceptable. Cultural theory would demand that we think the eco without making either mistake. If I belabor this point it is because of the risk that cultural theorists, who are well-practiced at defending the cultural against difficult odds, might see in my argument a claim that the eco exists outside, apart from, and wholly independent of discourse. But quite simply, I have not said that. Sadly, that practiced defense of the cultural has worked to keep cultural studies from developing a much needed way to think and talk about the necessary relatedness, the otherness, and the semi-autonomy of the human and other-than-human world. Laurie Whitt and I struggled to find that language in 1985 when we stated that

> What is uniquely human (as well as other-than-human) can then be recognized and respected, including what is of particular concern to us here — that characteristic mode of human being in which life is conducted in discursive conditions not of our own making. These discursive conditions or articulations can assert interconnectedness (interdependence) or deny it. But on the level of the biotic, no denial of interdependence can conjure it out of existence, or succeed in making it 'go away.' (Slack & Whitt 1992, p. 585)

I will put this another way: No matter how successful the discourse of Holocaust deniers might be in convincing people that the Holocaust was a hoax, and organizing culture to embody that, there is no way to bring back those millions of lives. Discourse is simply not the final court in every and all situations. We desperately need a cultural studies that knows how to deal with that possibility in every and all situations.

Cultural studies has been significantly encouraged to trouble the binary distinction between the human and the other-than-human with the image of the cyborg. Popularized by Donna Haraway (1985) in 'A Manifesto for Cyborgs,' the cyborg is posed to break down three boundaries: the boundary between the human and animal, the boundary between organism and machine, and the boundary between the physical and the non-physical (pp. 69–71). The cyborg world, Haraway argues 'might be about lived social and bodily realities in which people are not afraid of their joint kinship with animals and machines' (p. 72), a fusion of 'animal and machine' (p. 95). In her later article 'The Promises of Monsters,' Haraway (1992) claims for science studies what culture studies might acknowledge:

> ... what science studies as cultural studies do, by showing how to visualize the curious collectives of humans and unhumans that make up naturalsocial (one word) life. To stress the point that all the actors in these generative, dispersed, and layered collectives do not have human form and function — and should not be anthropomorphized. (p. 333)

While Haraway's hybrid cyborg promised enormous potential to rethink culture, it brought with it three limiting features: the idea that the cyborg was new, the idea of the cyborg as an identity; and the sci-fi potential of the cyborg.

By casting the cyborg as 'a matter of fiction and lived experience that changes what counts as women's experience in the late twentieth century' (Haraway 1985, p. 66), Haraway misses the opportunity to *foreground* the insistence that we have all always been cyborg and that cyborgs do not always have a human component. More recently and more convincingly, cognitive scientist Andy Clark, in *Natural-Born Cyborgs* (2003), argues, 'our sense of our own bodily limits and bodily presence is not fixed and immovable. Instead, is it an ongoing construct, open to rapid influence by tricks and ... by new technologies' (p. 59). We have always been hybrid: Bodies have always entered 'into deep and complex relationships with nonbiological constructs, props, and aids' (p. 5). Unfortunately, Clark is clearly unprepared to follow the implications of his own insight. His argument peters out, as though he resists accepting that being naturally cyborg entails some awesome responsibilities: that we ought to look far more critically at the reasons and ways those 'machine-parts' of us are developed, implemented, and regulated. Clark's argument could benefit greatly from understanding political economy and cultural theory. Reading Haraway and Clark together can work to enhance awareness that the cyborg, as a moving target, is not always glamorous, blasphemous, playful, resistant, or liberating.

Another important limiting feature of Haraway's cyborg is the emphasis on identity. Identity designates things, persons, subjects, and substances. Identities are points of origin and final destinations. Even when an identity is hybrid, it is a spaciotemporal point formed by the connection of two or more points. If the cyborg is formed by connecting the organic and the machinic, the resulting thing is something: an articulated thing, not an articulating process. Contrast the idea of the cyborg thing with Deleuze and Guattari's emphasis on lines over points, haecceity over identity: Haecceity is not identity, but a mode of individuation. It is a way of understanding, not things, persons, subjects, and substances, but the flows that shape bodies under given relations: 'relations of movement and rest between molecules or particles, capacities to affect and be affected' (Deleuze & Guattari 1987, p. 261). Haecceities assemble, aggregate, combine, and articulate content and expression in ways that matter. The lines of becoming that constitute haecceity are not defined by points, by identities. Rather, a line of becoming 'passes *between* points, it comes up through the middle, it runs perpendicular to the points first perceived, transversally to the localizable relation to distant or contiguous points' (p. 293). When an ecoculturalism is based on identity, it gets caught up in a politics of identity: polluters set against environmentalists, pristine wilderness set against civilization, development set against planning, cyborgs set against one another. When someone 'gets' that they are cyborg, the work can too easily stop there: 'I am cyborg. So what?' By focusing on the flows among the human and the other-than-human, cultural studies can more productively address what is empowered and what is disempowered, what is possible, and what is not. We can consider what new assemblages we might applaud, revel in, support, or see as a way to genuine multiplication. Recognizing that we are cyborg simply is not enough. When articulation and assemblage are recognized as process, there is simply no stopping point.

Nowhere is the cultural commitment to cyborg identity clearer than in popular science fiction. In these images, the cyborg is reduced to a particular kind of thing: a blend of human organism and machine, a human-hardware hybrid that either threatens 'real' humanness or enhances it (or both). With the prevalence of this cyborg in popular film, fiction, and everyday discourse, any theoretical attempt to recruit the cyborg in service of a transformed cultural studies is fighting an uphill battle. The failure of Clark's book to fully recognize the political implications of having always been cyborg is instructive.

Haraway's attempt to use the cyborg to shock, transgress, and startle us into rethinking the relation between the human and the unhuman, what she calls the naturalsocial (1992) or later naturecultures (2003), has its limits.

In main, the cyborg has become an unfortunately precious image with which to take pleasure in the machine components in our still very human lives.[4] By 2003, Haraway realizes that the cyborg can no longer 'fruitfully inform livable politics and ontologies in current life worlds .... By the end of the millennium, cyborgs could no longer ... gather up the threads needed for critical inquiry' (2003, p. 4).

Not tolerating inelegant stuttering

What does it take then to gather up the threads needed for critical inquiry? The best critical theorists are those who most elegantly handle the multiplicity of complex threads of the context and weave them into a convincing text. In the world of academic cultural studies, critical inquiry is practically synonymous with writing. The 'better' the weaving/writing, the more we value the theorist. Stuart Hall's enormous skill at weaving threads and writing elegantly provides a case in point. Without in any way diminishing those skills, I would like to suggest that in coming to expect them, cultural theorists often miss significant opportunities to examine, experience, and think about culture in new ways, to weave, as it were, relevant threads. In particular there are opportunities to think through the eco that will not be found in either academic discourse or in widely circulated forms of popular discourse. As Haraway (2003) teases, 'Anyone who has done historical research knows that the undocumented often have more to say about how the world is put together than do the well pedigreed' (p. 88). There is a lot to learn from the cultural 'mutts.'

For example, I am thinking here of what I call *becoming-with-horse*, which is suggested popularly in the 'listening to horses' movement. In a much debased form, the movement is expressed in popular media in *The Horse Whisperer* – both the book (Evans 1995) and the movie (1998). It is more adequately characterized in Monty Roberts' best-selling book *The Man Who Listens to Horses* (1997). But there are many, less popular books that cover similar territory in less elegant but effective ways. For example: Tom Dorrance's *True Unity* (1987), Ray Hunt's *Think Harmony With Horses* (1997), Pat Parelli's *Natural Horse-Man-Ship* (1993), Gawani Pony Boys' *Horse, Follow Closely* (1998), and Mark Rashid's *Considering the Horse* (1993) and *A Good Horse Is Never a Bad Color* (1996). These less accessible books, and the workshops on 'joining up' with horses that are held all over 'horse country' (which is anywhere there are horses) reveal a movement of far more significance than is represented in its more popular (more expressively elegant) versions, such as *The Horse Whisperer*. In fact, the far less visible workshops probably constitute the most effective part of the movement.

The movement is exciting for two reasons. First, it suggests a genuine – and promising – transformation in understanding cultural relations among heterogeneous species. Second, it is a popular movement with possibilities for far-reaching consequences. It is not that the insights offered by the listening-to-horses movement are particularly new. They are, however, being articulated in new ways as part of an emerging cultural assemblage.

The listening-to-horses movement has many different manifestations. At the one extreme (the easiest to grasp within language and the least interesting), it reproduces the problematic of identity. It goes like this: Horses have a language. Humans can learn that language and learn to speak it by performing minor acts of translation. So, for example, walking in a zig-zag fashion as you approach a horse communicates herbivore-grazing rather than predator-stalking. Communication here is nothing more than the connection formed between two identities with two distinct languages, and as such it hardens up those points rather than opening them to multiplicity. If anything, communication in this formulation enhances the power of human identity to exert power over the other. We now have power to cross the species divide, to translate and understand horse language, to communicate to them, and exert a new form of mastery. Horses lose their mystery, their otherness. They are merely the prey animal seeking comfort from predators. The terms are all fundamentally human and language is the language of identity.[5]

There is, however, a much more interesting thread in the listening-to-horses movement. In this thread, there is an attempt to move in the world *with horse*. Communication is not a connection between points or identities. Rather, it looks more like what Deleuze and Guattari call 'transversal communications between heterogeneous populations' (1987, p. 239) or a 'passage between heterogeneities'(1987, p. 250). In this case an active line transforms 'other becomings entirely different'; it induces a 'transformation of all of the preceding assemblages'(1987, p. 251). New haecceities assemble, combine and articulate expression and content in ways that open to multiplicity. Horse language is not reduced to human language, horse and human do not become horse–human (like cyborg). Instead a new herd forms, perpendicular to those identities, escaping them. This is not a transformation of essential forms (that would be a problem of identity), but a transformation of what can be expressed and lived, a *becoming-with-horse*. The transformative potential can be glimpsed in the listening-to-horses movement in its practice of 'joining up' with horses as opposed to training them. Horses are not trained into being some other imagined identity (the well-trained horse). Rather, horse and human 'join up' and *become* – releasing new possibilities, new ways of being and living.

It is difficult to either explain or know what this becoming-with-horse looks or feels like. As the line of flight escapes expressions that 'make sense' to us from within the escaped assemblage, language, as Deleuze maintains, 'stutters' (Deleuze 1994, p. 23). When it does not stutter, language is regulatory. Then, as explained by Christa Albrecht-Crane, language 'functions as an ordering mechanism through a process of normalizing and streamlining variables that are made to function as order-words in support ... of social processes.' It 'provides a (conceptual) vocabulary with which to make a certain sense of the world and with each other' (Albrecht-Crane 2005, p. 123–124). When, however, language stutters, it 'ushers in the words that it affects' (Deleuze, 1994, p. 23); it uses old and new words in ways that upset the ordering mechanism and open new possibilities. Great writers stutter, Deleuze argues, for they are strangers in the language within which they are required to express themselves (1994, p. 25). Their use of language will seem variously strange, for they are actively drawing new, unfamiliar lines. But not everyone with a line of flight to express may be as talented poetically. Because they may not be great writers, we must work even harder to see through the potentially revealing stuttering. Sometimes, just when you think you are going to get the explanation, the author cannot or does not explain. The words set out, fall short, and are sometimes pulled back – reterritorialized – in terms returned to the abandoned territory. In spite of these 'failures,' momentary glimmers open up possibility, multiplicity, and powerful affect. In the listening-to-horses literature, they open up ways of thinking and theorizing the role of the eco in culture in a non-anthropocentric way.

My favorite example of the halting, stuttering explanation of becoming-with-horse is expressed in the writing of Tom Dorrance (1987). I choose him because he stutters the hardest with superficially the least success.[6] His discourse is the most inelegant. Repeatedly in his books he suffers over his inadequacy with words to explain. His stuttering attests to the failure of existing discourse to characterize a line of flight. Yet he has something important to say. I greatly admire his 'failed' attempts at the same time that I glimpse the power of possibility in his idea of 'unity.' He writes:

> There can be some direction, or support and encouragement, but the *feel* itself can come from no one but themselves; they will know when the feel actually becomes effective, and when they are understanding.
>
> I've looked in dictionaries for the definition for the word *feel*. I haven't been really satisfied with the definitions I've found for this thing I'm talking about with the horse – this thing *between the horse and the person*.
>
> If I could tell people, just go through the motions here, and then they could pick this up and do it, I wouldn't do anything else but work with people and horses; but I can't do that. There is something more. It is something that has to come in the unity between the horse and the rider. And there is a delicate line that makes the difference. (Dorance 1987, pp. 12, 17)

People like Dorrance give workshops all over the country, working with horses and people in face-to-face interactions to teach the 'feel' he speaks of here. Although I have never attended a Dorrance workshop, I suspect that he is more effective at performing relations across heterogeneous species than he is at expressing them in written discourse. I have, however, experienced moments of becoming-with-horse that feel like what Dorrance describes.

Another, more poetic, example of stuttering to draw this transformative line of communication 'running perpendicularly to points first perceived' was written in 1954 and has been revived as part of this new movement.[7] Its revival suggests again that while the insights themselves are not new, they are participating in a process of transforming the concept of culture as anthropocentric as manifest in everyday life – in ways not especially visible in more popular media. It also makes clear that the listening-to-horses movement is not just about horses, but about the possibilities of affective trajectories involving animals generally. This example also illustrates that drawing lines of flight appears 'beyond the pale,' as magic, as hokum, as the ravings of weirdos – no matter how serious the efforts. Deleuze and Guattari refer to the 'passage between heterogeneities' as 'how we sorcerers operate' (1987, p. 250). In this example, J. Allen Boone (1976) tries to describe learning to become-with-dog. It is, delightfully, the language of sorcery:

> The most memorable of our silent talks took place out under the stars, where he and I would sit shoulder to shoulder in shared contemplation like a couple of cogitating philosophers. We would first saturate ourselves with distance. We would watch the lovely designs and purpose operating in all things, and we would wonder, and marvel, and ponder. We would listen to the Voice of Existence as it silent spoke in that language which knows no barriers of time, space or species. The magic of the Universe flowed through us, and the dog and I realized our individual and necessary places in that glorious cosmic expression. (p. 79)

More recently, the highly accomplished stutterer, Donna Haraway, after abandoning the cyborg, uses dogs as the vehicle to argue for rethinking the relationship between nature and culture. In her provocative manifesto, *The Companion Species Manifesto* (2003), she makes the case for 'constitutive relationships' (p. 12) between dogs and human 'all the way down': hence her designation 'naturecultures' (p. 12). That relationships are constitutive acknowledges a kind of co-evolutional development, or evo-devo, a evolutionary developmental interdependence, such that we (who and what we have become and are becoming) are co-dependent with the evolutionary development of dogs. As with those writing about, teaching, and performing becoming-with-horse, Haraway explores the historically specific, 'joint lives of dogs and people, who are bonded in significant otherness' (2003, p. 16), but she is out to reveal more than the co-dependence of dogs and humans. She considers the companion species: 'A bigger and more heterogeneous category than companion animal, and not just because one must include such organic beings as rice, bees, tulips, and intestinal flora, all of whom make life for humans what it is – and vice versa' (p. 15). Beyond her insight that all species are companion species, she counts the machinic and the textual, for they are 'internal to the organic and vice versa in irreversible ways' (p. 15).

In more explicitly academic forms of stuttering, research on the body suggests an especially potent site of both difficulty and possibility in rethinking the co-evolutionary interdependence of the human and the other-than human, in that the body (any body) is both human and other-than-human. This work challenges the idea that the body is 'fixed' in any way; not even the boundaries of the human body have been consistently drawn. Rosi Braidotti (2002) claims that the body is 'not an essence, let alone a biological substance, but a play of forces, a surface of intensities' (p. 21). Body boundaries are permeable (Bowen 2005, Hashimoto 2005), constituted in ongoing flows and relations among the material and discursive, organic and inorganic, human and other-than-human vectors, factors, bodies. If even the 'human' body is both human and other-than-human – throwing into deep suspicion the very designation 'human' – how can cultural studies ever parse the other-than-human as outside of, or insignificant to, the project?

Cultural approaches to studying technology, including Haraway's work on the cyborg, have taught us to recognize the co-evolution of the organic and the machinic. Cultural approaches to text and body have sensitized us to the co-evolution of the organic, the machinic, and the textual. Relatively arcane movements, such as listening-to-horses and companion animal training, reveal cultural sites where important cultural work is undertaken. We need only to put this all together and map out the implications. Because we co-habit an active history, as Haraway puts it (2003, p. 20), living ethically in relations of significant otherness requires 'ongoing alertness to otherness-in-relation' (p. 50) – an otherness that must include the technological, the textual, and the body, as well as the components of the eco: environment, ecology, biology, and nature.

Ecoculturalism isn't what it is about after all

The weight of the arguments brought together here compel cultural theorists to acknowledge that culture is the site of co-evolutionary development involving factors, vectors, or bodies with a variety of forms: what in inadequately but effectively territorialized language we characterize as organic and inorganic, discursive and non-discursive, machinic and spiritual, human and-other-than human (or unhuman in Haraway's terms), the said and the unsaid – expanded vastly beyond the concept of discourse. Just as feminists argued that ignoring gender perpetuates a silence with profound political effects, so too do we ignore technology and the eco with profound political and ethical effects.

My objection to ecoculturalism is this: like cyberfeminism, feminist cultural studies, ecofeminism, technoculture, technoscience, nature/cultures, or environmental cultural studies, ecoculturalism foregrounds one factor, vector, or body as primary, as especially significant. It is akin to labeling cultural studies through time as class cultural studies, race cultural studies, feminist cultural studies, ethnic cultural studies, difference cultural studies, power cultural studies, techno cultural studies, eco cultural studies, or queer cultural studies. While, especially in the case of feminism, there have been strategic reasons for staking out these prepositional grounds, the strategy has become an almost magical solution to a much more complex problem. We do not really solve the problem of rethinking culture when we simply add a new preposition to claim a new space: cyber, techno, eco, queer, etc. As cultural theorists, we ought to wrestle with the knowledge that it is impossible to contextualize culture without considering the co-evolution of all these significant articulating vectors, factors, or bodies.

Further, by foregrounding one factor, vector, or body, desirable as well as undesirable baggage is brought along. 'Feminist' and 'queer' threaten to limit the issue to gender (although they do not necessarily); 'environment' requires acknowledging the trajectory of a particular environmental movement (although it does not necessarily); eco, bio, and techno insist on engaging the versions of these from a positivistic scientific perspective (although they do not necessarily); 'nature' raises the need to confront the nature/culture split all over again, even in the midst of denying the split. So why foreground these terms? Why not just engage in a new, transformed practice of cultural studies?

There are those who call for abandoning cultural studies, in part because the specificity of cultural studies has been lost. Cultural studies has become almost anything — if, that is, you acknowledge the claims of the variety of voices who claim to practice it. My argument here might suggest that we abandon cultural studies on the grounds that the term 'cultural,' like 'nature,' raises the need to confront—unproductively — the nature/culture split yet again. Furthermore, 'culture' does suggest the anthropocentric. I do not advocate that path, however. Let me be clear. I want to jettison ecocultural studies, but not cultural studies. As problematic as the term 'culture' has been, there is reason to embrace it, to insist on the lineage, specificity, and possibilities of it. The term 'cultural studies' has won us space, given us a legitimate academic platform from which to observe, learn, communicate with one another, and teach. That is worth building on. But I would urge that we take on the essential and difficult task of specifying what we mean by the 'cultural.' To do that I insist that we must make a leap into the age we really inhabit, where there is so much at stake in the ways that culture is an active process of articulating flows within which relations of power are reproduced, resisted, and transformed. There are no neatly parsed, fixed 'humans' or 'other-than-humans,' or for that matter, cyborgs, in this concept of culture. There are only intermingling modalities, configuring bodies, geomorphs, biorhythms, herds. If we insist on culture in this non-anthropocentric sense as what constitutes the specificity of cultural studies, then we will have transformed cultural studies and revitalized its potential to describe and intervene in the world.

Acknowledgement

I extend thanks to Patty Sotirin for generous readings and thoughtful insight.

Notes

1. Slack & Whitt (1992) called for an 'ecoculturally informed cultural studies' that acknowledges a necessary inconnectedness between the cultural and the biotic (or the other-than-human world), abandons anthropocentrism, and rethinks its project in light of human relations with the other-than-human world. In what was a correct assessment, we wrote then, 'We anticipate the reluctance of cultural theorists to enter this ecoculturalist terrain based on a fear that to reorient cultural studies thus would be to change its project' (p. 589).
2. Cultural theorists who have for some time been attending to environment, ecology, and nature include Jody Berland (1994) Andrew Ross (1991), Carole Stabile (1994), Jennifer Daryl Slack and Laurie Anne Whitt (1992, 1994), and Mackenzie Wark (1994).
3. Athusser (1970) posits a fourth, the scientific, which does not hold up very well in his analysis and, like other scholars, I choose to leave it out of the equation.
4. In spite of these cultural limitations it is still possible to use the cyborg to develop an academically responsible (feminist) ethic, as Joanna Zylinska does in *The Ethics of Cultural Studies* (2005, pp. 138–158).
5. Pat Parelli's *Natural Horse-Man-Ship* (1993) exemplifies this approach. Although I do not contest his horsemanship, his 'keys to a natural horse-human relationship' reads like an operations manual. Is the horse here machine, the human the organic, and horse-man-ship merely cyborg identity? It may be that Parelli is simply so committed to his mission and to selling books as a measure of his success that he speaks in the language of an operations manual to make inroads. It is an improvement to treat horses with the kind of acknowledgment Parelli gives them, but the discursive text does not look like becoming-with-horse.

6   Dorrance (1987) is taken to task severely by Amazon.com reviewers for failing to explain 'his method.' I take this as an unreasonable demand to speak from within the very assemblage Dorrance is trying to escape.
7   Amazon.com recommended this text (Boone 1976) as one I would probably be interested in given the several books on horses that I purchased from them. This suggestion alone draws a link between it and the listening-to-horses movement.

References

Albrecht-Crane, C. (2005) 'Style, stutter', in *Gilles Deleuze: Key Concepts*, ed. C. J. Stivale, Stocksfield, Acumen Publishing, pp. 121–130.
Althusser, L. (1970) *For Marx*, trans. B. Brewster, New York, Random House.
Berland, J. (1994) 'On reading "the weather"', *Cultural Studies*, vol. 8, no. 1, pp. 99–114.
Boone, J. A. (1954) *Kinship With All Life*, San Francisco, Harper San Francisco. (Originally published 1954).
Bowen, L. M. (2005) 'Reconfigured bodies: the problem of ownership', *Communication Theory*, vol. 15, no. 1, pp. 23–38.
Braidotti, R. (2002) *Metamorphoses: Toward a Materialist Theory of Becoming*, Malden, MA, Blackwell.
Clark, A. (2003) *Natural-Born Cyborgs: Minds, Technologies, and the Future of Human Intelligence*, Oxford, Oxford University Press.
Cultural Studies (1994) 'Special section on cultural studies and the environment', eds J. Berland and J. D. Slack, *Cultural Studies*, vol. 8, no. 1, pp. 1–141.
Deleuze, G. (1994) 'He stuttered', in *Gilles Deleuze and the Theater of Philosophy*, eds C. V. Boundas & D. Olkowski, New York, Routledge, pp. 23–29.
Deleuze, G. & Guattari, F. (1987) *A Thousand Plateaus: Capitalism and Schizophrenia*, trans. B. Massumi, Minneapolis, MN, University of Minnesota Press.
Dorance, T. (1987) *True Unity: Willing Communication Between Horse and Human*, Clovis, CA, Word Dancer Press.
Evans, N. (1995) *The Horse Whisperer*, New York, Delacorte Press.
Foucault, M. (1980) *Power/Knowledge: Selected Interviews and Other Writings, 1972–1977*, ed. C. Gordon, New York, Pantheon Books.
Grossberg, L. (1988) 'It's a sin: politics, post-modernity and the popular', in *It's a Sin: Essays on Postmodernism, Politics & Culture*, L. Grossberg, T. Fry, A. Curthoys & P. Patton, Sydney, Power Publications, pp. 6–71.
Grossberg, L. (1997) *Dancing in Spite of Myself: Essays on Popular Culture*, Durham, NC, Duke University Press.
Hall, S. (1973) 'The determinations of news photographs', in *The Manufacture of News: Social Problems, Deviance and the Mass Media*, eds S. Cohen & J. Young, London, Constable, pp. 176–190.
Hall, S. (1977) 'Re-thinking the "base-and-superstructure" metaphor', in *Papers on Class, Hegemony and Party*, ed. J. Bloomfield, London, Lawrence and Wishart, pp. 43–72.

Hall, S. (1980a) 'Encoding/decoding', in *Culture, Media, Language*, eds S. Hall, D. Hobson, A. Lowe & P. Willis, London, Hutchins, pp. 128–138. (Originally published 1973).

Hall, S. (1980b) 'Race, articulation and societies structured in dominance', in *UNECSO, Sociological Theories: Race and Colonialism*, Paris, UNESCO, pp. 305–345.

Hall, S. (1981) 'Notes on deconstructing "the popular"', in *People's History and Socialist Theory*, ed. R Samuel, London, Routledge and Kegan Paul, pp. 227–240.

Hall, S. (1985) 'Signification, representation, ideology: Althusser and the post-structuralist debates', *Critical Studies in Mass Communication*, vol. 2, no. 2, pp. 91–114.

Hall, S. (1992) 'Cultural studies and its theoretical legacies', in *Cultural Studies*, eds L. Grossberg, C. Nelson & P. Treichler, New York, Routledge, pp. 277–294.

Hall, S. (ed.) (1997) *Representation: Cultural Representations and Signifying Practices*, London, Sage.

Hall, S. & Jefferson, T. (eds) (1976) *Resistance Through Rituals: Youth Subcultures in Post-War Britain*, London, Hutchinson.

Haraway, D. (1985) 'A manifesto for cyborgs: science, technology, and socialist feminism in the 1980s', *Socialist Review*, vol. 80, pp. 65–107.

Haraway, D. (1992) 'The promises of monsters: a regenerative politics for inappropriate/d others', in *Cultural Studies*, eds L. Grossberg, C. Nelson & P. Treichler, New York, Routledge, pp. 295–337.

Haraway, D. (2003) *The Companion Species Manifesto: Dogs, People, and Significant Otherness*, Chicago, IL, Prickly Paradigm Press.

Hashimoto, S. D. (2005) 'Technology, corporeal permeability, ideology', *Communication Theory*, vol. 15, no. 1, pp. 10–22.

Hebdige, D. (1979) *Subculture: The Meaning of Style*, London, Methuen.

Hoggart, R. (1969) 'Contemporary cultural studies: an approach to the study of literature and society', Mimeograph.

Hoggart, R. (1970) *The Uses of Literacy*, New York, Oxford University Press. (Originally published 1957).

Hunt, R. (1997) *Think Harmony With Horses: An In-Depth Study of Horse/Man Relationship*, Fresno, CA, Pioneer Publishing.

Latour, B. [as Jim Johnson] (1988) 'Mixing humans and nonhumans together: the sociology of a door-closer', *Social Problems*, vol. 35, no. 3, pp. 298–310.

Latour, B. (1996) *Aramis, Or the Love of Technology*, trans. C. Porter, Cambridge, MA, Harvard University Press.

McRobbie, A & Garber, J. (1976) 'Girls and subcultures', in *Resistance Through Rituals: Youth Subcultures in Post-war Britain*, eds S. Hall & T. Jefferson, London, Hutchinson, pp. 209–222.

McRobbie, A. (1981) 'Settling accounts with subcultures: a feminist critique', in *Culture, Ideology and Social Process: A Reader*, eds T. Bennett, G. Martin, C.

Mercer & J. Woollacott, London, Batsford Academic and Education Ltd, pp. 111–123. (Originally published 1980).
Parelli, P. (1993) *Natural Horse-Man-Ship*, Colorado Springs, CO, Western Horseman.
Pony Boy, G. (1998) *Horse, Follow Closely: Native American Horsemanship*, Irvine, CA, BowTie Press.
Rashid, M. (1993) *Considering the Horse: Tales of Problems Solved and Lessons Learned*, Boulder, CA, Johnson Books.
Rashid, M. (1996) *A Good Horse is Never a Bad Color*, Boulder, CA, Johnson Books.
Roberts, M. (1997) *The Man Who Listens to Horses*, New York, Random House.
Ross, A. (1991) *Strange Weather: Culture, Science and Technology in the Age of Limits*, New York, Verso.
Sandywell, B. (2004) 'The myth of everyday life: toward a heterology of the ordinary', *Cultural Studies*, vol. 18, nos 2/3, pp. 160–180.
Sawchuk, K. (2001) 'Bioturism: travels in the bioscape', in *Digitized Bodies, Virtual Spectacles*, ed. N. Czeglady, Budapest, Ludwig Museum Budapest/Museum of Contemporary Art, pp. 57–71.
Slack, J. D. (1985) 'The development and use of communication technologies: critical issues', *The Journal of Communication Inquiry*, vol. 9, no. 1, pp. 17–27.
Slack, J. D. (1989) 'Contextualizing technology', in *Rethinking Communication: Volume 2, Paradigm Exemplars*, eds B. Dervin, L. Grossberg, B. J. O'Keefe & E. Wartella, Newbury Park, CA, Sage, pp. 329–345.
Slack, J. D. (2005) 'Environment/ecology', in *New Keywords: A Revised Vocabulary of Culture and Society*, eds T. Bennett, L. Grossberg & M. Morris, Malden, MA, Blackwell Publishing, pp. 106–109.
Slack, J. D. & Whitt, L. A. (1992) 'Ethics and cultural studies', in *Cultural Studies*, eds L. Grossberg, C. Nelson & P. Treichler, New York, Routledge, pp. 571–592.
Slack, J. D. & Wise, J. M. (2005) *Culture and Technology: A Primer*, New York, Peter Lang.
Stabile, C. A. (1994) '"A garden inclosed is my sister", ecofeminism and eco-valences', *Cultural Studies*, vol. 8, no. 1, pp. 56–73.
The Horse Whisperer (1998) Dir. Robert Redford, Touchstone Pictures.
Thrift, N. (2004) 'Electric animals: new models of everyday life?', *Cultural Studies*, vol. 18, nos 2/3, pp. 461–482.
Wark, M. (1994) 'Third nature', *Cultural Studies*, vol. 8, no. 1, pp 115–132.
Whitt, L. A. & Slack, J. D. (1994) 'Communities, environments and cultural studies', *Cultural Studies*, vol. 8, no. 1, pp. 5–31.
Williams, R. (1961) *The Long Revolution*, London, Chatto and Windus.
Williams, R. (1992) *Television: Technology and Cultural Form*, Hanover, Wesleyan University Press. (Originally published 1974).
Wilson, A. (1992) *The Culture of Nature: North American Landscape from Disney to the Exxon Valdez*, Cambridge, MA, Blackwell.
Zylinska, J. (2005) *The Ethics of Cultural Studies*, London, Continuum.

Dr Vandana Shiva, an interview by Andy Opel

FROM WATER CRISIS TO WATER CULTURE

Fresh water has gone through some significant changes over the past twenty years. What once had been sold by the gallon as an emergency storm supply in grocery stores in the U.S. is now marketed by the pint by global corporations. Public water supplies are increasingly pressured to privatize their services as local fresh water sources are bought by these same companies, and global trade agreements and international development organizations increasingly promote the privatization of fresh water supplies. Dr. Vandana Shiva has been a leading voice in the efforts to defend local water rights and promote new forms of "public-public" partnerships to protect fresh water supplies. For this issue of Cultural Studies, *Dr. Andy Opel interviewed Dr. Shiva about the connections between culture and water, how our cultural attitudes shape our water use and how we might change those cultural habits to ensure clean water for the future.*

Fresh water has gone through some significant changes over the past 20 years. What once had been sold by the gallon as an emergency storm supply in grocery stores in the US is now marketed by the pint by global corporations; Coca-Cola, Pepsi-Co and Nestle. Public water supplies are increasingly pressured to privatize their services as local fresh water sources are bought by these same companies. Global trade agreements and international development organizations [International Monetary Fund (IMF), World Bank] increasingly promote the privatization of fresh water supplies. Although water resource issues have received relatively little attention from the mainstream media,[1] these corporate moves have been coupled with increased attention from journalists, activists and scholars.[2] Dr Vandana Shiva has been a leading voice in the efforts to defend local water rights and promote new forms of 'public–public' partnerships to protect fresh water supplies. Dr Andy Opel has written about the bottled water industry (Opel 1999) as well as the intersection of environmentalism and popular culture. For purposes of this issue of *Cultural Studies*, they spoke across continents in December 2005 to exchange ideas about the connections between culture and water, how our cultural attitudes shape our water use and how we might change those cultural habits to ensure clean water for the future.

Opel: You have written the book *Water Wars* (Shiva 2002) as well as many articles, given numerous interviews and spoken publicly about global water resource issues.[3] Can you give us an update about where we are as a planet with regard to fresh water supplies?

Shiva: We are at a very precarious time with regard to global fresh water supplies because water is being treated like a non-renewable resource. Even though water can be available forever in adequate quantities according to the ecosystems and their water endowment, all of the technology of the last 50 years has been breaking out of the water cycle and breaking out of the culture of conservation and awareness of the water cycle. The entire system of industrial agriculture is based on obstructing rejuvenation of rivers, rejuvenation of aquifers. Basically, the 'so-called' additional food that is being produced is really additional water sucked out of the earth and sent off to the marketplace. I think industrial agriculture has done the maximum harm to fresh water and everywhere in the tropics, wherever industrial agriculture has spread, in countries like India, wherever green revolution technology has spread, that is where we have a water crisis.

Opel: So industrial agriculture is *the* leading cause of fresh water scarcity?

Shiva: Industrial agriculture and rampant industrialization, which could only be viable if it treated pollution as zero cost and treated the river as the place to carry the pollution. Just look at what's happened in China in the last few weeks, where river after river has had an accident, with the release of chemicals from industrial plants. From the Bhopal industrial disaster of 1984, the ground water is still contaminated there. The Yamuna the river on which Delhi has been built and has lived for millennia, in the last 20 years of industrialization, the Yamuna has become an industrial sewer, it is just carrying the waste of industry. This externalization of polluting industries is the second big burden on our fresh water. In my lifetime, really just 20 years ago, I could go travel anywhere in my country, go on treks, go in villages, just bend down and drink from any stream and any river and not get sick.

Opel: You have also used the term 'water cultures.' What do you mean by this term and how does a cultural perspective shed light on what many view as an economic commodity?

Shiva: When the awareness and consciousness of our living in the water cycle dies, that is when water culture dies. To me, water culture is the consciousness of water, the consciousness of being immersed in a water cycle, the consciousness of knowing that we are 70 percent water, and that the planet is 70 percent water, and to tread extremely lightly to ensure that water balance is not destroyed. Heightened water awareness creates water culture and water cultures build into them cultures like the sacredness of India's rivers. If Indian's could have such a long-term evolution of civilization in the Ganges basin, it is because the Ganges was related to as a sacred mother nourishing the entire basin. The culture that that creates is extremely different from the culture which sees water running into the sea as wasted and sees rivers as wild women to be tamed and creates the most violent technologies for rerouting rivers, imprisoning rivers and drying out rivers. That idea of control that develops technologies that disrupt the water cycle and impair the water culture goes hand-in-hand and are leading to the current thinking that water is just another commodity on the planet, you don't have to give it any special respect. And every right wing think tank that is promoting and supporting water privatization repeatedly states that water is just another commodity.

Opel: Could you describe what you mean when you say water cycle?

Shiva: The water cycle is the process through which water recycles itself. Water can never run out as long as it is allowed to recycle itself. As long as the forests evaporate the water, moves up into the clouds, forms precipitation, falls as snow, falls as rain, comes back to the ground, the ground welcomes those raindrops, welcomes the snow and in that welcoming, recharges the aquifers, realizes the rivers. That perennial reach out of water is the water cycle, the most efficient way of renewing water resources on the planet.

We are disrupting that water cycle by first destroying the places where water is held, catchments of our beautiful rivers. My first involvement with an environmental movement was working with the women of the high Himalayas who launched the 'chipko' movement.[4] Chipko means to embrace and they embraced trees to prevent logging. When they were hugging the trees to stop them from being logged, they were also embracing water because they recognized that forests are the protectors of water and it was their struggle over 10 years that led to a ban on logging in the catchment and changed water policy and changed water thinking. It did not come out of the scientists, it came out of peasant women who recognized the water cycle and that the cradle of recharging of our water sources on the planet are our catchment forests, that their stands are the biggest dams. Here we think of dams as concrete, but they prevent water from recharging the ground, they prevent water from recharging along the entire basin. That is another disruption of the water cycle. And the third disruption of the water cycle is our mad romance with concrete. Look how we are paving over the world, blocking every drop from going back into the earth where it belongs. And it is no accident that we have. Combined with climate change, and climate change destabilizing the amount of water we receive in periods so we get too much rain when we shouldn't and too little when we should, combined with the blocking of drainage, the blocking of leaching of the ground water, we have increasing flood disasters. Bombay was drowned in floods this last June, Chennai (Madras) is under flood water now. We have become experts at disrupting the water cycle. We treat that as technological progress. Every step of destroying the water cycle is treated and defined as a step in progress.

Opel: You have written about a concept you call ecological democracy. Can you describe what you mean by ecological democracy? How do you think our cultural attitudes about natural resources such as water are connected to our larger political cultures? Does one need to be changed before the other? Can they be changed independent of one another?

Shiva: Ecological democracy or earth democracy means three things. It means, firstly, a democracy of all life, not just human life — all life, plant life, animal life, microbial life because all life has a right to have a share in the planet's water. All beings need water and ecological democracy recognizes our duty to other beings, not just to provide the human community with water. But earth democracy and ecological democracy for me is also democracy from the ground up. It's the democracy of the earth that has the highest decision-making powers in the places closest to where people live, use natural resources, have to handle ecosystems and have to handle the consequences of their actions. The third meaning for me of ecological democracy is a democracy that recognizes our ecological nature, our ecological identity and therefore recognizes that we are a biological species that needs water, that needs food and that these essentials are the most fundamental human rights, that they are everyday rights, everyday responsibilities that have to be looked after.

How do we connect it to the larger issue of political culture, political democracy? Well, we've just had the World Trade Organization (WTO) meetings in Hong Kong and these WTO meetings have increasingly grasped more and more spheres of life, so the trade relations in intellectual property rights agreement took over control of biodiversity by introducing patents on life forms, piracy of traditional knowledge. The new general agreements on trade in services (GATS) and the whole services text that has been adopted in Hong Kong includes among other things the privatization and commodification of water. Earth democracy basically addresses this worldview of the world as a supermarket, the world as a place where things are bought and sold, the recognition that where there is no ecosystem, there is no culture. Earth democracy addresses this narrowing of our political culture both by reclaiming democracy for people and reclaiming democracy for all of life so that we are able to re-embed our actions – our economic actions, our ecological actions – within the earth family, within the diversity of species on this planet.

Opel: I appreciate what you are saying. We need to democratize the trade agreement process because we know that they have been anti-democratic from the beginning.

Shiva: And there are certain things that you cannot democratize at that distant level. You cannot have, as we have seen again and again, 150 countries trying to represent their millions of citizens. They can not then make appropriate decisions about how water should be used, how water should be managed at a global level, driven by the trade and commodification paradigm. They will eventually sign on to an inappropriate decision driven largely by those who would commodify our fundamental needs.

Opel: 'Globalization' and 'the marketplace' are the new meta-narratives of our time. You have made a distinction between the market paradigm and an ecological paradigm. Can you describe this distinction and give us any examples of movement toward an ecological paradigm?

Shiva: All the work I have done over the past two decades is really to not just talk and think about alternatives to the market paradigm and an ecological paradigm but to actually shape it, shape it on action. If you think about water, the places where we are making a difference and where we are building a water democracy and building an ecological paradigm, is in cases for example of creating alternatives to the privatization being pushed by the World Bank. In Delhi, we have managed to stop that privatization, first by mobilizing communities all along the Ganges from where the water was to be brought to then be commodified and sold by Suez, the world's biggest water corporation. We've also continued to work with the Delhi communities on conservation. We have enough water in Delhi as long as it is conserved and as long as it is shared.

Scarcity is a product of the market paradigm. Scarcity is a product of the market thinking, 'Oh, the river Yamuna is there as a sink, let's throw all our waste into it.' It creates scarcity by polluting our rivers. It creates scarcity by allowing some people to get their water and others to have none. Ecological paradigm recognizes that everyone has an equal access to water, an equal right to water, and those equal rights allow us to make sure we can share and conserve what is there. Our work in Delhi and the water democracy movement we have built there, shows that if communities engage in conservation and recycling, there is no scarcity, there is no need for corporations to enter our water economy.

The other place where the ecological paradigm in water is really built beautifully is in agriculture. I mentioned the largest waste of water is in industrial farming. We don't need a lot of water for growing good food. Chemicals need a lot of water. It is chemical farming that needs intensive water and intensive irrigation. We have reduced water use, through organic farming, by 60–70 percent and still maintaining crop yields and sometimes even increasing crop yields because it means a deeper agriculture of care. And one of the most beautiful movements that has evolved over the past few years in India is the movement to threat the ecological paradigm as a paradigm of living democracy. The villages declare themselves as earth republics. Republics in which the family is the trees, the plants, the animals, the goats, the buffalo, everything together, one family. And within that earth family, is a clear recognition that you have to protect all life and you have to use your resources in ways that all life has a share. Which means that you have to change your farming systems from chemical farming that destroys the earthworms, that pollutes the water, to organic farming. You have to shift your ways of doing forestry from monocultures for the pulp industry to ecological forestry for the needs of all. The living democracy movement focuses on the conservation of biodiversity, the production of ecological foods and the conservation and sharing of water. And it is able from the ground to address the passing laws of WTO and say, 'We are sorry, we have higher laws. We cannot think of biodiversity as the property of some corporation so we are compelled to not obey the WTO laws. We have higher laws with respect to water and our water culture says we must share and we cannot commodify. We will continue to hold our water as sacred, a sacred resource to be shared for all life.' I feel extremely empowered and extremely hopeful with the emergence of these new movements shaping a new ecological paradigm and a new earth democracy.

Opel: Last summer, Indian photographer Sharad Haksar created a billboard from a photo of water jugs lined up at a pump in front of a Coca-Cola billboard.[5] This pictured served as a commentary on the water shortages in India, drawing attention to the 500,000–1.5 million liters of water a day used by Coke to manufacture soft drinks in the bottling plant in the Palakkad district of Kerala. This sign also drew attention to the fact that it takes seven times the amount of fresh water to manufacture one bottle of Coke. You have been a vocal critic of Coke as well and I wanted to ask what you thought of this form of 'culture jamming' and how this type of activism might play into broader efforts to change the 'water cultures?'

Shiva: For me, it was culture jamming when I went in 2002 to join the women of Pallakad who were fighting the Coca-Cola plant which was destroying 1.5 million liters of water a day. And here they were, the women who were having to walk extra miles because Coke had polluted and destroyed their water. Their culture of water verses the Coke commodification of water, in a way that movement itself was cultural jamming. And now, Sarad Haksar's photograph as you describe it, in a way reflects an imagery that of the real life political culture jamming these women have done. They have shut down that plant and I say three cheers to them and three cheers to Sarad Haksar.

Opel: In many ways, cultural habits around water use are driven by infrastructure – our toilets in the West use 1.5–2 gallons with every flush and faucets and showerheads rarely restrict water flow. In your book *Water Wars* you write about the community construction of Johads, water retention pods that capture monsoon rains. Can you talk about the connection between material infrastructure and the habits of water use? How much of our 'water culture' is determined by the tools we surround ourselves with? Do you think we need to change the way people think or rather change the material conditions that shape their actions?

Shiva: I think we need to change both and both feed each other. I think if we think of water as a very precious gift that we have to nurture, conserve and recycle, then we will not use it in a wasteful, careless way. Then we will build the caring through conserving it with the Johads, we will take that extra walk in order to not have millions of gallons flushing down toilets. We will make news designs that do not assume abundant water in order to be able to recycle our own waste – to turn it into a replenishment for the soil. We have an ancient bit of wisdom that says everything is food, everything is something else's food. We need to recognize that we too need to recycle ourselves in order to be able to recycle water. The way we think decides the material conditions we make, what technologies we shape. If we think of water as a gift we must care for, we will have a decentralized system of low water use technologies. If we think of water as a non-renewable resource whose access is determined by how much you can pay for it and you don't have to care about how far it came from, how much it's exploitation led to crisis for someone else, we will then support large dam building, we will support building canals and mad projects like the one in India that is being supported now by the World Bank called the river linking project that is basically a river rerouting project. Corporations that get into water privatization are actually civil engineering companies. They've made their money building; the Suez Canal, Bechtel making giant sized dams. They will continue to shape the material infrastructure that creates a carelessness with respect to water because they thrive on that carelessness. That carelessness in fact takes away our sovereignty. If we have to care for water, we have to take responsibility for water, we have to reclaim democracy.

Opel: Keeping with the idea of changing 'water cultures' — I want to ask about the pathways to change. In the US, we don't hear about the case studies you are talking about and we are increasingly saturated with commercial, corporate media who derive significant advertising revenue from the companies working the hardest to privatize water supplies (Pepsi-Co, Nestle and the Perrier Group, Suez/Vivendi). What role will the global media play in changing 'water cultures?' Is there a media strategy you would recommend to local activists?

Shiva: The corporate media is designed to create consumers. It is designed to silence the narrative of what is happening to real people in their lives. Corporate media presents the image that water comes from these corporations rather than that it comes from the earth and is cared for by us. The role of the corporate media is increasingly to create water illiteracy and to create and support a water dictatorship. How do we have a media strategy? By pluralizing our communication system, recognizing that what corporate media says is not the only way to talk to each other. We don't have to talk via the corporate media, there are lots of other ways of talking and other ways of knowing about reality. The fact that you are talking to me today is part of the alternative beyond corporate media. This is communication beyond the communication of corporate control.

Opel: The public resistance to Bechtel's attempt to privatize the water supply in Cochabamba Bolivia resulted in canceling Bechtel's contract and renewed support for maintaining a public water utility. This was fueled in part by news that Bechtel would raise water prices by 35 percent. While the outcome of this story is encouraging for local communities attempting to defend their natural resources from multinational corporations, the impetus to action could be argued to be the result of financial self-interest. Do you think financial pressures are the primary forces that will mobilize local communities? If so, how do you reconcile this with the economists who claim the only way to safeguard water is to attach a monetary value to it? Are these two sides of the same coin?

Shiva: Wasters of water are those who can pay lots of money to buy it. Conservers of water are those who have no money. The most important water conservers are those who walk miles to collect a pot of water. They cannot afford to waste that water. Those who can build swimming pools in desert areas and irrigate golf courses and manage to pay that high price will never ever conserve a drop of water. High prices and high value are not the same thing. You can have very high prices for water and value it very low by treating it as just another commodity, not as the basis of life itself. And in that context, I would say it is not true that the people of Cochabamba only responded in financial terms when the price of water was going up. The slogan of the movement was 'water is life.' Water is Life – it was a cultural statement and of course the high prices was the ground for resistance but was not the basis for thinking about water.

Opel: Economist, engineer and ranking World Bank's ranking water advisor John Briscoe argues for a mix of public and private supervision of water supplies. In the US, most of us pay for metered water from a public utility that acts as a monopoly in most cases. Briscoe (2005a) argues that one alternative is 'to assign property rights to users and then allow them to trade those rights. This is not a "free market." Indeed, it requires a great deal of regulation. Informal markets have long existed wherever there has been water scarcity. But in recent decades, there has been enormous progress in establishing formal markets in places like California in the United States, Chile, Australia and Mexico' [online]. What do you see as the tensions or balance between public and private management of water supplies?

Shiva: We know John Briscoe because he keeps recommending privatization. The real tension in what is called public–private partnerships is that these arrangements are all about the public bearing the cost and the private walking away with profit from water treaties. I am among those who believe that the only way you can really sustain the water on this planet and sustain human life on the basis of converting water is to recognize that water by its very nature is a public good. And it must be managed as a public good and of course, each of as a part of the community, are also individuals and so society has public and private built right into it. But the idea that giant, private corporations and small, tiny municipal authorities can have an equal partnership, particularly under the pressure of the World Bank financing policies, is totally false. And is made so clear in the case of Delhi, where every step of the way since 1998, the World Bank twisted the arms of the local public utility and forced the utility to farm out contracts, increasing the costs 10–20 times more, increasing the financial burden of the public utility. That sort of public–private partnership is leading to socialism for capital, socialism for corporations. They are supported by the public utilities, they are supported by public finance, and they are supported by public resources and common resources. The public has been marginalized in making these decisions. Briscoe's statement that 'the greatest benefit of getting the private sector involved is precisely that it brings greater public scrutiny, openness and accountability' is also a total lie, because all of these contracts are secret contracts. Never are they made public. The World Bank's own loans are not public knowledge. The contracts they force our governments to sign with companies are not public knowledge. The cases that were brought against us when we fought these companies to leave our countries were conducted in secret courts in London, and Bechtel dragged Bolivia to a court in Amsterdam, these are not public.

These are systems based on secrecy. These are systems based on exclusion and these are systems based on corruption and lack of accountability. Private players have always fixed our tap and laid the pipeline. That is a whole different contractual arrangement than giant corporations being brought in by the World Bank clout and that being called a public–private partnership. The alternative to that is what I call public–public partnership. The citizens as public, working with the public utilities, to manage water as a public good and conserve water as a common property resource for all people and for the good of all. In the report that John Briscoe (2005b) released for India about two to three months ago, they have very clearly attacked the concept of water as a commons and communities having rights to water. For us, that is the pillar of a water culture – that water is a commons and communities have rights. It will be interesting to watch over the next decade which paradigm wins, the water privatization paradigm or the water democracy paradigm that we fight for.

Opel: Briscoe (2005a) has also argued that 'the greatest benefit of getting the private sector involved is precisely that it brings greater public scrutiny, openness and accountability' [online]. Clearly, efforts to privatize water are eliciting greater public scrutiny and more often outrage. In many ways privatization attempts are serving to mobilize local communities. In a globalized world where national sovereignty is often trumped by global trade agreements, what advice do you have for local communities working to defend their public water supplies?

Shiva: My first suggestion is to just look at the record. Privatization is failing. Even though the propaganda machinery is so intense, on the ground more privatization projects have failed than succeeded. Second, we don't just have a right to water; we have a duty to water. We have a duty to conserve water. That duty I believe is one of our highest duties as human beings on this planet. Other species do not have the capacity to destroy water as much as we do. And therefore, as a species, we have to be part of shaping movements for ecological democracy, for ecological renewal of our resources. From the work I have done over 30 years, and the fact that I have been a physicist and I am scientifically literate, I can tell you one thing. The more we conserve water, the better quality of life we create for ourselves. The idea of progress based on the destruction of water as a measure of progress is obsolete. It does not belong to this century. This century has to be based on recognizing that the more we protect our water, the more evolved we are as a species.

Opel: Thank you Dr Shiva for taking the time to speak with me.

Acknowledgements

Andy Opel would like to thank Dr Michelle Laurents, Eric Welch and WVFS 89.7FM for their production assistance with this interview.

Notes

1   Water privatization was the number one most censored story in 2000, according to Project Censored [online].
2   Glennon (2004), Barlow and Clark (2003), and Ward (2002).
3   See Vandana Shiva's ZNet Homepage [online] and the Navdanya Homepage [online].
4   For a brief description of the movement, see Chipko Movement, India [online].
5   For more information on Haksar and this billboard, see Sharad Haksar [online] and India Resource Center [online].

References

Barlow, M. & Clark, T. (2003) *Blue Gold: The Fight to Stop the Corporate Theft of the World's Water*, New York, New Press.
Briscoe, J. (2005a) 'Who pays the pipe? Who calls the tune?', UNESCO article, [online] Available at: http://www.unesco.org/courier/1999_02/uk/dossier/txt21.htm
Briscoe, J. (2005b) 'India's water economy: bracing for a turbulent future', World Bank Report, [online] Available at: http://www.worldbank.org.in/WBSITE/EXTERNAL/COUNTRIES/SOUTHASIAEXT/INDIAEXTN/0,,contentMDK:20668501 ~ pagePK:141137 ~ piPK:141127 ~ theSitePK:295584,00.html
Chipko Movement, India [online] Available at: http://www.iisd.org/50comm/commdb/desc/d07.htm
Glennon, R. (2004) *Water Follies: Groundwater Pumping and the Fate of America's Freshwaters*, Washington, DC, Island Press.
India Resource Center (2005) 'Coca-Cola threatens top Indian photographer with lawsuit', [online] Available at: http://www.indiaresource.org/news/2005/1077.html

Navdanya Homepage [online] Available at: http://www.navdanya.org/
Opel, A. (1999) 'Constructing purity: bottled water and the commodification of nature', *Journal of American Culture*, vol. 22, no. 4, pp. 67–76.
Project Censored [online] Available at: http://www.projectcensored.org/publications/2001/index.html
Sharad Haksar [online] Available at: http://www.sharadhaksar.com/
Shiva, V. (2002) *Water Wars: Privatization, Pollution and Profit*, Cambridge, MA, South End Press.
Shiva, V. ZNet Homepage [online] Available at: http://www.zmag.org/bios/homepage.cfm?authorID=90
Ward, D. R. (2002) *Water War: Drought, Flood, Folly and the Politics of Thirst*, New York, Riverhead Books.

Notes on Contributors

Eeva Berglund taught anthropology at Goldsmiths College, London from 1998 to 2002. Her doctoral thesis on German environmentalism and the problems of scientific knowledge was published in 1998 as *Knowing Nature, Knowing Science: An Ethnography of Local Environmental Activism*, by White Horse Press, Cambridge. With David G. Anderdon, she also co-edited a collection of essays in 2004 titled *Ethnographies of Conservation: Environmentalism and the Distribution of Privilege*, by Berghahn Books, Oxford. Since then she has written on various environmental issues, science and technology, and academic life. She does unpaid work for several London-based cultural and environmental organizations.

Jody Berland is Associate Professor of Humanities, York University, Toronto, Canada. She has published widely on cultural studies, Canadian communication theory, music and the media, culture and the environment, and the cultural technologies of space. She is co-editor of *Cultural Capital: A Reader on Modernist Legacies, State Institutions and the Value(s) of Art*, McGill-Queen's University Press, Montreal (2000), and editor of *Topia: A Canadian Journal of Cultural Studies* (http://www.yorku.ca/topia). Her book *North of Empire* is forthcoming with Duke University Press, Durham, NC.

Catriona (Cate) Mortimer-Sandilands is Canada Research Chair in Sustainability and Culture at York University, Toronto, Canada. Her current research focuses on the ways in which lesbian writers have, historically and in the present, used ideas of nature, environmental philosophies, and conventions of nature writing to explore, challenge, and problematize sex and sexual identities. She also writes about Canadian parks, eco-politics, and literatures.

Andy Opel teaches critical media studies as well as documentary and experimental video production as an Assistant Professor in the Department of Communication at Florida State University, Tallahassee, FL. His recent books include *Micro Radio and the FCC: Media Activism and the Struggle Over Broadcast Policy* (2004) and a volume he co-edited, *Representing Resistance: Media, Civil Disobedience and the Global Justice Movement* (2003). He recently wrote and directed *Cargo Bike*, a short eco-horror film about a bicycle that eats SUV drivers, out in Spring 2006.

Phaedra C. Pezzullo is an Assistant Professor of Rhetoric and Public Culture in the Department of Communication and Culture, as well as adjunct faculty of Cultural Studies and American Studies at Indiana University, Bloomington, IN. She currently is completing two book projects, *Toxic Tourism: Rhetorics of*

Pollution, Travel, and Environmental Justice (University of Alabama, Tuscaloosa, AL, 2007) and *Environmental Justice and Environmentalism: The Social Justice Challenge to the Environmental Movement*, co-edited with Ronald Sandler (MIT Press, Cambridge, MA, 2006).

Jean P. Retzinger is a lecturer in the Group Major in Mass Communications at the University of California, Berkeley, CA. Her research explores popular culture representations (primarily in film and advertising) and press coverage of agriculture and food. Her interest lies in examining the environmental implications of food production and consumption at the interstices of nature, culture, science, and technology.

Dr Vandana Shiva is a physicist, ecologist, activist, editor, and author of many books. In India, she has established Navdanya, a movement for biodiversity conservation and farmers' rights. Her recent books include *Earth Democracy: Justice, Sustainability, and Peace* (2005), *Water Wars: Privatization, Pollution, and Profit* (2002), and *Stolen Harvest: The Hijacking of the Global Food Supply* (2000).

Jennifer Daryl Slack is Professor of Communication and Cultural Studies in the Department of Humanities at Michigan Technological University, Houghton, MI. Her most recent book, co-authored with J. Macgregor Wise is *Culture and Technology: A Primer* (Peter Lang, New York, 2005). She has also edited *Animations (of Deleuze and Guattari)* (Peter Lang, 2003) and John T. Waisanen's posthumous *Thinking Geometrically: Re-Visioning Space for a Multimodal World* (Peter Lang, 2002). Her work on cultural studies and environment has appeared in the journals *Cultural Studies*, *Topia*, and *Communication Theory* and in the books *The New Keywords*, edited by Tony Bennett *et al.* (Blackwell, Oxford, 2005) and *Cultural Studies*, edited by Lawrence Grossberg *et al.* (Routledge, New York, 1992).

Margaret Werry is an Assistant Professor at the University of Minnesota, Twin Cities, MN, in the Department of Theatre Arts and Dance. She writes predominantly on the relationship between tourism, performance, ethnic politics, (neo-) liberal statehood, looking at cultural policy and tourism practice in the South Pacific at the turn of the twentieth century, and the turn of the twenty-first. Her work has been published in *Public Culture*, *Theatre Journal*, and *Essays in Theatre*.

Index

Page numbers in **Bold** represent figures

academia 56
Acland, C.R. 5
Adam, B. 52, 62, 66; moonlighting 62
agriculture: conventional 24; production 23
Alaimo, S. 103
Althusser, L. 123; social structure 123
American pet owners: survey 78–9
animal 71; attitudes 73; bodies 77; cruelty 71; images 73; metaphors 89; photography 86; social history 79; space language **91**; status 71
animal taxonomy 83
animal-internet locale 72
anthropocentric 123
Anzaldua, G. 4
Armesto, F. 11
Artificial Intelligence (Spielberg) 21
Auge, M. 55

Bagemihl, B. 99
Baker, S. 76, 89–90
balneology 39–40; philosophy 39; therapeutic science 39
Barry, A.: et al 35
Barthes, R. 87
Battlefield Earth (Christian) 15, 20
Bauman, Z. 55
Bechtel, S.C. 145
Beck, U. 55; cosmopolitanism 55
Berger, J. 77, 87
Berglund, E. 52–70
Berland, J. 71–94; and Slack, J.D. 2
binary 125
bio-political: differentiations 41; intervention 42; program 45
body boundaries 132
Boone, J.A. 131

Boswell, A. 10–11
boundaries of land 54
Bouthillette, A.M. 112
A Boy and his Dog (Jones) 16, 22–3
Braidotti, R. 132
Braun, N.: and Castree, N. 98
Brazil (Gilliam) 17
Brennan, T. 52–3, 63, 66
Briscoe, J. 146–7; public scrutiny 147
Buck, P. 40
Bullock, M. 44
Butler, J.: study 99

cannibalism 23
capitalism 65–6
Castells, M. 55
Castree, N.: and Braun, B. 98
cat 73; cultural identification 75; cyber **84**; de-naturalization 79; disposition 85–6, **86**; domestic life 80, **81**; dual role 81; images 72, **73**; proliferating 76; representation 76; satanic **82**; thought-practice 84; totem 72
cat images: mass production 83
cat and mouse 71–94
cat overpopulation 85
cat-human networks 85
Certeau, M. de. 74; space-power relations 75
chipko movement 140
Chris, C. 72, 89
Clark, A. 126–7
climatological practice 40
climatology 40
co-dependance: dogs and humans 132
communication: transversal 129
consumer desires 54
cool cats 84

INDEX

corporate media 145
corporeal conflict 106
Crane, C.A. 129–30
critical theorists 128
cultural studies 3
cultural studies 117–18, 126; holistic perspective 96; limitations 2–3
culture: three aspects 119
culture jamming 144
The Culture of Nature (Wilson) 123
cyborg: boundaries 126; identity 127; natural 126

de facto: impact 119; resistance 120
Deleuze, G.: and Guattari, F. 76–7
democracy movement 143
Derrida, J. 76
Desert of the Heart (Rule) 103–4, 109; Anne 103–4
differences: cultural or individual 20
digital kitties 87; photographic performance 87
Doniger, W.: and Wolfe, C. 90
Dorrance, T. 130; workshop 131
dystopian visions 11

earth: democracy 142; republics 143
eco: terms 125
ecocultural studies 97–8, 117–37
ecoculturalism 117
ecological: democracy 141; paradigm 142–3; totality 97; unity 96
economic globalization 53
electronic cat images 88
environment *see* nature
environmental: identity 4–5; matters 3
environmental matters (Berland and Slack) 2
Escobar, A. 65
ethical incompleteness 38
Ethics and Cultural Studies (Daryl and Whitt) 95
ethnic stereotypes 15
ethno-historical: method 34
ethnographic 34

fabulation 12
fetishism 88
The Fifth Element (Besson) 15
Finland 52; environmental futures 52; fieldwork 53; forestry 57; forests 52–70; recession 61
flood disasters 141

food 10–11; gruel 18–19; moral lessons 21; and science fiction films 9–30; technology's role 11
food preferences 20
food scenes 10–11
forests: Finland 52–70
Forster, L. 20
Foucault, M. 34, 45, 122

Galiano 108–9; Island 108; Mount 109
Ganges: basin 140
Gattaca (Niccol) 19
gay ghetto 112
general agreement on trade in services (GATS) 141–2
geographic information system (GIS) 98
global communications 65
global competitiveness 56
governmental analysis 46
Grossberg, L. 120, 122
Guattari, F.: and Deleuze, G. 76–7

haecceities 127
Haksar, S. 143–4
Halberstam, H. 99, 111; queer space 99
Hall, S. 122; and Williams, R. 118–19
Haraway, D.J. 54, 78, 132
Harvey, D. 52
health: construal 39; hydropathy 39
Herderian rule 40
heteronormative relations 99
Himanen, P. 61
Hoggart, R. 118; *The Uses of Literacy* 118
holistic health regimen 39
home formation 88
homophobic relations 99
horse language 129
housing reform 36
human communities 110
human-animal: distinctions 80; relations 74
human-cat networks 85
Hunter, I. 45; aesthetics 45

iconographic cat 77
identity 127
imperialist nostalgia 44
industrial agriculture 139
information society 55–6
Ingram, G.B. 112
inter-species domestic kinship 78
International Monetary Fund (IMF) 138

INDEX

Jameson, F. 10
Jay, R. 79
Jessop, B 62
juxtaposition 14

Kainuu 57; forests 58; province 53; slogan 57
Kainuu Rural Advisory Centre 63
Kainuu schools forest week 63–5; exchanging ideas 63–4; state-owned forests 64
Kember, S. 86–7
Kete, K. 82
Keywords (Williams) 2
King, G.: and Krzywinska, T. 11
Kirsch, S. 59
Krzywinska, T.: and King, G. 11

La Voyage dans la Lune (Melies) 9
language: stutters 130
The Last Man (Ralston) 15
The Lathe of Heaven (Loxton and Barzyk) 16
Latour, B. 41, 124
Leach, E. 75; research 75
Lefebvre, H. 84
Leopold, A. 4
lesbian separatism 103
liberal citizenship 43–4

McLuhan, M. 9
McRobbie, A. 119
The Man Who Listens to Horses (Robert) 128
Maori 32–3; collectivities 36; communal livelihood 32; liberal subjects 41–2; lifeways 35; new homes 38
Marchak, M.P. 57
massacres: eighteenth century 81–2
material infrastructure: connection water habits 144
The Matrix (Wachowski) 12–13
Melies, G. 9
Miller, T.: and Yudice, G 38
mindfulness 103
Minh-ha, T.T. 4
Minority Report (Speilberg) 14
modern constitution 41
modernity 53, 66; boundary-imposing 54
Moore, D.S.: *et al* 98
Morris, D. 84
municipalities 57
Muses, R. 85

natural world 110
nature: documentaries 90; inaccessible 41; relationships 58; titanic force 32
nature relationship society 41
negative prophecy 17
New Zealand 47; liberal pluralism 47; liberal state-formation 47
nostalgia 12–14, 16

Opel, A. 138–51
Osborne, T. 36
overture 1–8

Paasi, A. 57
parody 15
pet: animosity 77–8; keeping 78
Pezzullo, P.C. 1–8, 52
political rationalities 46
Pollock, D. 3
popular culture 119, 121; discourse 121–2
post-apocalyptic films 17
post-cyborg theorists 66
post-humanist 88
postmodernism 97
Povinelli, E. 43
Pratt, M.L. 43
Probyn, E. 24
protagonist body 104–5
public-private partnerships 146
public-public partnership 147

queer 98; community 111; family 108; nature 98–9, 104; theory 98–9
queer ecocultural politics 111
queering families 101

racial fascination 43
rationalization process 80
reductionism 123
relative autonomy 124
Retzinger, J.P. 9–30
rhetorical ambiguity 76
Roberts, A. 12
Robins, K. 87
Robocop (Verhoeven) 20
Roger, K.M. 80
Rose, N. 45
Rosoldo, R. 1
Ross, A. 97
Rotorua 31–4; tourism 33–4; touristic bio-politics 33; touristic laboratory 40
Rule, J. 101; *Desert of the Heart* 103–4; *The Young in One Another's Arms* 101–4

INDEX

Said, E. 88; study of history 66
Sanatorium: government 37; reserve 37–8
Sandilands, C.M. 95–116
Sandywell, B. 122
Sawchuk, K. 119
scarcity 142–3
Schama, S.: natural landscapes 58–9
Schlosser, E. 24
Schofield, M.A. 11
Scholes, R. 12
Schuster, M. 106
science fiction 9–10, 12; cinema 9–10; comfort foods 13; familiar foods 16; films 9; food scenes 12; hunger 12, 18
Seed, D. 13, 17
semi-autonomy 124
Sennett, R. 55
Serpell, J. 78
sexuality 101; implication 101
Shimakawa, K. 43; bio-poetic spatial process 43
Shiva, Dr V. 138–51
Silent Running (Trumbull) 29
Simon, C. 79; woman-cat relationship 79
ski-tunnel 59–60
Slack, J.D. 117–37, 121; and Berland, J. 2; and Whitt, L.A 96, 125
slavery motif: master-slave relation 78
Sobchack, V. 16
social equilibria 35
social reproduction tension space of flows 56
society relationship nature 41
Soper, K. 54
Sotkamo 59
Soylent Green (Fleischer) 13, 23
space flow 55, 56
Sparks, P. 83
spatial: experiments 44; identification 43; practice 36
Spirn, A.W. 4
Staiger, J. 17
Survin, D. 10

technological assemblage 124–5
technological culture 125
The Terminator (Cameron) 19
Tester, K. 80
thermal phenomena 42
thermal reserve 42–3
A Thousand Plateaus (Deleuze and Guattari) 89
Thrift, N. 119

THX 1138 (Lucas) 18
The Time Machine (Pal 1960 Film) 22
top-down measures 54
tourism: conduct 46; ethnic 47; landscape 45–6; Rotorua 33; techniques 37
tourism and race 31–51
tourist habitus 44
trade agreement: democratize 142
The Trial (Kafka) 89

unfamiliar foods 16–20
urban: redevelopment 106; sadness 107; traumas 106–7
The Uses of Literacy (Hoggart) 118

Vancouver: gay/nude Wreck Beach 112–13
Virtanen, S. 60–1; verbal image 63

water: cultural habits 144; cycle 139–40; dams 140–1; fresh 138; high price and value 146; non-renewable resource 144; privatization 147; resource issues 138
water cultures: changing 145
water habits (connection) material infrastructure 144
Water Wars (Shiva) 139, 144
Weber, F.P.: and Weber, Sir H. 40
Werry, M. 31–51
Whakerewarewa 43; environment 43–4
Wheeler, R. 104
Whitt, L.A: and Slack, J.D. 96, 125
Williams, R. 11, 24; and Hall, S. 118–19; *Keywords* 2
Wilson, A. 123
Wise, G. 124
Wittgenstein, L. 80–1
Wohlmann, A.S. 39
Wolfe, C.: and Doniger, W. 90
working-class people 118
World Bank 146–7
World Trade Organization (WTO) 141, 143; laws 143

The Young in One Another's Arms (Rule) 101–4; characters 105; dynamics 105
Yudice, G.: and Miller, T 38

zoos 77
Zylinska, J. 97

History of Photography

EDITOR:
Graham Smith, *University of St Andrews, UK*

ASSOCIATE EDITOR:
Peggy Ann Kusnerz, *Ann Arbor Michigan, USA*

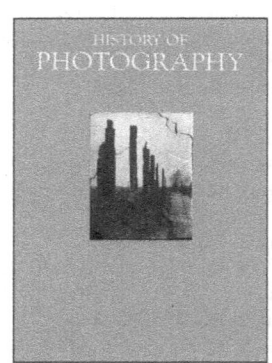

History of Photography is an international journal devoted exclusively to the history and criticism of the basic semantic unit of all modern media - the photograph. It covers the uses of photography from the earliest times to the present day, and is open to all critical approaches, whether historical, art historical, sociological, or anthropological. It is designed to supply the needs of curators, scholars, and critics, and to support the work of graduate students entering this developing field of study. It is also an indispensable repository of documentary texts, indexes, and bibliographies of all periods. *History of Photography* is a fully peer reviewed journal.

SUBSCRIPTION RATES
2008 - *Volume* 32 (*4 issues per year*)
Print ISSN 0308-7298
Institutional rate (print only): US$497; £299; €398
Personal rate (print only): US$262; £157; €210

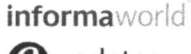

A world of specialist information for the academic, professional and business communities. To find out more go to: **www.informaworld.com**

Register your email address at **www.informaworld.com/eupdates** to receive information on books, journals and other news within your areas of interest.

For further information, please contact Customer Services at either of the following:
T&F Informa UK Ltd, Sheepen Place, Colchester, Essex, CO3 3LP, UK
Tel: +44 (0) 20 7017 5544 Fax: 44 (0) 20 7017 5198
Email: tf.enquiries@informa.com
Taylor & Francis Inc, 325 Chestnut Street, Philadelphia, PA 19106, USA
Tel: +1 800 354 1420 (toll-free calls from within the US)
or +1 215 625 8900 (calls from overseas) Fax: +1 215 625 2940
Email: customerservice@taylorandfrancis.com

www.informaworld.com/thph

Third Text

EDITORS:
Rasheed Araeen, London, UK
Ziauddin Sardar, London, UK

Third Text is an international scholarly journal dedicated to providing critical perspectives on art and visual culture. The journal examines the theoretical and historical ground by which the West legitimises its position as the ultimate, arbiter of what is significant within this field. Established in 1987, the journal provides a forum for the discussion and (re)appraisal of theory and practice of art, art history and criticism, and the work of artists hitherto marginalised through racial, gender, religious and cultural differences. Dealing with diversity of art practices - visual arts, sculpture, installation, performance, photography, video and film - *Third Text* addresses the complex cultural realities that emerge when different worldviews meet, and the challenge this poses to Eurocentrism and ethnocentric aesthetic criteria. The journal aims to develop new discourses and radical interdisciplinary scholarships that go beyond the confines of eurocentricity.

SUBSCRIPTION RATES
2008 - *Volume 22 (6 issues per year)*
Print ISSN 0952-8822
Online ISSN 1475-5297
Institutional rate (print and online): US$490; £324; €392
Institutional rate (online access only): US$465; £307; €372
Personal rate (print only): US$138; £83; €110

informaworld — A world of specialist information for the academic, professional and business communities. To find out more go to: **www.informaworld.com**

@updates Taylor & Francis Group — Register your email address at **www.informaworld.com/eupdates** to receive information on books, journals and other news within your areas of interest.

For further information, please contact Customer Services at either of the following:
T&F Informa UK Ltd, Sheepen Place, Colchester, Essex, CO3 3LP, UK
Tel: +44 (0) 20 7017 5544 Fax: 44 (0) 20 7017 5198
Email: tf.enquiries@informa.com
Taylor & Francis Inc, 325 Chestnut Street, Philadelphia, PA 19106, USA
Tel: +1 800 354 1420 (toll-free calls from within the US)
or +1 215 625 8900 (calls from overseas) Fax: +1 215 625 2940
Email: customerservice@taylorandfrancis.com

View an online sample issue at:
www.informaworld.com/ctte

Photographies

NEW IN 2008

EDITORS:
David Bate, *University of Westminster, UK*
Sarah Kember, *Goldsmiths, University of London, UK*
Martin Lister, *University of the West of England, Bristol, UK*
Liz Wells, *University of Plymouth, UK*

Photographies seeks to construct a new agenda for theorising photography as a heterogeneous medium that is changing in an ever more dynamic relation to all aspects of contemporary culture. *Photographies* aims to further develop the history and theory of photography, considering new frameworks for thinking and addressing questions arising from the present context of technological, economic, political and cultural change.

Photographies will investigate the contemporary condition and currency of the photographic within local and global contexts. The editors seek research papers and innovative visual essays, shorter papers engaging new debates, review essays evaluating publications, cultural events, key developments, exhibitions and conferences.

CALL FOR PAPERS

The Editors of *Photographies* are now inviting the following kinds of submissions:

- Research papers and innovative visual essays (6000–8000 words)
- Shorter papers engaging new debates (circa 4000 words)
- Reflective review essays evaluating publications, cultural events, key developments, exhibitions and conferences.

Papers and proposals should be sent to: photographies@plymouth.ac.uk
Enquiries and submissions are welcome throughout the year.

SUBSCRIPTION RATES

2008 - Volume 1 (*2 issues per year*)
Print ISSN 1754-0763
Online ISSN 1754-0771
Institutional rate (print and online): US$224; £115; €179
Institutional rate (online access only): US$212; £109; €170
Personal rate (print only): US$58; £30; €46

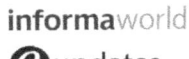

A world of specialist information for the academic, professional and business communities. To find out more go to: **www.informaworld.com**

Register your email address at **www.informaworld.com/eupdates** to receive information on books, journals and other news within your areas of interest.

For further information, please contact Customer Services at either of the following:
T&F Informa UK Ltd, Sheepen Place, Colchester, Essex, CO3 3LP, UK
Tel: +44 (0) 20 7017 5544 Fax: 44 (0) 20 7017 5198
Email: tf.enquiries@informa.com
Taylor & Francis Inc, 325 Chestnut Street, Philadelphia, PA 19106, USA
Tel: +1 800 354 1420 (toll-free calls from within the US)
or +1 215 625 8900 (calls from overseas) Fax: +1 215 625 2940
Email: customerservice@taylorandfrancis.com

www.informaworld.com/rpho